Essentials of F

Everything you need to know to administe

MW00653240

I'd like to order the following **Essentials of Psychological Assessment**.

Essentials

of **Psychological Assessment** Series

ORDER FORM

Please send this order form with your payment (credit card or check) to:
Wiley, Attn: Customer Care, 10475 Crosspoint Blvd., Indianapolis, IN 46256

QUANTITY	TITLE	ISBN	PRICE

Shipping Charges:	Surface	2-Day	1-Day
First item	$5.00	$10.50	$17.50
Each additional item	$3.00	$3.00	$4.00

For orders greater than 15 items, please contact
Customer Care at 1-877-762-2974.

ORDER AMOUNT _____

SHIPPING CHARGES _____

SALES TAX _____

TOTAL ENCLOSED _____

NAME_____

AFFILIATION_____

ADDRESS_____

CITY/STATE/ZIP _____

TELEPHONE _____

EMAIL_____

❑ Please add me to your e-mailing list

PAYMENT METHOD:

❑ Check/Money Order   ❑ Visa   ❑ Mastercard   ❑ AmEx

Card Number _____ Exp. Date _____

Cardholder Name (Please print) _____

Signature _____

Make checks payable to **John Wiley & Sons.** Credit card orders invalid if not signed.
All orders subject to credit approval. • Prices subject to change.

To order by phone, call toll free 1-877-762-2974
To order online: www.wiley.com/essentials

WILEY

Essentials of Gifted Assessment

Essentials of Psychological Assessment Series

Series Editors, Alan S. Kaufman and Nadeen L. Kaufman

Essentials

of Gifted Assessment

Steven I. Pfeiffer

WILEY

Library of Congress Cataloging-in-Publication Data:

Library of Congress Cataloging-in-Publication Data has been applied for and is on file with the Library of Congress.

ISBN 978-1-118-58920-5 (paper); ISBN 978-1-118-70564-3 (ePDF); ISBN 978-1-118-87316-8 (ePub)

Printed in the United States of America

FIRST EDITION

PB Printing 10 9 8 7 6 5 4 3 2 1

CONTENTS

SERIES PREFACE

In the Essentials of Psychological Assessment series, we have attempted to provide the reader with books that will deliver key practical information in the most efficient and accessible style. Many books in the series feature specific instruments in a variety of domains, such as cognition, personality, education, and neuropsychology. Other books, like *Essentials of Gifted Assessment*, focus on crucial topics for professionals who are involved in any way with assessment—topics such as specific reading disabilities, evidence-based interventions, or ADHD assessment. For the experienced professional, books in the series offer a concise yet thorough review of a test instrument or a specific area of expertise, including numerous tips for best practices. Students can turn to series books for clear and concise overviews of the important assessment tools and key topics in which they must become proficient to practice skillfully, efficiently, and ethically in their chosen fields.

Wherever feasible, visual cues highlighting key points are utilized alongside systematic, step-by-step guidelines. Chapters are focused and succinct. Topics are organized for an easy understanding of the essential material related to a particular test or topic. Theory and research are continually woven into the fabric of each book, but always so as to enhance the practical application of the material rather than to sidetrack or overwhelm readers. With this series, we aim to challenge and assist readers interested in psychological assessment to aspire to the highest level of competency by arming them with the tools they need for knowledgeable, informed practice. We have long been advocates of *intelligent testing*—which incorporates the notion that numbers are meaningless unless they are brought to life by the clinical acumen and expertise of examiners. Assessment must be used to make a difference in the child's or adult's life, or why bother to test? All the books in this series—whether devoted to specific tests or general topics—are consistent with this credo. We want this series to help our readers, novice and veteran alike, to benefit from the intelligent assessment approaches of the authors of each book.

We are delighted to include *Essentials of Gifted Assessment* in our series. Dr. Steven Pfeiffer is, in our opinion, among the small group of the world's leading experts in the field. He is an unusually articulate spokesperson on the varied topics that make up the broad domain of gifted education and gifted assessment. *Essentials of Gifted Assessment* introduces the theory and practice underlying gifted assessment within the context of the history that produced this important field. This book provides an overview of who the gifted are, the reasons why we should identify gifted students, and the purposes of gifted assessment. Key principles of gifted assessment are discussed and an up-to-date overview on gifted assessment measures is provided. Topics include the use of local norms, measuring creativity and motivation, nonverbal measures, the importance of recurring gifted assessment, multipotentiality, gifted testing and minority group students, and evaluating the twice-exceptional student. This book provides practitioners with the tools needed for ethical, evidence-based, and informed clinical practice with high-ability students.

Alan S. Kaufman, PhD, and Nadeen L. Kaufman, EdD

Series Editors

Yale Child Study Center

Yale University School of Medicine

ACKNOWLEDGMENTS

I want to thank Alan Kaufman and Nadeen Kaufman, editors of the Essentials of Psychological Assessment Series, for inviting me to write this book. It has been a great intellectual pleasure. Having spent a long and very satisfying professional career working with high-ability students—beginning with my dissertation on creativity, followed by my work at Duke University and later at Florida State University as an administrator, clinician, consultant, and researcher—it has been extremely gratifying writing this book as part of the Wiley assessment series.

I gratefully acknowledge the many high-ability students and also parents, psychologists, and educators that I had the privilege of working with and learning from during my tenure as executive director of the Duke University Talent Identification Program and later, as professor and director of clinical training at Florida State University and codirector of the Florida Governor's School for Space Science and Technology. I appreciate, value, and hold in reverence the many lessons learned from the extremely bright students whom I have worked with over the past thirty-five years. I owe special thanks to Professor James Gallagher for sparking my initial interest in the gifted and serving as an early mentor and role model while I was still a doctoral student at the University of North Carolina-Chapel Hill. It saddened me to learn, as I was writing this book, that Jim had passed away. I had looked forward to sharing a draft and inviting his feedback.

Others who have inspired my thinking about gifted assessment and who deserve mention for ideas that appear in this volume include Professor Michael Wallach (the importance of "what we measure"), Professor Louis Hsu ("respecting psychometrics"), clinical psychologist Andy Burka ("appreciating and searching for the uniqueness in every client"), test author Jack Naglieri (my mentor early in my career in "test development 101"), and Dr. Maureen Neihart (National Institute of Education, Singapore) and Dr. Pauline Dixon (Newcastle University, England) for helping me experience firsthand the "impact of culture." Special thanks are due to Susie Raiford at Pearson Assessment for her invaluable input into the new WISC-V. Finally, thanks to Elspeth MacHattie for her exquisitely valuable editing and to Emilee Valler, one of my doctoral students, for her dogged sleuth work in locating missing references and citations.

I continue to appreciate and respect the support of my wife, Jan, who graciously permitted me many evenings and weekends away from bike rides, tennis games, and trail runs to write this book.

I dedicate this book, as I did my last book, *Serving the Gifted*,[1] to practitioners who hold an interest in identifying and working with students of high ability. For far too long, school psychologists and other professionals working in the schools have focused the great majority of their time, effort, and creative resources on those students who fall at the lower end of the ability continuum. I hope that *Essentials of Gifted Assessment* helps to focus greater attention on the identification and assessment needs of students of uncommon ability and high potential. I also hope that this volume contributes in some meaningful way to best practices in gifted assessment. One final point: this book isn't about assessing intelligence. It is about the theory and practice underlying assessing giftedness.

---

1. *Serving the Gifted* was published in 2013 by Routledge in its School-Based Practice in Action Series.

Essentials of Gifted Assessment

One

INTRODUCTION TO GIFTED ASSESSMENT

WHO ARE THE GIFTED?

At first blush, it might seem as though we can quickly dispense with the question, exactly who are the gifted? If you work in the schools, then you know exactly who they are. The gifted are those students who meet the eligibility criteria that your school district and state have stipulated for this group. And if you are a graduate student in psychology, then you also know who the gifted are. They are those students who have obtained an IQ test score that exceeds a certain threshold, according to what you learned in your assessment of intelligence course. These are the views of a great many practitioners and graduate students, according to a recent national survey (McClain & Pfeiffer, 2012) and as gathered from informal conversations at school psychology conferences and workshops here in the United States and also internationally.

As you will quickly learn, however, this book departs from the traditional and some might argue outdated and even archaic view of who the gifted are and suggests a more nuanced perspective of what is meant by giftedness. *High IQ equals gifted* was the view that dominated twentieth-century thinking in both psychology and education. But we are now in a new millennium and have learned much from research in developmental psychology, the cognitive neurosciences, and the talent development field since the early days of gifted education, and this new information better informs our understanding of high-ability students—the gifted (Pfeiffer, 2002, 2003). In the next chapter, we will examine a few models of giftedness that lead to different ways to conceptualize giftedness and define the gifted student. Most would agree that the young child who is reading at age 3, excelling at competitive chess by age 6, or playing the violin in an orchestra at age 10 is gifted. These examples are indicative of children who are developmentally advanced, one hallmark of giftedness (Pfeiffer, 2002, 2012). Most authorities on giftedness agree that academically gifted students are those in the upper 3–5% to 10–15% (the exact range depending on the authority) compared to their same-age peers in general intellectual ability, distinguished performance in one or more academic domains, and evidence of creative work (Pfeiffer, 2003, 2012). Not surprisingly, there is a genetic influence in the expression of giftedness, at least at the high end of the IQ continuum (Plomin & Spinath, 2004). For example, the fields of music and mathematics are particularly rich with examples of child prodigies. Evidence also comes from the emergence of eminence among young children from impoverished environments (Nisbett, 2009). However, most developmental psychologists and behavioral geneticists also agree that the unfolding of gifts requires a nurturing and supportive environment, available resources, certain personality characteristics, and even good fortune (Nicpon & Pfeiffer, 2011; Pfeiffer, 2012, 2013b). More on the topic of who exactly the gifted are will be presented in Chapter 2.

What follows are working definitions that begin to answer the question of who the gifted are. These definitions are based on my tripartite model of giftedness, which I will explain shortly. The first is a definition of the *gifted child*:

> The gifted child demonstrates a greater likelihood, when compared to other students of the same age, experience and opportunity, to achieve extraordinary accomplishments in one or more culturally valued domains [Pfeiffer, 2013b].

According to this definition, a child's gifts can be in any culturally valued domain, such as academics, athletics, the performing arts, leadership and student government, or even community volunteerism. The list of gifts is almost inexhaustible, limited only by what the community and the culture value and deem important. In most cultures and societies, as the child gets older there is increased opportunity for exposure to a growing number of domains in which the adolescent and young adult can come to excel and even gain expertise and eminence. For example, the young girl who demonstrates precocious mathematical abilities at age 6 or 7 will likely find a wide variety of academic and career domains to excel and become distinguished in as a young adult.

This definition of the gifted child reflects the view that this child demonstrates a greater likelihood of achieving extraordinary accomplishments in one or more culturally valued domains than other children of the same age and with the same opportunity (Pfeiffer, 2013b). The next definition describes the *academically gifted student*. It is conceptually similar to the definition of the gifted child, and fully consistent with the tripartite model of giftedness that you will be introduced to shortly. This second definition of the gifted is intentionally more narrowly focused on academics and schooling:

> The academically gifted student demonstrates outstanding performance or evidence of potential for outstanding academic performance, when compared with other students of the same age, experience and opportunity, . . . and a thirst to excel in one or more academic domains . . . . [T]he academically gifted student is likely to benefit from special educational programs or resources, especially if they align with their unique profile of abilities and interests [Pfeiffer, 2013b].

Frequently the academically gifted student's academic needs are not being substantially met in the classroom or school, and quite often this student requires specialized programs, services, or activities not ordinarily provided in the regular classroom—not always, but oftentimes. This failure points to what really should be the primary rationale and justification for gifted assessment in the schools—*to determine whether a student has uncanny intellectual abilities and/or outstanding academic performance or evidence of potential for outstanding academic performance, frequently indicative of a need for special educational programs or resources not presently available in the regular classroom.*

BRIEF HISTORY OF GIFTED EDUCATION

Much has been written about the history of giftedness and gifted assessment (e.g., Mönks, Heller, & Passow, 2000; Robinson & Clinkenbeard, 2008; Tannenbaum, 1983, 2000). Anyone working with high-ability students should take the time to become familiar with this literature. I am reminded of the warning that those who don't study or respect history are more likely to repeat the mistakes of the past. The same is true for gifted assessment and gifted education. An appreciation of the history of gifted education over the past one hundred years will enlighten the practitioner about what has been tried and has worked, as well as what has been tried and has failed. With this knowledge we can avoid repeating the mistakes of the past!

As far back as Confucius in China and Plato in Greece, philosophers wrote about "heavenly" (gifted) children. Their writings not only theorized about what constituted high ability but also provided practical recommendations for how society should go about identifying and nurturing these special young citizens (Mönks et al., 2000). Early philosophers embraced views that giftedness constituted a set of special attributes that we today would view as aspects of cognitive ability (Pfeiffer, 2013b).

In the United States we trace the early roots of attention to the gifted to the research conducted by Lewis Terman, a professor at Stanford University. Terman conducted a large longitudinal study in California that followed a cohort of students who had tested with IQ scores at or above 140. Terman collected tons of data on these students over the course of fifty years. He stated that the "twofold purpose of the project was, first of all, to find what traits characterize children of high IQ, and secondly, to follow them for as many years as possible to see what kind of adults they might become" (Terman, 1925, p. 223; Terman & Oden, 1951, p. 21). Terman concluded that children of high IQ (140 or higher) were healthier, better-adjusted, and higher achievers than unselected children (Robinson & Clinkenbeard, 2008). This early work set the stage for establishing within the education and psychology community what Dai (2010) calls a *gifted child focus*.

There are other early scientific studies and writings on the gifted, such as Galton's *Hereditary Genius* (1869) and Cattell's *A Statistical Study of American Men of Science* (a series of articles published from 1906 to 1910) (Whipple, 1924). However, nothing quite captured the imagination of the public as Terman's *Genetic Studies of Genius* did (Mönks et al., 2000). More than any other individual, Terman helped to define and conceptualize giftedness as high IQ. Almost one hundred years later, Terman's influence on the gifted field remains prominent. The gifted child focus emphasizes general intelligence and assumes that the gifted constitute a clearly demarcated and fixed category of exceptional individuals who differ in a number of quantitative *and* qualitative ways from their nongifted peers. The gifted child focus dominated twentieth-century thinking. It has been the major zeitgeist in gifted education up until the last ten to fifteen years. A relatively new focus is now emerging and is beginning to challenge the predominant gifted child focus. This new focus has been labeled a *talent development perspective* (Dai, 2010; Pfeiffer, 2013b). More will be said about this second perspective shortly and in the next chapter.

Another influential figure in the history of gifted education, and one of my former professors and mentors at the University of North Carolina-Chapel Hill, is James Gallagher. In 1960 Gallagher submitted a report to the Illinois state legislature whose purpose was "to review and summarize all of the information now available relating to the education of gifted children" (Gallagher, 1960, p. 3). Gallagher's report, *Analysis of Research on the Education of Gifted Children*, concluded that "special programming for gifted children requires additional personnel and services" (p. 131). Gallagher pointed out that only 2 cents out of every 100 dollars spent on K–12 education in the United States supports the gifted, and that existing programs for the gifted do not reach nearly enough of the

≡ Rapid Reference 1.1   Federal Expenditur Gifted Education

In 2006, the U.S. Department of Education allocated 1/100 of 1% of its total education budget expenditures for the education of the gifted.

gifted students in America's schools. He added that special programs for the gifted are a low priority at all levels of government, that the federal role in services to the gifted is all but nonexistent, and that "gifted students have been relatively ignored in educational programs such as No Child Left Behind" (Gallagher, 2008, p. 7); this is also true of the more recent federal Race to the Top initiative. In 2006, for example, the U.S. Department of Education spent nearly $84 billion. The only program specifically funded to address the education of the gifted got $9.6 million, 1/100 of 1% of federal education expenditures. Like many authorities in the gifted field, Gallagher embraced the gifted child focus. His illustrious career (which, sadly, ended in 2014) included passionately advocating for meeting this group's unique needs.

A number of other individuals have been influential in the history of gifted education in the United States, and most of those who worked during the twentieth century have adopted a gifted child focus. Leta Hollingworth (1886–1939), for example, played an important early role with her case studies of high IQ students in the New York City schools. Hollingworth was a psychologist who practiced in New York City at about the same time that Terman was a professor at Stanford. Hollingworth is the author of the first textbook on gifted education, *Gifted Children: Their Nature and Nurture* (1926).

The United States has been slow to respond to the educational needs of students of high ability. This lack of attention has also been true globally. Many authorities feel that the ambivalence and disinclination of federal governments, and of many states in the United States, to address the unique learning needs of high-ability students is the result of society's perception that they are already a privileged group who will do quite well without special funding or services (Stephens, 2008, 2011). There is also a sense that the principle of equity trumps the principle of excellence in driving educational policy. And yet the National Science Board (2010) recognizes this dilemma in American education. It has stated in a report that "the opportunity for excellence is a fundamental American value and should be afforded to all" (p. 5). A recent editorial in the *New York Times* mirrored this point with the headline, "Even gifted students can't keep up"; the editorial bemoaned the performance of U.S. students on the 2012 Program for International Student Assessment test, which was poor compared to that of students from many other countries (The Editorial Board, 2013).

One final point bears mentioning in this intentionally brief overview of the history of gifted education and gifted identification. A recent survey indicates that substantial changes in definitions and categories of giftedness have occurred over the past decade. States vary considerably in how they identify gifted and talented students in their schools. A majority of states still anchor gifted assessment to Terman's view that giftedness equates to high IQ, although they don't use quite as high a threshold or cut score as Terman did for demarcating giftedness. States also frequently endorse a multiple cutoff or averaging approach to decision making about who the gifted are (McClain & Pfeiffer, 2012). More will be said about different decision-making models in Chapter 7. It is fair to conclude that states continue to embrace a gifted child focus and have not yet considered a talent development perspective that downplays general intelligence, is more domain or specific talent centered, and less exclusive (Dai, 2010).

GIFTEDNESS AS A SOCIAL CONSTRUCTION

There exists in education and among educators of the gifted the myth that giftedness is something real. It is a popular belief among both professionals and the lay public alike. Many educators and psychologists continue to believe that giftedness is real, something concrete, analogous to height, weight, or hair color or similar to biomedical conditions such as diabetes, spinal meningitis, or arteriosclerosis. This belief is the hallmark of the gifted child focus. Many in the gifted field still believe, as Annemarie Roeper (1982) first advocated, that the gifted "think, feel, and experience" the world differently; "giftedness is a greater awareness, a greater sensitivity, and a greater ability to understand and transform perceptions into intellectual and emotional experiences" (p. 21). The reality is that, in Borland's words, "giftedness is not a fact of nature, but, instead, a social construction" (2009, p. 237). It is not akin to weight, hair color, or diabetes. The concepts of normal, subnormal, and supernormal (or gifted) are human inventions, not discoveries of nature. Although we often talk in the schools about giftedness as something real, something that children either are or, sadly, are not, something with an existence independent of our naming of it, it is nothing more than a social construction. It is an invented way of categorizing children (Borland, 2005). In my opinion, this is an extremely important point—that giftedness is a social construction, not something real. Anyone who is involved in assessing giftedness needs to appreciate that he or she is measuring or gauging a psychological construct that is a human invention. Assessing the height or weight or visual acuity of a child is a less subjective enterprise. We need to respect that when we talk about gifted-ness, we are considering *a created con-*

> ## DON'T FORGET
> ....
> Giftedness is a social construct, a human invention; it is *not* something real.

cept that is useful and can be operationally defined and measured, but not something real in nature. Juvenile diabetes, for example, is something real, with clear signs and (biophysiological) indicators that differentiate children with and without this disease. There is a clear etiology, set of symptoms, course over time, and (we hope, effective) treatment regime for those with the disease. And there is a fairly clear distinguishing line (or *joint,* as it is called in medicine) that differentiates the patient with diabetes from the patient without it. The same is not quite true for giftedness. Those of us who work in the schools should never forget this important and not insignificant distinction.

Historically, each society has used the concept of giftedness as a label to explain and recognize those individuals who perform exceptionally well in whatever domains that society values. Cultural anthropologists remind us that what constitutes giftedness in a, for example, hunting and gathering society, differs markedly from what is viewed as giftedness in an industrial or postindustrial information- and service-driven culture. It is not difficult to envision that an individual considered gifted in one society—for example, an innovative and highly successful Silicon Valley software programmer—might not possess the requisite attributes or abilities to merit the gifted label in other societies or regions of the world (Pfeiffer, 2013b).

This myth that giftedness is something real and not a social construction is no minor influence. It has had huge implications for how we view students of uncommon or exceptionally high ability—whom we label the gifted (S. B. Kaufman, 2013; Nicpon & Pfeiffer, 2011; Treffinger, 2009). It has had huge implications for how we go about assessing gifted students in the schools. And it has had huge implications for the rules and regulations we establish for providing programs and services for those students whom our assessments deem as gifted. Much more will be discussed on these very topics throughout this book.

TRIPARTITE MODEL

This discussion of giftedness as a social construction and not something that is real logically leads to the question, well then, who exactly are the gifted, and how

≡ *Rapid Reference 1.2 Tripartite Model of Giftedness*

- Giftedness through the lens of high intelligence
- Giftedness through the lens of outstanding accomplishments
- Giftedness through the lens of potential to excel

should we conceptualize giftedness? This is a very important question, and I will discuss it next.

There are many different ways to conceptualize giftedness. There are educational conceptualizations, political conceptualizations, philosophical conceptualizations, and psychometrically driven conceptualizations. No one conceptualization is correct. They are all simply different ways to view individuals who are in some way special or unique. In Chapter 2 we will examine a few leading conceptualizations, or models, that have been proposed by authorities in the gifted field. Each of these gifted models presents unique ideas that can help practitioners more easily understand and communicate what is meant by students of uncommon or exceptional ability and promise. As I will discuss in the next chapter, these models differ in important ways.

I have proposed a conceptual model for academic giftedness that I call the *tripartite model of giftedness* (Pfeiffer, 2013b). This model provides three different ways to view students with uncommon, advanced, or exceptionally high ability. The model also offers three different ways to assess and array special educational programs for these three different types of high-ability students. The tripartite model incorporates three distinct but complementary lenses through which one can view academic giftedness. The three views that are the foundation of the tripartite model are simply three alternative ways to consider assessing and grouping students of uncommon or high ability.

- Giftedness through the lens of high intelligence
- Giftedness through the lens of outstanding accomplishments
- Giftedness through the lens of potential to excel

The first perspective, the *high intelligence* viewpoint, will be familiar to most readers. When we view giftedness through this first lens, a test of intellectual ability or its proxy is used to assess students who are functioning at a certain level considerably above average intellectually. Other tests or procedures can supplement or replace the IQ test, but the criterion for high intelligence giftedness is based on compelling evidence that the student is advanced intellectually when compared to his or her peers. This first gifted perspective can follow a general (g)

or multidimensional view of intelligence (e.g., Cattell-Horn-Carroll [CHC], structure of intellect, or multiple intelligences). It can even be based on a neuroanatomical model of giftedness; recent work, for example, has postulated that more intelligent children demonstrate a more plastic cortex, with an initial acceleration and prolonged phase of cortical increase, followed by a period of vigorous cortical thinning by early adolescence (Shaw et al., 2006).

Adherents of this first perspective have historically tended to de-emphasize the role of learning or the acquisition of skills over time and through experience. More recent theorists who embrace this perspective, however, recognize the importance of experience and learning (e.g., Gottfredson, 1997, 1998).

The rationale for gifted programs based on viewing giftedness through the lens of high IQ is that students with superior intelligence need and/or are entitled to advanced, intellectually challenging, and/or faster paced academic material not typically found in the regular classroom. Gifted education based on a high intelligence perspective consists of a highly accelerated and/or academically advanced and challenging curriculum. Another assumption underlying the high intelligence perspective is that students of superior intelligence should be entitled to special gifted education throughout their education (Pfeiffer, 2013b).

The second perspective, the *outstanding accomplishments* viewpoint, does not deride or criticize the importance of high intelligence. Many advocates of this second perspective, in fact, consider an IQ test score one useful but not necessarily central measure when identifying academically gifted students. However, this second perspective does emphasize performance in the classroom and on academic tasks as the central or defining characteristic of academic giftedness. According to this second perspective, evidence of academic excellence is the sine qua non to qualify as a gifted student and to qualify for admittance into a gifted program, not high IQ (Pfeiffer, 2013b).

Psychologists and educators who embrace this alternative and second perspective would rely on direct academic performance measures to assess gifted students, not tests of intellectual ability that measure cognitive skills but not necessarily direct evidence of "authentic" academic excellence. The importance of creativity is often emphasized when viewing giftedness through this second lens. Also, the importance of assessing motivation, drive, persistence, and academic passion—clearly nonintellectual factors—is emphasized by many advocates of this alternative way of conceptualizing giftedness (Pfeiffer, 2012, 2013b). These nonintellectual factors, of course, affect the learning and talent development of all students, not only students of exceptionally high ability (S. B. Kaufman, 2013).

The rationale for gifted programs based on an outstanding accomplishments perspective is that students who excel academically have earned and deserve special academic programs because of their outstanding effort and superior classroom accomplishments. Gifted education based on an outstanding accomplishments perspective is slightly but not radically different from gifted education guided by a high intelligence perspective. In gifted programs designed for students demonstrating outstanding accomplishments, programs would consist of highly enriched and academically challenging curricula (Pfeiffer, 2013b).

The third lens through which one can conceptualize academic giftedness, based on the tripartite model, is what I call *potential to excel*. Some students—for any number of reasons—have not been provided enough opportunity or the proper intellectual stimulation to develop what remains latent and as yet undeveloped or underdeveloped intellectual or academic gifts (Pfeiffer, 2013b). This third perspective is based on my experience working with many students of high potential, the experience of countless others, and an abundant body of research (Irving & Hudley, 2009; Nisbett, 2009).

I think most knowledgeable individuals agree that not all students start out on an equal footing. Some children being raised in poverty, children in families in which intellectual and educational activities are neither encouraged nor nurtured in the home or in which English is not the primary language spoken in the home, and children growing up in rural or overcrowded or dangerous communities where intellectual stimulation and educational opportunities are rare are all at a distinct disadvantage for developing their gifts (Ford & Whiting, 2008; Nisbett, 2009; Pfeiffer, 2002, 2012, 2013b).

Psychologists, educators, and parents who advocate for this third perspective view the potential to excel as a defining characteristic of what I have termed the *almost or potentially gifted student.* From this third perspective, the student with high potential to excel is seen as very likely to substantially increase his or her cognitive abilities and academic performance when provided with special resources or placement in a special gifted program. The assumption underlying this third perspective is that with time, an encouraging and highly stimulating environment, and the proper psychoeducational interventions, these students will eventually actualize their yet unrealized high potential and distinguish themselves from their peers as gifted.

In other words, when identifying students with a high likelihood of gifted status, the premise is that with enough nurturance, stimulation, and encouragement, these students will demonstrate significant increases in their IQ and/or significant increases in their academic performance—considerably more than what one would expect from students with less potential. Gifted education based on a potential to excel perspective should consist of a highly motivating and enriched curriculum that may include compensatory interventions.

It is useful to think of academically gifted students in the schools as falling within one or more of these three categories based on the tripartite model of giftedness. The three categories serve to eliminate much of the acrimony often found when local schools or state departments of education try to adopt only one, typically narrowly defined conceptualization of giftedness (e.g., the psychometric or high IQ model, in which a student needs to score above a predetermined cut score to qualify as gifted). The three categories are quite easy to understand. And perhaps more important, each of these three categories lends itself to distinct gifted identification/assessment and curriculum and instruction schemes (Pfeiffer, 2002, 2013b).

Individuals in the first category of the gifted, *students with exceptionally high intelligence*, typically have IQ scores in the top 2% to 5% when compared to other children of the same age.[1] In the early years, these students obtain IQ scores of 135–150 or higher, and in middle school, when tested *above-level* by the regional talent search programs,[2] they obtain SAT or ACT scores in the top 1% to 2% of the population. It is important to emphasize that there is nothing scientific or exact about a 2% or 5% threshold or cut score demarcating intellectually gifted from not intellectually gifted. The myth that giftedness and high IQ are synonymous contributed to the early belief that there is some magical cutoff that separates gifted from not-gifted individuals. Nothing is further from the truth. If we accept that giftedness is a social construction, not something actually real in nature, then we also can appreciate and remember that where we draw the line separating gifted from not-gifted is also arbitrary (Pfeiffer, 2012, 2013b).

The second category of gifted in the tripartite model, *academically gifted learners*, are academically precocious, do exceptionally well in classroom activities and assignments, enjoy learning and academic challenges, and demonstrate persistence and high motivation when facing academic challenges. When tested, they are found to have above average IQs, most typically 120 to 130 or higher, to enjoy school and schooling, and to be highly enthusiastic about learning. They are characteristically among the most capable students and are top-performing students in the class. Teachers love

DON'T FORGET

There is no scientific basis for one particular cut score correctly demarcating students who are gifted from students who are not gifted.

---

1. In many countries the designated cut score is higher, for example in Singapore and Hong Kong giftedness is defined by intellectual functioning in the top 1%.

2. The talent search model, founded at Johns Hopkins University, is an above-level testing program. Regional talent searches have been conducted at Johns Hopkins, Duke, and Northwestern Universities for over thirty years.

to have these students in their classroom. IQ tests are not necessary—although often helpful—to identify this group of gifted learners. Performance in the classroom and on academic tasks is the hallmark that identifies these academically capable learners.

The third category of gifted within the tripartite model consists of *students with high potential to excel.* They are often recognized by their teachers and others as bright or quick learners, hardworking, and highly curious about the world around them. They may not test exceptionally well on standardized aptitude or achievement tests. Their IQ test scores may fall short of established thresholds or cut scores for gifted consideration, sometimes as low as 110–115. Their achievement test scores and classroom performance may also fall short of the outstanding performance demonstrated by academically gifted learners. Yet there is something about these students that conveys latent, partially hidden, and underdeveloped high ability. They are the uncut and unpolished "diamonds in the rough" (Pfeiffer, 2013b).

Ratings by teachers on standardized instruments such as the Gifted Rating Scales (GRS) (Pfeiffer & Jarosewich, 2003) often pick up characteristics that suggest a youngster with considerable untapped potential. The following items are frequently rated by teachers as "way above average" (8 or 9 on the 9-point GRS Likert scale) for students in this third category, students with high potential to excel: learns difficult concepts easily, learns new information quickly, completes academic work unassisted, understands complex academic material, displays an active imagination, strives to achieve, works tenaciously, and takes on new and difficult tasks. Many experienced teachers are often quite perceptive and adept in identifying behaviors and attitudes observed in the classroom that indicate a youngster may have unusually high potential, as yet unrealized or untapped. Successful athletic coaches often see this same type of gifted youngster among young athletes, one with little experience or savvy for the sport but loads of untapped potential to excel if provided the right opportunity and training experiences (Pfeiffer, 2013b).

The unique challenge with the third category of gifted, those with high potential to excel, is that it is always a speculative classification. The classification is based on observational and test data, classroom and contextual information that is integrated to *infer* that if life circumstances had been different, the child would very likely appear as a student of high intelligence and/or a student who is an academically gifted learner. The inference is that, if given a different home and thus different familial, cultural, economic, and/or community circumstances, the child would resemble—and qualify as—a student with high intelligence and/or a student who is an academically gifted learner (Pfeiffer, 2013).

This third category of gifted also carries with it a *prediction*. The prediction is that if the stu-dent is provided with well-conceived, comprehensive, intensive, evidence-based psychoeducational interventions—often requiring a home component—then he or

> **DON'T FORGET**
>
> A student's profile of cognitive abilities and relative standing on measures of IQ can change over time and, in some instances, dramatically.

she will ultimately appear indistinguishable from, or at least very similar to, any student who is already identified as falling within one of the other two gifted categories, high intelligence or academically gifted learner. This remains a highly speculative and untested hypothesis in the gifted education field. It is, however, the principle underlying many gifted programs designed specifically for students of color and cultural diversity whose test scores don't meet minimum school district criteria for gifted consideration (Ford & Whiting, 2008; Worrell & Erwin, 2011).

In summary, these three categories of gifted students constitute different groups of children, with different levels and profiles of abilities and different skill sets and even personality characteristics, although they are not necessarily mutually exclusive. There is, of course, considerable overlap. For example, there are many students with exceptionally high IQ scores who are academically gifted learners with a burning passion to learn. This should come as no surprise to the reader.

However, there are also many extraordinarily academically gifted learners with tested IQ below 120. And there are many students with tested IQ at 130 and above who have not distinguished themselves academically in the classroom, for any number of reasons. The gifted field historically has focused considerable attention on gifted students with high intelligence but undistinguished classroom performance, often known as underachievers (Pfeiffer, 2002, 2013b; Rimm, 2008).

SHOULD WE IDENTIFY GIFTED STUDENTS?

I conclude this part of the discussion by affirming the value and importance of gifted assessment: it provides an opportunity to identify students who will likely benefit the most from the allocation of limited (and often costly) resources to students of uncommon intellectual and academic ability—the gifted. All too often the gifted student's academic needs are not being substantially and appropriately challenged in the classroom or school, and quite often the specialized programs, services, or activities not ordinarily provided in th classroom—not always, but frequently. The tripartite model reminds administrators, educators, psychologists, and policymakers that there are multiple ways of viewing giftedness. And as a result, there is more than one type of special program for the gifted student (Reis, 2006).

There is great value in gifted assessment. I propose an even more radical position: *gifted assessment should be recurring.* Similar to procedures used in most elite sports and performing arts selection situations, procedures for students identified as gifted in the schools should call for them to be reevaluated at least every two years to demonstrate continued outstanding performance when facing increasingly challenging academic hurdles. The assessment should also be open to students who have not been identified as gifted at an earlier time. Recurring gifted assessment represents a more valid prediction of ultimate, out-of-school, real-world success. Recurring gifted assessment also increases the base rate for success of the gifted identification enterprise from a talent development perspective (Ackerman, 2013; Pfeiffer, 2012, 2013b).

Programs for the gifted should reflect the unique learning needs of high-ability students, and should derive from the gifted literature and national and state standards and legislation (Landrum, Callahan, & Shaklee, 2001). There are many different gifted curriculum models and programs (Dixon, 2009; Karnes & Bean, 2009; Rakow, 2011). Gifted assessment should always consider the type of programs, services, and/or resources offered by the school district and available in the community or online. Otherwise, gifted assessment is an intellectual exercise that may lead only to the cherished label of "gifted" for a child—one often sought after by many parents but otherwise not leading to any real, beneficial outcome or change in the curriculum or instruction for the child. When gifted assessment (and gifted classification) is linked to a quality gifted program—often marked by an academically rigorous and more challenging and fast-paced curriculum with high-order analytical and critical thinking skills and hands-on discovery learning (Berger, 2008; Pfeiffer, 2013b)—there follows the potential for real benefit to the youngster and society. Many children in the top 5, 10, and even 20% of the intelligence distribution will have a huge and disproportionately large influence on our culture, economy, institutions, and quality of life in the future. In essence, our future depends in large measure on how successfully we identify and educate our next generation of gifted students.

PURPOSES OF GIFTED ASSESSMENT

Up to this point, we have focused on *gifted assessment as a means of identifying high-ability students*, as evidenced by uncanny intellectual abilities, outstanding classroom performance, or evidence of potential for outstanding academic perform-ance. The primary rationale for gifted identification is to recognize and serve those students of exceptional ability or potential who frequently need special educational programs or resources not presently available in the regular classroom. This remains the number one purpose for gifted assessment in the schools. However, there are other reasons for gifted assessment, including the following:

- Providing information to support admission to special schools or gifted programs
- Understanding the unique strengths and weaknesses (asynchronies) of an exceptionally bright child or ascertaining the degree of giftedness
- Assessing growth in areas such as creativity or critical thinking with implications for curriculum modification, student "fit" within a gifted program, and program evaluation
- Assisting in the diagnosis of twice exceptionality
- Discerning factors potentially contributing to underachievement and/or low motivation
- Providing information on homeschooling
- Determining appropriate grade placement and/or making decisions about acceleration

We turn next in Chapter 2 to different conceptions of giftedness and how these conceptions can lead to different, although not necessarily incompatible, ways to assess giftedness.

🪶 TEST YOURSELF 🪶

1. **There is a genetic influence in the expression of giftedness:**
   a. True
   b. False

2. **The author's definition of giftedness explicitly excludes mention of culture to reinforce the idea that giftedness is culture-free:**
   a. True
   b. False

3. **The author contends that academically gifted students are likely to benefit from special educational programs or resources that align with their unique profile of abilities and interests:**
   a. True
   b. False

(continued)

(*continued*)

4. **Lewis Terman identified youngsters with IQ test scores at or above 120 in selecting the group of gifted children that he followed:**
    a. True
    b. False

5. **James Gallagher pointed out that we spend very little money in the United States to support gifted students in the schools:**
    a. True
    b. False

6. **The author disputes the view that the concept of gifted is a social construction:**
    a. True
    b. False

7. **The tripartite model of giftedness consists of three parts: intelligence, creativity, and motivation:**
    a. True
    b. False

Answers: 1. True; 2. False; 3. True; 4. False; 5. True; 6. False; 7. False.

Two

CONCEPTIONS OF GIFTEDNESS GUIDE GIFTED ASSESSMENT

A s mentioned in the preceding chapter, there are many different ways to conceptualize giftedness. Sternberg and Davidson (2005) edited a volume that includes contributions from more than twenty authorities in the field describing a wide variety of conceptions of giftedness. In a recent book I provide a discussion and synthesis of a number of models (Pfeiffer, 2013b). The interested reader may want to review these resources for more a more in-depth discussion of different conceptions of giftedness.

In this chapter, I discuss four conceptions of giftedness that presently dominate thinking in the gifted field. Many authors have proposed their own models, which have unique and theoretically relevant elements. However, most of the widely cited models in the gifted field fit nicely into one of the four groups described in this chapter. It is important to emphasize that these different models imply somewhat different ways to assess gifts. I describe key elements within each of the four models so that the reader can begin thinking about how different models lend themselves to the selection of different gifted assessment procedures and even specific tests. This is one important theme that is a central thesis of this book: although practitioners might wish otherwise, there unfortunately is *not* one correct assessment protocol for high-ability students. As will be discussed throughout this book, the choice of tests or procedures to use in a gifted assessment battery depends on a number of factors. These factors include the conception of giftedness that the practitioner (and school district) holds as "true" or finds most useful; the vision, mission, goals, and curriculum of the gifted program that the student is being evaluated for; and even factors such as school district and state education policy.

The different ways that giftedness has been conceptualized by different authors vary in their level of sophistication, and also vary in how easily they can be translated into psychological and psychoeducational assessment. They also vary in their relative emphasis on the role of individual differences, developmental

≡ *Rapid Reference 2.1   Four Conceptions of Giftedness*
....

- Traditional psychometric view (high IQ model)
- Talent development model
- Expert performance model
- Multiple intelligences model

antecedents, genetics, and the impact of the environment (Ackerman, 2013; Simonton, 2013; Wai, 2013). It is important to emphasize that to the extent that assessment is guided by theory, the different models lend themselves to different gifted assessment procedures and tests. The four gifted models that I introduce in this chapter are the *traditional psychometric view*, *talent development models*, the *expert performance perspective*, and the *multiple intelligences* model.

These four models are not contradictory to my *tripartite model*, which was introduced in the first chapter. In fact, they are in some ways complementary. And they share some degree of overlap among one another as well.

Julian Stanley's mathematically and verbally precocious model, for example, reflects thinking that cuts across two groups, the traditional psychometric view of high intelligence and talent development models (Stanley, 1976, 1990, 2000). Françoys Gagné's developmental, differentiated model of giftedness and talent (Gagné, 2005), Joseph Renzulli's three-ring conception of giftedness (Renzulli, Siegle, Reis, Gavin, & Ree, 2009; Renzulli, 2005b, 2011), and Rena Subotnik's developmental model (Subotnik, 2003; Subotnik, Olszewski-Kubilius, & Worrell, 2011) all fit within the second way of viewing giftedness (talent development models) and are fully compatible with my tripartite model. Finally, the work of my colleague K. Anders Ericsson at Florida State University epitomizes a somewhat novel way of thinking about giftedness, with a strong emphasis on the environment, from an expert performance perspective (Ericsson, 1996, 2013; Ericsson & Charness, 1995).

Before discussing the four models or ways of viewing giftedness, it is important to mention that there is growing consensus among most authorities within the gifted field that giftedness is best viewed as *specific*, that the expression of giftedness occurs within a particular domain (Mayer, 2005). I agree with this viewpoint, at least when we consider students of high ability beginning around the 3rd or 4th grade (Pfeiffer, 2013b). In preschool and in the early grades,

DON'T FORGET
....
The tripartite model of giftedness offers three different ways to proceed with a gifted assessment.

≡ Rapid Reference 2.2   Julian Stanley's Talent Search Model

- Based on above-level assessment (also known as out-of-level assessment).
- Incorporates academically challenging and fast-paced educational programs.
- Regional talent search programs exist at Johns Hopkins, Duke, and Northwestern Universities.

one could make a compelling argument, in my opinion, that giftedness—or rather the prediction of academic giftedness— is not yet necessarily specific to one particular domain but rather more a reflection of general intellectual ability

CAUTION

No one theory or model of giftedness is correct!

and potential to excel. For example, most would agree that a 3-year-old child who is reading at a 2nd-grade level is gifted.

TRADITIONAL PSYCHOMETRIC VIEW

Most readers are probably familiar with the traditional psychometric view of giftedness, which in large part conceptualizes high intellectual ability as the hallmark and defining feature of giftedness. This view is almost always presented in graduate school courses on IQ testing. In essence, this perspective views high tested intelligence and giftedness as synonymous (Pfeiffer, 2002, 2012, 2013b). Many of the earliest researchers in the gifted field investigated the scientific basis of giftedness from a domain-general perspective, using the terms *gifted*, *genius*, and *talented* interchangeably. Francis Galton's book *Hereditary Genius* (1869) intro- duced the notion of intellectual genius to the public. Galton analyzed the family lineage of distinguished men and found that genius ran in families and concluded that genius must be genetically inherited. His estimations of genius were subjective, not based on psychometric measures, but nonetheless his work set the stage for the scientific study of giftedness (Ackerman, 2013; S. B. Kaufman & Sternberg, 2008).

Galton's work was followed by Charles Spearman's (1904) investigations. Spearman used the newly developed statistical technique of factor analysis to determine that there was a significant amount of shared variance across a great many cognitive tests. He called this ubiquitous shared ability g, or general intelligence (recently labeled *psychometric g*). The factor analyses that he ran on the set of cognitive tests he had obtained also uncovered specific abilities unique to one or two of the tests, and he labeled each of these specific abilities *s*. At around the same time as Spearman was using factor analysis to discover the ubiquitous *g* factor, Alfred Binet and Theodore Simon (1916) developed a mental scale to identify students struggling in the Paris schools who might need alternative education. Binet and Simon's scale was perhaps the first test to include assessment of higher-level cognitive skills.

Lewis Terman adapted Binet and Simon's scale and created the Stanford-Binet Intelligence Scale, one of the first tests used to identify gifted students (Terman, 1916). This scale yielded a global score that viewed giftedness from a domain-general perspective and intelligence as a single entity. Terman proposed a classification system for use in the schools in which a student who obtained an IQ score of 135 or above was considered *moderately gifted*, above 150 *exceptionally gifted*, and above 180 *severely and/or profoundly gifted* (Terman, 1925; Webb, Meckstroth, & Tolan, 1982; S. B. Kaufman & Sternberg, 2008). This classification is still popular today, both in the United States and internationally.

Psychometric *g* or IQ continues to be the leading indicator for gifted identification in a great majority of gifted programs in the United States and internationally (Sternberg, Jarvin, & Grigorenko, 2011; McClain & Pfeiffer, 2012). There are several reasons for this. IQ as a single indice is easy to understand. The IQ score is a straightforward yet elegant and even sophisticated solution to the question of what is meant by giftedness. Another reason for the appeal of the IQ score as representative of giftedness is that it provides an exact number of apparently mathematical precision; as a single, quantified number, it appears to be a fair, impartial, objective, and even unarguable arbiter for practitioners to use when deciding which students fall at or above a set cut score demarcating giftedness. Of course there also is a huge research literature supporting the validity of the IQ test score. Arguably, the validity of the IQ construct is supported by more published research than any other psychological construct is (Neisser et al., 1996; Nisbett, 2009). It is undeniable that IQ predicts school performance moderately well. IQ also predicts many other important life outcomes. However, there are measures of other psychological constructs that have also shown promise in predicting school performance and life success (Simonton, 2013; Sternberg et al., 2011). We will return to this point shortly, when discussing the talent development model.

Another reason for the high appeal of the IQ test in gifted assessment is that it is objective and relatively easy to administer, score, and interpret, at least for professionals who have received training and supervision in individual cognitive assessment. We tend to select tools designed to measure things that we understand, and IQ and related proxies for general intellectual ability, or *g*, are easy to understand. Finally, IQ enjoys a long and storied history and great familiarity. Many people remain comfortable viewing IQ and giftedness as synonymous. Test publishers contribute to the widespread acceptance of the psychometric view of giftedness because of their significant commitment to successfully marketing and selling their most prized products.

There are many researchers and test publishers within the psychometric camp who don't necessarily endorse a domain-specific model of intelligence. Louis Thurstone (1938) was perhaps the first researcher who challenged the prevailing domain-general model and proposed the notion of *specific abilities* as an alternative way of conceptualizing intelligence. Thurstone used a different method of factor analysis than Charles Spearman did, and identified seven primary and independent mental abilities. A debate between Spearman and Thurstone continued for a time, but ultimately a growing body of studies supported hierarchical factor models of intelligence. The hierarchical models had general ability at the very top, more general higher cognitive abilities at the next level, and various more specific cognitive skills lower in the hierarchy. The hierarchical model that has gained greatest acceptance in the psychometric community is Carroll's (1993) three-stratum theory. In Carroll's model, Stratum I consists of highly specialized cognitive skills, Stratum II has somewhat less specific and broader domains of intellectual abilities, and Stratum III, at the apex, has only one ability, the *g* factor.

Recently, Carroll's model and another hierarchical model, the Horn and Cattell (1966) model of fluid and crystallized intelligence were synthesized into the Cattell-Horn-Carroll (CHC) theory (Flanagan & Harrison, 2005). Although the CHC model includes *g* at the apex, its main emphasis is on the measurement of those factors and cognitive abilities in the middle stratum (S. B. Kaufman & Sternberg, 2008). The CHC theory has influenced the development and revision of a number of IQ tests used in gifted identification, including the fifth edition of the Stanford-Binet (Roid, 2003), the second edition of the Kaufman Assessment Battery for Children (KABC-II) (Kaufman & Kaufman, 2004a), and the third edition of the Woodcock-Johnson Tests of Cognitive Abilities (WJ III) (Woodcock, McGrew, & Mather, 2001). More will be said about these and other ability tests in Chapter 4.

TALENT DEVELOPMENT MODELS

Quite clearly, the most familiar and still the most popular conceptualization of giftedness reflects the traditional psychometric view. However, a growing minority of recent theorizing about giftedness falls within a second conceptualization of giftedness, which I label talent development models. I will briefly discuss three talent development models within this second grouping to illustrate the richness of the talent development models and how they depart from the traditional psychometric view. Respecting the principle of full disclosure to the reader, I admit that my heart belongs to this second conceptualization.

Differentiated Model of Giftedness and Talent

Professor Françoys Gagné conceptualizes giftedness as natural abilities that are transformed through learning and training into high-level skills in particular occupational fields. In this regard, he views gifts as residing within the child, the result of favorable genetics, prenatal environment, and neurobiological status. Gagné's conceptualization is unique in distinguishing gifts from talents (Gagné, 2005, 2009).

His model, which he calls the DMGT (differentiated model of giftedness and talent), proposes four broad aptitude domains: intellectual, creative, socioaffective, and sensorimotor. Each of these four aptitude domains can be subdivided. Gagné acknowledges that many different and competing classification systems exist at this next level (e.g., the intellectual domain could be subdivided according to verbal and nonverbal intelligence, fluid and crystallized intelligence, Carroll's [1993] three-level system, Howard Gardner's [1983,1993] popular and provocative theory of multiple intelligences, Robert Sternberg's triarchic and expertise theories [Sternberg, 2001; Sternberg & Davidson, 1986], or any one of the many other views on intelligence). The same is true for the other three broad aptitude domains in the DMGT model.

Gagné proposes that talents progressively emerge from the *systematic transformation* of aptitudes—in the case of the gifted, high aptitudes transform into well-developed skills characteristic of a particular field or domain. This conception of giftedness clearly reflects an appreciation for development over time, viewing "the talent development process consisting of transforming specific natural abilities into the skills that define competence or expertise in a given occupational field" (Gagné, 2005, p. 103). In this regard, his talent development ideas are compatible with the ideas proposed by other theorists supportive of a developmental view, such as Rena Subotnik and her colleagues (Subotnik, 2003; Subotnik et al., 2011), and with my own thinking on the tripartite model of giftedness (Pfeiffer, 2013b).

Gagné does not shy away from confronting the thorny question of who the gifted are, and by implication, how to assess giftedness in the schools. His DMGT conceptualization posits a five-level system of cutoffs for giftedness. He sets the first threshold at 10%, which he labels *mildly gifted*. This equates to an IQ of approximately 120, with, on average, one in ten students considered mildly gifted. This cutoff is consistent with Joseph Renzulli's model, which I will discuss shortly. Gagné sets his second threshold at 1%, which he labels *moderately gifted* and which accommodates students with IQ scores of 135. The next three levels are for the *highly gifted* (145 IQ), *exceptionally gifted* (155 IQ), and *extremely gifted* (165 IQ). Of course, most of us who work with high-ability students have very few opportunities to evaluate a student at the highest levels (1 in 10,000 for an IQ of 155) and 1 in 100,000 for an IQ of 165. In my practice over the last thirty-five years, I've evaluated fewer than a dozen students who tested at this level. A helpful resource when working with this highly rare group of extremely intelligent students is Gross (1994).

There is both a heuristic appeal and simple elegance to Gagné's developmental model. It is one of the first developmental models formulated in response to the field's early overemphasis on wholly genetic determinants of giftedness (S. B. Kaufman & Sternberg, 2008). I might add that Françoys Gagné is a charming, gracious, and persuasive theorist whose ideas have captivated many in the gifted field. I consider him a colleague and friend and, although we disagree on some points, respect his passionate efforts to explicate for the field the concepts of natural abilities and the developmental process.

Subotnik's Developmental Transitions in Giftedness and Talent

Next I turn to Rena Subotnik, whose ideas on talent development in many ways parallel the DMGT model proposed by Gagné. Subotnik is director of the Center for Gifted Education at the American Psychological Association. Her work has had a profound impact on my own thinking about high-ability individuals. During my tenure as executive director of Duke University's Talent Identification Program (TIP), I invited her to speak on the Duke campus because I was so impressed by her compelling and provocative ideas on how a talent development model helps those who work in the gifted field understand how general and specific abilities transform into competencies, then expertise, and ultimately outstanding performance (Subotnik, 2009). I was particularly persuaded by how Subotnik's firsthand experience in observing and studying gifted artists helped formulate her thinking on talent development. In many ways it paralleled my own personal experience of observing and working with gifted athletes, which I will briefly share before providing a description of Subotnik's views.

My own story provides insights into why Subotnik's ideas on talent development so personally resonate with my own thinking and views on the gifted. My youngest daughter, now an adult, was identified at age 5 as having precocious athletic ability—analogous to the early identification of intellectual giftedness. By age 10, my daughter had been identified by and invited to train with the U.S. Youth Soccer Olympic Development Program, known as the ODP (Vincent & Glamser, 2006). Her elite youth career began as a player on the ODP "under 13" soccer team. A few years later, she was selected to the ODP regional team, which is the feeder for the U.S. national soccer team. She was a young girl with a whole lot of natural athletic ability.

As a psychologist with already considerable experience in working with young kids of extraordinarily precocious and distinct intellectual ability, it was a revelation to be exposed to the world of elite youth athletics. I learned a great deal shepherding my young daughter through the world of competitive youth sports. My experience broadened my view on talent development in the world of competitive sports (Côté, Baker, & Abernethy, 2003; Wolfenden & Holt, 2005). My experience as a parent of an elite athlete expanded my appreciation for what is required to develop expertise at the highest levels of performance (Durand-Bush & Salmela, 2002; Ericsson, 1996). My experience on the sidelines of soccer fields, in the locker rooms of highly competitive soccer teams, and in talking with elite soccer coaches introduced me, firsthand, to the importance of motivation, coaching, deliberate practice, mentors, supportive team members, and the ways that competition can be helpful but also detrimental to a high-ability athlete's motivation and self-esteem (Pfeiffer, 2013a, 2013b). It also helped me to formulate my thinking on gifted assessment. Much of what I learned while on the sidelines influenced my thinking about the development of intellectual gifted-ness—the importance of grit, motivation, passion, persistence, opportunity, precise feedback, and good fortune. These lessons applied to highly gifted, world-class athletes. Much of what I learned through my involvement with elite youth athletics influenced my views on what it takes to be successful and ultimately make your mark in any field, including the classroom, lab, courtroom, or surgical suite. What I learned on the sidelines of playing fields influenced my own thinking on gifted students in the classroom, which is consistent with Rena Subotnik's ideas.

My experience observing and spending time with young elite athletes radically changed my view of giftedness—from a view that giftedness was a primarily static and innate ability that a few kids had and most did not have, to a view that gifted-ness is a much more complex developmental process. I came to view giftedness as the unfolding of God-given general abilities and domain-specific skills along with distinct personality characteristics and attitudes toward learning, challenge, and competition. And these necessary conditions unfolded within the context of environmental support over time marked by tons of practice; precise, facilitative instruction and feedback; supportive mentors; and an unswerving passion for what you're learning in harmony with ambition to reach your full potential. My experience on the sidelines began as early as 1990 to shape my own views of giftedness within a developmental perspective (Pfeiffer, 2013a). My personal experience helped me appreciate that a youngster with extraordinary ability could be viewed as gifted at one point in time but, due to any number of compromising factors or bad luck, not necessarily continue along a developmental trajectory that would lead that individual to be viewed later in life as gifted (Pfeiffer, 2012, 2013a).

Now let's get back to Rena Subotnik. Subotnik reminds us that giftedness is a dynamic construct, that giftedness develops over time, and that giftedness is not the same as high IQ. Her developmental model posits that gifted children transition first from broad educational experiences in the early years to more narrowly focused domains in colleges, institutes, and conservatories. And if these same learners continue on a trajectory of talent development, they will engage in experiences and opportunities that afford them "the pursuit of scholarly productivity, innovation, or artistry." In other words, her model views "talent development as the transformation of abilities into competencies, competencies into expertise, and expertise into outstanding performance or seminal ideas" (Subotnik, 2009, p. 155).

Subotnik's developmental model is similar in some ways to Gagné's conceptualization. One notable difference is that Subotnik's model expands and extends the vision of gifted education and takes a long view in articulating the ultimate goal of our efforts with high-ability kids. Her position emphasizes that the goal of gifted education should be recruiting a large number of bright kids of uncommon ability and providing them with a range of facilitative opportunities and experiences over childhood, adolescence, and even young adult life to maximize the likelihood that as many as possible will ultimately reach the highest levels of expertise, creativity, or eminence in their various fields. The reader will note that this model is very similar to the youth soccer development model that I described earlier. I wholeheartedly agree with and endorse this developmental model for high-ability kids, not only in sports but also in the intellectual and educational realm.

From a gifted assessment perspective, it is worth noting a few key concepts in Subotnik's talent development model. She envisions talent development as consisting of a series of transitions and stages, with environmental factors and psychosocial variables including motivation, persistence, drive, the will to overcome obstacles, and interest in a field playing central roles in helping to propel the child along the talent development path. At each stage of development, her model suggests that different factors come into play. For example, in Stage 1 which is a "transition from ability to competency," high levels of intrinsic motivation, persistence, responsiveness to external rewards, and teachability are critical factors (Subotnik, 2009). This is consistent with my work with young soccer players who successfully transition from general athletic ability to gaining a considerable soccer-specific skill and knowledge. *Note that motivation, persistence, and what I term* teachability *are three constructs within Subotnik's model that should be measured as part of a gifted assessment protocol.*

Subotnik recognizes that not every domain or field follows exactly the same trajectory, and that future research will, we hope, illuminate age and gender differences across various domain trajectories. For example, there are likely significant differences in the age of onset and the relative influence of facilitative factors that promote soccer expertise versus gymnastics expertise or, indeed, expertise in aerospace physics versus surgical medicine. Subotnik expects that future research will also illuminate differences in the relative contributions and roles that family, school, mentors, psychosocial variables, personality, and community play in the unfolding of talents across different domains. It is exciting to imagine that at some future time we may actually have algorithms for developmental trajectories across different fields.

Subotnik believes that definitions of giftedness must change over the course of a child's development and path toward eminence in a specific field or domain. She also believes that *giftedness should be defined in terms of actual accomplishment* (Subotnik, 2003; Worrell, Subotnik, & Olszewski-Kubilius, 2013). This is not an insignificant point. It is, in fact, a rather contentious position for many in the gifted field who hold strongly to the view that giftedness and high IQ are the same and that any person with a very high IQ should be recognized as gifted, irrespective of his or her ultimate accomplishments or lack thereof in later life. I will provide an admittedly overly simplified example to illustrate this point. Assume that an intellectually bright 19-year-old who was a National Merit semifinalist in high school, with a tested IQ on the Stanford-Binet of 144 and SAT scores in the 95th percentile, drops out of a small, elite liberal arts college in his freshman year. He finds himself living at home and working delivering pizza for Domino's. Many in the gifted field would argue that this young man is unquestionably still gifted. They might go on to argue that he is, in fact, a perfect example of a "gifted underachiever." I am fairly confident that Subotnik would disagree with this position. I imagine that she would say that this young man demonstrated, at an earlier time in his life, unequivocally sterling intellectual potential and great promise, based on his high school academic performance and tested IQ and SAT scores. I further suspect that she would go on to argue that, nevertheless, for any number of possible reasons—medical, psychological, family, sociocultural, and/or environmental—this young man either didn't or wasn't able to take advantage of his potential talents. She in fact states that "giftedness in children is probably best described as potential." Her point is that maintaining the label of gifted in adolescence and adulthood requires turning (or transforming, to use Gagné's model) potential into actual outstanding performance or accomplishment (Subotnik et al., 2011; Worrell et al., 2013).

I created this fictional case of the 19-year-old college dropout to illustrate a point. I suspect you can guess that my view on the construct of giftedness is in line with the position I have attributed to Subotnik. I would still consider this young man very bright intellectually. I have no argument at all with that view. But I see no value or utility in continuing to label this young man as gifted. I agree that definitions of giftedness should change over the course of development. And for this reason, I am not so sure that it is helpful to go beyond stating that our fictional pizza delivery man is very bright and employed in a job that is obviously far below his intellectual capability. Is he still gifted? Well, according to Subotnik's model, perhaps not. This gets back to a point that I made in the first chapter. I advocate and strongly believe that *gifted assessment in the schools be a recurring, periodic process*. I suggest that it occur at least every two years. This is consistent with a talent development model. It is also consistent with the "successive hurdles approach" to assessment, recommended by Meehl and Rosen (1955) over fifty years ago to mitigate errors of prediction when base rates are low—which they are by definition among high-ability students.

Stanley's Talent Search Model

In the introduction to this chapter, I suggested that Julian Stanley's model incorporates features of both the traditional psychometric view and a talent development model. His work is too important to ignore, which is why I've included it in this discussion of conceptions of giftedness. During my tenure as executive director of the Duke University Talent Identification Program, I had the good fortune of visiting with Julian Stanley at Johns Hopkins University and became intimately familiar with the talent search model that he developed (Stanley, 1976). His *talent search model* is based on an above-level testing program that is both simple and elegant. Stanley was familiar with Leta Hollingworth's use of above-level testing, in which a student is administered a test designed for students several years older (Stanley, 1990). Stanley initially piloted his model with math prodigies, who were given the mathematics section of the Scholastic Aptitude Test (now the SAT-I); he followed this initial pilot with large-scale testing of bright 7th and 8th graders, who took a test designed for college-bound 11th and 12th graders (Assouline & Lupkowski-Shoplik, 2012).

The talent search model is predicated on a highly ingenious idea proposed by Stanley. He recognized that administering an above-level test (in other words, a test designed for older students) to already identified bright students (in the top 3–5% on grade-level standardized tests) would provide a much higher ceiling for further differentiating the range of abilities among a cohort of bright children. Using above-level testing, he was able to cherry pick the very brightest from among an already select group of high-ability students.

Stanley recognized in his work at Johns Hopkins with these extraordinarily bright middle school students that discovering uncommon ability was not enough. One also needed to provide these uniquely gifted youngsters with a different type of educational experience. A second component of his talent search model was formulating academically challenging and fast-paced educational programs for these students. On the campuses of Johns Hopkins and, shortly thereafter, Duke and Northwestern Universities, summer programs were developed for young students who scored at the highest levels on the above-level testing program. At this writing, the talent search model has expanded exponentially with summer programs—and now weekend, home study, and online educational programs—offered on campuses nationwide and globally for students identified through regional talent searches.

The talent search model is perhaps the best-researched model of talent development (Subotnik et al., 2011). For example, many talent search students complete one or more years of mathematics in a three-week summer program (Brody & Benbow, 1987; Kolitch & Brody, 1992; Stanley, 2000). There is considerable empirical support as well for the predictive validity of the domain-specific identification system used by talent search programs (Olszewski-Kubilius, 2004). Youth identified before age 13 as demonstrating profound mathematical or verbal reasoning abilities have been tracked longitudinally for nearly three decades. And their outcomes, as a group, have been quite impressive (Kell, Lubinski, & Benbow, 2013). The Florida Governor's School for Space Science and Technology pilot program, for which I served as codirector, was designed specifically to incorporate Stanley's talent search model. Although we looked at general measures of intellectual ability in our admissions screening process, we put much greater weight on evidence of each applicant's specific abilities in science and mathematics. In selecting finalists for our STEM-focused summer academy affiliated with the Kennedy Space Center and NASA, however, we also considered each applicant's level of motivation, persistence, and passion for learning—added ingredients that we felt strengthened the recipe for predicting who would benefit most from our high-powered summer academy (Pfeiffer, 2013b). We also looked at personality characteristics among our large applicant pool. These additional constructs that we considered as part of the admissions packet—including constructs that I label *strengths of the heart*—are not considered part of the talent search model. We next turn briefly to the ideas of Joseph Renzulli, like Julian Stanley, another extremely influential figure in the gifted field.

Renzulli's Three-Ring Conception of Giftedness

One of the most familiar models of giftedness among educators is Joseph Renzulli's three-ring model (Renzulli, 1984, 2009). Renzulli contends that there are two types of giftedness, which he refers to as *schoolhouse giftedness* and *creative-productive giftedness*. Schoolhouse giftedness refers to high test scores and exceptionally good grades. It is the type of giftedness that most of us who work in the schools are familiar with. It resembles *giftedness through the lens of high intelligence* in my tripartite model. The second type of giftedness, according to Renzulli, is more indicative of what is seen in distinguished adolescents and eminent adults who actually produce creative and extraordinary things in culturally valued fields. In this regard, Renzulli's creative-productive giftedness is not dissimilar to the second type of giftedness in my tripartite model: *giftedness through the lens of outstanding accomplishments*.

Renzulli's three-ring conception of giftedness interfaces with his two types of giftedness. He contends that the basis for developing giftedness requires the intersection of three components: above average intellectual ability, task commitment, and creativity. Note that his conceptualization of giftedness does not require extraordinary IQ, as many other models do. It requires only substantially above average IQ, a lower threshold and a significant departure from most other conceptualizations in the gifted field. Also, according to this model a student could present with unbelievably through-the-roof IQ but low levels of task commitment and/or creativity and *not* be considered gifted.

In more recent writing, Renzulli has suggested, based on work that he labels Operation Houndstooth (Renzulli, 2005b), that giftedness requires, in addition to above average ability, creativity, and motivation, a number of other factors including optimism, courage, romance with a topic or discipline, sensitivity to human concerns, mental energy, and a sense of destiny (Sternberg et al., 2011). These other factors are similar to my own thinking about the importance of strengths of the heart (Pfeiffer, 2013a).

The foundation for Renzulli's gifted model employs markedly liberal thresholds for each of the components: students need only demonstrate above average ability, motivation, and creativity to be considered gifted. Operationally translating this model into an actual gifted identification decision-making rubric,

Renzulli contends that the talent pool for developing giftedness in the schools should consist of the top 15% to 20% of students in these three constructs (Subotnik et al., 2011).

Renzulli is an educator and most of his work has focused on how his triadic or three-ring conceptualization can be applied to the school curriculum. Renzulli and his collaborator (and wife) Sally Reis propose three types of enriched instruction that facilitate the development of talent among gifted students (Reis & Renzulli, 2009a, 2009b). In Stage 1, young students identified as gifted are introduced to high appeal and highly enriched educational activities in domains of interest. In Stage 2, gifted students are provided specific and advanced instruction in domains of interest. This is clearly a transition to more serious pedagogy. Finally, in Stage 3, students are presented with experiences that encourage creative productivity that may eventually lead to adult career contributions that benefit society. It is no exaggeration to state that Renzulli's writings have had a huge impact on the differentiated curriculum and instructional pedagogy for gifted learners. In my consultations and visits with school districts across the United States, I have been impressed by the number of gifted educators who are familiar with and have adopted parts of the Renzulli model for their work with high-ability students. Before concluding my brief discussion on Renzulli, I should add that his three-stage instructional model for gifted students is similar to the elite youth soccer talent development model that helped formulate my own thinking on talent development among gifted students.

EXPERT PERFORMANCE PERSPECTIVE

Anders Ericsson has enjoyed a highly successful career investigating the concept of expertise and expert performance and how it is accomplished. His research has focused on identifying and "specifying the mediating mechanisms that can be assessed by process-tracing and experimental studies" (Ericsson, Roring, & Nandagopal, 2007, p. 13). Ericsson does not believe that IQ tests play a useful role in predicting performance domains of expertise. He has built a career advocating attention to the power of environmental variables, including what he labels *deliberate practice* and its importance in explaining most of the variance in extraordinary accomplishments. He clearly downplays the relevance of innate ability, heritability, and individual differences in predicting which children will become gifted adults (Ericsson, 2013). Critics of his model label his position "the most extreme exemplar of the environmentalist viewpoint" (Ackerman, 2013, p. 1). Let's take a moment to discuss what Ericsson means by deliberate practice, because it is critical to his model.

In a widely cited study of elite chess players, Nobel Prize winner Herbert Simon and William Chase (with whom Ericsson studied) proposed a "ten year rule," based on their observations that it took a decade of intensive study and practice to reach the top ranks of chess. Even Bobby Fisher was no exception (Colvin, 2008). Ericsson agreed with Simon and Chase and has conducted numerous studies that corroborate the idea that deliberate practice makes all the difference between expert performers and average adults across almost all domains. Deliberate practice is characterized by several components: it is activity designed specifically to improve performance, often under the watchful eye and close supervision of a teacher, mentor, or coach; it includes a good deal of specific and continuous feedback; it must be repeated a lot; and it is highly demanding mentally—it isn't fun! (Colvin, 2008; Coyle, 2009). Deliberate practice is meant to stretch the individual beyond his or her comfort zone and beyond the current skills level; it requires that the learner and/or teacher identify and isolate very specific elements of performance that need to be learned or improved upon to further development toward expertise (Ericsson, Krampe, & Tesch-Romer, 1993; Syed, 2010). Deliberate practice is effortful, it requires feedback if the person is to improve, and, as Ericsson and his colleagues remind us, it is not inherently enjoyable (Ericsson, 1996, 2013).

The reader may be wondering if a section on Ericsson's work on deliberate practice and the acquisition of expert performance belongs in a chapter on different conceptions of giftedness. This is a fair question. Some authorities in the gifted field have embraced Ericsson's ideas as relevant to giftedness and talent development. This is in spite of his vigorous opposition to the significance of natural abilities. For example, Ericsson et al. (2007) write, "With the exception of fixed genetic factors determining body size and height, we were unable to find evidence for innate constraints to the attainment of elite achievement for healthy individuals" (p. 3). Some in the gifted field find this conclusion misguided and even heresy. Although I don't personally get upset with Ericsson's de-emphasizing individual differences or with his extreme environmental position, I don't agree with many of his ideas. They run counter to my own experience working with high-ability children and youth for over thirty years. And I think that his extreme environmental view ignores considerable research supporting the importance of natural ability, individual differences, early experiences, and critical periods (Ackerman, 2013). Irrespective of one's feelings about Ericsson's position, his focus on the importance of deliberate practice, sustained effort in the face of frustration, and years of effortful practice if one aspires to reach a level of expertise provides the gifted field with important ideas to consider.

MULTIPLE INTELLIGENCES MODEL

The fourth model was proposed by one of the most widely recognized names among school psychologists in the gifted field, Howard Gardner (Robertson, Pfeiffer, & Taylor, 2011). Howard Gardner is a professor at Harvard who caught the attention of the public in 1983 with the publication of his groundbreaking and highly popular book *Frames of Mind* (Gardner, 1983). In this book Gardner proposed the idea of multiple intelligences. In his model, multiple intelligences are perceived as independent cognitive systems, *not* hierarchically nested under one general ability factor (Gardner, 1983, 1993). Gardner's theory of human intelligences was formulated through a selective analysis of the research literature, not psychometric techniques such as factor analysis. His review and synthesis of a wide-ranging literature in support of his theory of multiple intelligences included studies of patients with brain damage, idiot savants, and prodigies; evolutionary history; and findings from psychometric and experimental psychology studies. Gardner concluded that there was compelling evidence for at least eight separate intelligences: linguistic, logical-mathematical, spatial, musical, bodily-kinesthetic, interpersonal, intrapersonal, and naturalist. He has recently added a ninth intelligence—existential intelligence—to his list (Dai, 2010; S. B. Kaufman & Sternberg, 2008).

Gardner's theory of multiple intelligences has had a profound impact on the educational field, although much less influence on the gifted field. His ideas have played a substantial role in greatly expanding educators' views on intelligence—and not just in the United States. In my international travels I have found that his theory of multiple intelligences is often among the first topics that colleagues in other countries want to discuss. Among the most significant aspects of Gardner's revolutionary theory is the idea that intelligence is not a single, unitary construct. This single idea, and his highly engaging and distinctly readable writing style, made Gardner and his theory akin to a rock star and his music for some in gifted education. Many intervention programs have been published by followers of the multiple intelligences model. The public and lay media have been infatuated with his appealing theory, particularly since many incorrectly interpreted it as suggesting that everyone is gifted in something.

Gardner's theory has not gone without criticism, however. First and foremost, there is no published research that has tested the theory of multiple intelligences as a whole. Second, the intelligences that Gardner proposes were based on highly selective reviews of the literature that he cites in support of his theory. Studies that did not support his theory were not included in his synthesis of the literature on human intelligence. Third, he omits a considerable amount of the psychometric literature on intelligence, which arguably should be included in any unifying theory of intelligence. Fourth, there exist only a handful of measures of his eight (or nine) intelligences, and many of those that do exist display less than adequate psychometric rigor. This makes it difficult to evaluate the efficacy of classroom interventions based on a multiple intelligences model (S. B. Kaufman & Sternberg, 2008; Pfeiffer, 2013b). It also leaves the practitioner at a loss for a way to measure the different intelligences! Irrespective of these criticisms Gardner's theory of multiple intelligences has had a profound impact on the educational field, and even on pop culture. It doesn't, however, lend itself easily to operationalizing exactly who the gifted students in the schools are and how a practitioner might go about identifying these students applying Gardner's model.

THEORY OF SUCCESSFUL INTELLIGENCE: WICS

Before I conclude this chapter, I thought the reader might enjoy a brief description of a recent proposal by Robert Sternberg for an alternative way to look at intelligence. I won't muddy the waters by treating his proposal as a fifth model. It's not quite a model. But his *theory of successful intelligence* is fascinating and provocative, as many of Robert Sternberg's ideas are, and worth mentioning before we close this chapter on alternative conceptions of giftedness.

Robert Sternberg conducted most of his research and writing on intelligence and giftedness while he was a professor at Yale University. However, he then left Yale to pursue higher education leadership positions as a dean, provost, and ultimately, president of a major university. Sternberg is a prolific author and has written on far-ranging topics beyond intelligence and giftedness, including leadership and love. Sternberg's theory of successful intelligence emphasizes the contention that three components of intelligence work harmoniously. The components are creativity, intelligence (both academic and practical), and wisdom. Sternberg writes, "Successfully intelligent people balance adaptation to, shaping of, and selection of environments by capitalizing on strengths and compensating for or correcting weaknesses" (Sternberg et al., 2011, p. 43).

His theory of successful intelligence is referred to as WICS: standing for wisdom, intelligence, and creativity synthesized. He believes that giftedness involves both skills and attitudes; the skills arise from developing competencies and expertise, similar to Subotnik's model and Ericsson's expert performance framework. The attitudes are how gifted individuals employ the skills that they have developed. Sternberg's theory contends that gifted individuals do not necessarily excel at everything. He believes that gifted individuals are well aware of their strengths and limitations and make the most of their strengths and find ways to compensate for their weaknesses. This is certainly a novel and intriguing idea in the gifted field.

By creativity, Sternberg means the skills and attitudes needed to generate relatively novel, high-quality, and appropriate ideas and products. I will provide more discussion of this topic in Chapter 3. Sternberg views intelligence as consisting both of those skills and attitudes that we think of when we consider conventional intelligence (or psychometric g) and of practical intelligence—the skills and attitudes that individuals rely on to solve everyday problems. Sternberg contends that academic skills and attitudes are important for giftedness, since gifted individuals need to be able to retrieve, remember, analyze, synthesize, and evaluate information. In this regard, his theory is complementary to Renzulli's three-ring conception of giftedness. However, he also argues that practical intelligence is important; gifted individuals need to be able to adapt to their environment, change the environment to suit their needs, or seek a different, more facilitative environment. There is a clear flavor of Piaget in this notion of practical intelligence. Sternberg contends that, ideally, gifted individuals need to be high in practical as well as academic intelligence. "Their creativity may help them generate wonderful ideas, but it will not ensure that (gifted individuals) can implement the ideas or convince others to follow the ideas. Many creative individuals have ended up frustrated because they have been unable to convince others to follow their ideas" (Sternberg et al., 2011, p. 44).

Wisdom is the thorniest and most elusive of Sternberg's three components in his theory of successful intelligence. He believes that individuals are wise to the extent that they use their successful intelligence, creativity, and knowledge to pursue ethical values, balance their own and others' interests, and seek to reach a common good. However, it is unclear how we are to operationalize or go about measuring wisdom or the synthesis of intelligence, creativity, and wisdom. In my view, wisdom is a highly valued virtue and character strength, but it should not necessarily be viewed as a component of giftedness per se (Pfeiffer, 2013a). I view wisdom as a highly valued strength of the heart—an important character strength or virtue, not a component of intelligence.

I have taught a seminar on the psychology of giftedness and routinely asked my students to participate in a class activity that had them rank order from a list of twenty or so adjectives those adjectives that they think most characterize or depict an ideally intelligent, creative, and wise individual. I've used this classroom activity to illustrate the concept of implicit theories of intelligence, creativity, and wisdom, based on a study Sternberg first conducted thirty years ago (Sternberg, 1985). What I've found in reviewing the rankings of my seminar students has been fairly consistent over the years, and these rankings suggest fairly distinct conceptions of how we view ideally intelligent, creative, and wise persons. On the one hand, for example, these seven characteristics are consistently selected most frequently as illustrative of an intelligent person: has good problem-solving ability, inquisitive, reasons clearly, is good at distinguishing between correct and incorrect answers, has a huge store of information, thinks quickly, and is perceptive. On the other hand, these six characteristics, year in and year out, are consistently selected most frequently by my students as depicting a creative person: imaginative, unorthodox, takes chances, is emotional, is intuitive, and is a free spirit. Finally, when considering an ideally wise person, students routinely select the following four signature characteristics: a good listener, thoughtful, listens to all sides of an issue, and considers advice. My classroom activity clearly falls well short of rigorous research, but it does lend some anecdotal support to Sternberg's proposal for three distinct components of successful intelligence.

SYNTHESIS OF DIVERGENT VIEWS OF GIFTEDNESS

This chapter has introduced different models and conceptions of giftedness. We explored four ways of viewing giftedness. We started with a traditional psychometric view, followed by a variety of talent development models. Included in the talent development models we briefly discussed are the ideas of Françoys Gagné, Julian Stanley, Joseph Renzulli, and Rena Subotnik. We then examined Ericsson's expert performance perspective, and concluded with Howard Gardner's multiple intelligences theory and Robert Sternberg's WICS ideas on successful intelligence.

Throughout, I have sought to highlight points of shared agreement among the various theorists. I have also sought to highlight ways in which many of these ideas conform to my tripartite model of giftedness. Finally, I have tried to indicate, when relevant, implications for gifted assessment. For example, the various talent development models all suggest that gifted assessment go beyond testing *general ability* to include measures of *specific abilities*, *motivation*, and *level of interest* in different subject matter/fields of study. *Teachability* (or coachability) and *persistence* along with *frustration tolerance* are two additional potential domains of gifted assessment aligned with talent development models.

I would be remiss and professionally discourteous if I didn't mention that a number of other theorists have extended important ideas on what giftedness is and how talent develops. I direct the interested reader to a volume edited by Sternberg and Davidson (2005) that includes many gifted models. A few theorists whose writings I am particularly attracted to and who offer different ideas on how to conceptualize giftedness and explain talent development include Bloom (1982,

1985), Feldhusen (2005), Feldman (1986, 1994), Piirto (1998, 2004, 2008), and Tannenbaum (1983, 2003).

Before concluding this chapter, I would like to briefly revisit the tripartite model of giftedness (Pfeiffer, 2008, 2010, 2013b). The tripartite model incorporates ideas proposed by many of the theories discussed in this chapter. The tripartite model was proposed to reconcile some of the seemingly irreconcilable and even acrimonious differences among the different models. The tripartite model is also designed to be practical. I developed it after consulting with many school districts, educators, school psychologists, and administrators nationwide.

The tripartite model conceptualizes giftedness from three vantage points: high intelligence, outstanding accomplishments, and potential for outstanding accomplishments. The three perspectives are not mutually exclusive, as examples will shortly illustrate. Within the tripartite model, the first category of gifted students is defined as having exceptionally high IQ scores, in the top 2% when compared to other children of the same age. In the early years, these students obtain IQ scores of 135–150 or higher, and in middle school when tested above-level by the regional talent search programs, obtain SAT scores that place them in the top 1% or higher of students their age. In this regard, the tripartite model borrows from Julian Stanley's ideas.

The second type of gifted students within the tripartite model are conceptualized as academically gifted learners who are scholastically precocious, do exceptionally well in classroom activities and assignments, enjoy learning and academic challenges, and typically demonstrate persistence and high motivation when faced with academic challenges. They typically have above average IQs, sometimes 120–130 or higher, enjoy school and schooling, and are enthusiastic about learning. They are characteristically among the most capable and top-performing students in the class. In this regard the tripartite model is compatible with ideas from Renzulli's three-ring conception of giftedness and, to a degree, Gagné's differentiated model of giftedness and talent.

One reason why I developed the tripartite model of giftedness was that none of the existing conceptions of giftedness satisfactorily resolved the practical question of whether a given student was gifted or not gifted. The tripartite model originated from my interest and professional involvement in the development of elite youth athletes. The tripartite model contends that one can view giftedness from three different perspectives, or through three lenses. The first perspective views giftedness as exceptionally high intelligence. Most authorities in the intelligence field agree that intelligence is a very general mental capability that includes the ability to recall, reason, plan, solve problems, acquire knowledge, learn quickly, learn from experience, and effectively adapt to one's environment. It is clearly more than book learning or "school smarts," and reflects important mental capabilities to make sense of things and figure out what to do in challenging situations (Gottfredson, 1997). Note the similarity to Sternberg's WICS model.

Viewing giftedness from this first perspective can involve any of the many different views of what constitutes intelligence. A practitioner in the schools, employing this first lens, could adopt a simple, straightforward view of general intelligence (psychometric *g*) and use any reliable and valid measure of general mental ability to identify gifted students. In this instance, the practitioner would operationally define giftedness as high general mental ability.

One could just as easily adopt a different, more complex and nuanced conception of intelligence, such as Cattell's (Sternberg, Lautrey, & Lubart, 2004) fluid-crystallized model of intelligence. One would then select an appropriate set of tests that demonstrates how well a student solves tasks that measure both fluid and crystallized aspects of intelligence (Blair, 2006).

Any number of different conceptions of intelligence can be used when viewing giftedness through the first lens, such as Guilford's (1967) structure of intelligence model or the now popular Cattell-Horn-Carroll model (Sternberg et al., 2004). The point is that giftedness is conceptualized as high intelligence, irrespective of whichever view of intelligence or whichever cognitive ability tests the practitioner prefers to use. In this regard the tripartite model is aligned with Gagné's view of "gifts" within his DMGT conceptualization of giftedness.

An IQ test or its proxy is used to identify gifted students when viewing giftedness through the first lens of the tripartite model. Other tests could be used to complement or replace the IQ test, as has been done in the gifted field (e.g., using Raven's Progressive Matrices or the Naglieri Nonverbal Ability Test to help identify gifted minority group students; Ford & Whiting, 2008). However, whichever view of intelligence is used, the engine driving this first perspective is a *reliable, fair, valid, and comprehensive estimate of a student's overall mental capability.* Intelligence testing is viewed as the sine qua non for identifying giftedness from this first perspective. One unique requirement for gifted assessment within this first perspective is that the ability test selected should have a *high ceiling.* A second requirement, important when selecting any test for educational or clinical decision-making purposes, is that the test's normative sample should include a representative number of individuals similar to the individual that you are evaluating for gifted eligibility.

The rationale for gifted programs based on using IQ and other ability tests to assess giftedness is that students cannot be expected to have their educational needs appropriately met in regular classrooms because they are too advanced intellectually to be appropriately challenged in the mainstream classroom. There is considerable evidence for this position, certainly among students with exceptionally precocious mental abilities in classrooms that do not provide differentiated curriculum and instruction (Dai, 2010; Pfeiffer, 2013b).

The second perspective in the tripartite model is outstanding accomplishments. Gifted assessment within an outstanding accomplishments perspective relies upon performance measures to identify gifted students, not measures of general ability. Measures can include portfolio assessments, tryouts, auditions, and interviews. When this model is applied to academic giftedness, student classroom performance and performance on academic tasks would be used to assess students to determine their eligibility for gifted programs (Pfeiffer, 2013b).

Gifted assessment selects students for gifted programs through procedures similar to those presently used to identify students for other select programs in the schools, including the debate team, chorus, band, orchestra, school plays, student newspaper, cheerleading, student government, and varsity athletic teams. Gifted assessment includes teacher ratings, class or grade rankings, rubric evaluation of classroom products, group or individual achievement test scores, and report card performance. IQ test scores are not required. But performance on an IQ test could certainly be included in an algorithm. Evidence of creativity is often considered an important component within this second view of giftedness. We will talk more about creativity and its measurement in the next chapter.

This second way of viewing giftedness does not necessarily contend that general ability or psychometric g is not important. I certainly don't advocate that general ability should be discounted when viewing giftedness through the lens of outstanding accomplishments. However, this second lens places a particularly high value and weight on the importance of actual performance and evidence of accomplishments, particularly when conducting gifted assessments in the later grades. Gifted assessment should include an evaluation of how students approach academic work, their level of motivation and passion for different academic subjects, and their persistence and level of frustration tolerance. Measures of self-confidence and self-efficacy can be useful as well. However, the most important factor is assessment of actual performance. Note a similarity here to the ideas proposed by Françoys Gagné, Rena Subotnik, and Joseph Renzulli and to Anders Ericsson's expert performance framework. This second perspective is consistent with a talent development model. Opportunities for students to earn a place in their school's gifted program are based on a *competitive-democratic model* of giftedness (Pfeiffer, 2013b). The most deserving or worthy students qualify for gifted programs because they have earned the privilege based on their effort, hard work, and actual accomplishments.

However, within this second view of giftedness, students should *not* necessarily be awarded the privilege of the gifted label for their entire schooling. In my opinion gifted assessment should be recurring over the course of a student's school career. In my experience it seems prudent for students to be reevaluated at least every two years. Gifted placement within this model should be flexible and fluid, open to the possibility of new students qualifying for entrance later in their school careers if they demonstrate, at a future time, extraordinary performance compared to their peers. And the model should also be open to some students exiting from the program if their academic performance wanes over an extended period of time—if there is evidence that planned interventions have proved unsuccessful. The axiom is that *not* all high-ability students benefit from specialized gifted programs and resources. Gifted assessment takes on a whole new outlook and greatly expanded role when a school adopts this second view of giftedness.

I should warn the reader that not all parent groups or gifted educators are enthusiastic about this idea. Some parents and educators get upset with the notion that some students could rotate out of a gifted program and no longer be considered gifted. I understand and am sympathetic to this reaction. But I believe that this idea is fair and equitable, and fully consistent with American values and ethics. The idea that a student can be asked to exit from an elite or special program or group is already in place in today's schools. High-performing students who are members of an elite team, club, or other group in their school often face the prospect of having to relinquish their membership if they exhibit a decline in their level of performance or show disinterest or low motivation.

The third perspective in the tripartite model, potential for outstanding accomplishments, is similar to the outstanding accomplishments model, with the slight difference that it recognizes that some students have not been provided an equal opportunity to develop their gifts, which have therefore not yet been actualized. This third perspective is based on an affirmative action model of giftedness when applied to minority group and typically underrepresented groups of gifted students (Pfeiffer, 2013b). Gifted assessment from this third perspective—*correctly identifying students of high potential*—is trickier than identification of gifted students from the other two perspectives. Assessment designed to predict future performance, of course, can never be quite as accurate as the assessment of present status. We can and should expect an appreciable number of false positives and false negatives when assessing giftedness from this third perspective. Many would argue, and I agree, that the greater risk is in false negatives—deciding, based on a gifted assessment, that a given student *does not* have uncanny potential when in fact he or she *does*. That obviously has more tragic implications for a student than falsely identifying a student as likely gifted who doesn't in reality have uncanny potential.

Gifted assessment measures can be of two types, and they are not mutually exclusive. Practitioners can use scores on performance measures that predict future performance. And practitioners can evaluate student performance on academic tasks that hopefully predict future scholastic performance. The implication of the affirmative action perspective is that the student of unusually high potential—the diamond in the rough—will substantially benefit, more than other students, from a highly enriched and nurturing academic environment (Pfeiffer, 2013b). The theory underlying this third perspective is that a select group of high-potential students will benefit to a much greater degree than their peers when provided an educational milieu that facilitates the full unfolding of their gifts. This is, quite frankly, a humanistic and politically meritorious but not well tested hypothesis in the gifted field. I admit that it is an aspirational view that I embrace.

According to Ceci and Papierno (2005), when special opportunities are provided to everyone rather than to a targeted group of students with a history of lower scholastic performance, achievement gaps will actually widen. Ceci and Papierno contend that it is incumbent on the field to identify the top 10% of the underrepresented segments of society and provide them with resources to develop their potential. This idea that we should identify and provide special resources for the top 10% of underrepresented students in our schools is consistent with the tripartite model's third lens for viewing gifted students, which seeks those with unusually high potential to accomplish great things if provided the right opportunities at a high enough dosage and over a long enough time.

Selection of students for gifted programs is tricky and open to contentious dispute among those parents whose children might come close but are ultimately not selected. Gifted assessment needs to be based on carefully selected instruments and procedures that reliably measure a student's performance based on at least two criteria: one, how closely the performance approximates the threshold established for identification in the outstanding accomplishments perspective, and two, whether there is any validity evidence, even local evidence, that the interpretation of the test scores or procedures used works as intended (Impara, 2010; Pfeiffer, 2013b).

CONCLUSION

Let me conclude this chapter by highlighting a few key points that are shared by many of the models discussed here and that have guided my thinking on gifted assessment and how we can best serve high-ability students in the schools:

- Giftedness is a social construct and not something that is real. Giftedness is not something that students have or don't have. It is a social construction, a potentially useful educational concept that educators can use in the schools to categorize a subset of students based on alternative criteria (such as high IQ or outstanding academic performance). There can never be a cut score that invariably separates gifted from nongifted students. The decision on where to draw the line will always be based on judgment—ideally, thoughtful, deliberate, and prudent judgment by professionals who are well acquainted with the issues surrounding giftedness.

- General intellectual ability matters in school performance and in real-world success. There are various ways to define and conceptualize the construct of intelligence and no one way is correct. General ability is almost always important to measure when conducting a gifted assessment and considering a student for gifted eligibility. Most, but not all, models acknowledge the importance of recognizing and assessing natural abilities in one or more culturally valued domains.

- In addition to general ability, specific abilities and skills; a constellation of attitudes, interests, and beliefs; opportunities provided and taken advantage of; and motivation, persistence, frustration tolerance, and passion contribute synergistically to the ultimate heights that bright students reach in terms of their accomplishments in a given field. Factors beyond the school and gifted program contribute to the calculus that ultimately determines one's success in life. Opportunities, personal choices, personality, unanticipated events, and good fortune all play a role at every stage in the talent development process. Gifted assessment can and should include collecting data and evidence beyond general ability on a number of cognitive, personality, and attitudinal factors that have been shown to play a role in the development of expertise, and even eminence, in various fields.

- There are many different ways to define and identify the gifted student; the tripartite model provides three different lenses through which a practitioner can conduct a gifted assessment. Although some in the gifted field argue that the number of students who are provided gifted services should be based on the actual need for services, I believe it is very difficult, if not impossible, to operationalize educational need in a

> # CAUTION
> ....
> - Giftedness is a social construction.
> - Giftedness is not real.
> - Giftedness is an idea invented by humans, not something that exists in nature.
> - Giftedness can be and often is a useful construct.

scientifically defensible way. Part of the reason for this difficulty is that the construct of giftedness is not something real. Giftedness is a concept that we humans have invented. All students, including students of uncommon or high ability, benefit from a differentiated curriculum and classroom instruction and activities that appropriately challenge them (Borland, 2005). How many of these students should be provided a special gifted program, however, is ultimately a political, philosophical, and practical decision guided by available resources and value judgments. Unfortunately, it is not a scientific question that can be answered by inserting data into a precise mathematical formula.

There are compelling economic, political, and cultural reasons for nations to provide significant financial and human resources for students of uncommon ability. And yet gifted education in the United States has a history of being appropriated extraordinarily limited resources (Gallagher, 2008; personal communication, February 17, 2013). In my opinion there are obvious long-range benefits to our society when the federal government, state legislatures, and local school districts amply fund resources for gifted education.

🖋 TEST YOURSELF 🖋
....

1. **Psychometric g or IQ is no longer used for gifted identification in most states:**
   a. True
   b. False
2. **The DMGT model discounts the role of natural ability:**
   a. True
   b. False
3. **The author discusses his experience with the U.S. Youth Soccer Olympic Development Program to illustrate how more than ability plays a role in the emergence of eminence:**
   a. True
   b. False

4. **The talent search model uses a full-scale IQ score to identify youth of extraordinary general ability:**
   a. True
   b. False

5. **Renzulli emphasizes intelligence, creativity, and motivation in his conceptualization of giftedness:**
   a. True
   b. False

6. **Sternberg's theory of successful intelligence includes wisdom, motivation, and creativity:**
   a. True
   b. False

Answers: 1. False; 2. False; 3. True; 4. False; 5. True; 6. False.

Three

Guiding Principles and Fundamental Beliefs

The approach to gifted assessment that I advocate is guided by a set of core principles and fundamental beliefs. This chapter provides an overview of these key principles and beliefs. They serve as the foundation and basis for *why* one undertakes gifted assessment, *how* one approaches gifted identification and assessment, *which* tests and procedures might be selected (or not included) as part of a gifted assessment battery, and *when* gifted testing should occur. Although the reader may be anxious to skip ahead to the next three chapters which includes more tangible, meat-and-potatoes material on traditional and alternative measures of intellectual ability, achievement, and creativity, the information in this chapter is arguably among the most important content in this volume. It is too often given little if any coverage in graduate intelligence and pyschoeducational assessment courses (Robertson, Pfeiffer, & Taylor, 2011). So sit back, relax, and take the time to mull over the ideas presented in Chapter 3. The seven guiding principles and four fundamental beliefs that follow are critically important considerations for any professional undertaking the assessment or identification of giftedness and talent.

FUNDAMENTAL BELIEFS OF GIFTED ASSESSMENT

The first of the four fundamental beliefs that guide my thinking about gifted assessment is that *giftedness is a useful construct* even if it is not something that is real. Recall from Chapter 1 that giftedness is a social construction. I explained that the concepts of intellectually normal, subnormal, and supernormal (or gifted) are human inventions, not discoveries of nature. We often talk about giftedness as something real, something that children

DON'T ～～～ ET
....
Giftedness is a soci～ ～～ ～
something real.

either are or are not, something with an existence independent of ou～ but the construct is really an invented way of categorizing children (Bo～ However, even though giftedness is not something that is actually real, ～ that giftedness is a highly useful concept created by humans. In my experi～ thirty-five years of working with high-ability students, the gifted construc～ times serves a beneficial and constructive purpose. It serves to direct much-n～ resources and services to high-ability students in the schools. It is also a valu～ psychological construct in encouraging and structuring research on high-abili～ individuals (Pfeiffer, 1980, 2013b).

Recall my definition of the academically gifted student as one who "demon-strates outstanding performance or evidence of potential for outstanding academic performance . . . [and] *is likely to benefit from special educational programs or resources, especially if they align with their unique profile of abilities and interests*" (Pfeiffer, 2013b). Frequently, many very bright students' academic needs are *not* being substantially met in the classroom—not always but often because of the great challenge today's schools face in serving large numbers of students who vary tremendously in terms of their ability, interest, motivation, preparedness, and passion for learning. Gifted identification is valuable and important because it provides an opportunity to direct resources—advanced programs and curricula— to exceptionally bright, "special needs" students. This is one reason why giftedness is a useful and beneficial construct. It creates a category of learners in the schools who often require specialized educational interventions to do well, not to mention thrive and excel.

The second belief that guides my thinking about gifted assessment is a conviction that *we can differentiate high-ability and high-performing students (i.e., the gifted) from other, less bright and less accomplished students* in the schools. Recall that the tripartite model conceptualizes giftedness from three alternative vantage points (Pfeiffer, 2013b). Practitioners can differentiate gifted from non-gifted students by adopting the *high intelligence perspective.* We simply need to establish some IQ score or range of scores, for example scores on multiple measures of cognitive ability falling in the top 2% or 5% when compared to scores of other students of the same age and opportunity. There is no one correct or "true" cut score or even range that distinguishes gifted from not-gifted of course. But this does not mean that a school district or state can't justify establishing a set of criteria and decision rules for a gifted categorization based on high intelligence, especially if the decision rules are based on a clear, coherent, logical, and educationally justifiable rationale.

The second type of gifted within the tripartite model, you will recall, is the *academically outstanding student*. These students are scholastically precocious, do exceptionally well in the classroom, enjoy learning and academic tasks, and often demonstrate unswerving persistence and high motivation when faced with academic challenges. They are characteristically among the most capable and top-performing students in the class. Practitioners can reliably differentiate gifted from nongifted students by adopting this second perspective as well; for example, a school district could operationally define the gifted as those students in their district who are consistently the top two or three performers in their respective classes (e.g., criteria could be based on GPA and statewide group achievement test scores). Alternatively, a school district could define academically outstanding gifted students as the top ten performers in each grade. There is no one best or scientifically correct algorithm for establishing decision rules or inclusion and exclusion criteria for this or any other gifted category; schools can decide to be conservative or liberal in the number of high-performing students they would like to see with this label and, therefore, selected to receive special gifted programs, resources, or services. A school district might decide, for example, to be more liberal and use a larger "net" in the earlier grades, while employing a more conservative set of criteria for older students in the upper grades.

Finally, we can differentiate gifted from nongifted students by viewing gifted-ness through the third lens of the tripartite model: students with the greatest *potential for outstanding accomplishments*. Remember that this third perspective is the most diagnostically challenging, since the practitioner is now making predictions about future behavior rather than assessing present ability or performance. Nevertheless, although this is more diagnostically difficult, the practitioner can assess students with the goal of identifying those students of unusually high potential and promise, the diamonds in the rough (Pfeiffer, 2013b). Colleagues and I used this very approach in a pilot study that measured change over time in a student's profile of abilities, using the Gifted Rating Scales as one means of identifying the diamonds in the rough (Pfeiffer, Kumtepe, & Rosado, 2006).

A third belief that guides my thinking about gifted assessment is that *there are different types/domains and different levels of giftedness*. The number of different gifts is limited only by what culture and society value. As pointed out in Chapter 1, a student's gifts can be expressed in academics, the performing arts, leadership and student government, athletics, and even community volunteerism. This list of different gifts is almost inexhaustible. Howard Gardner pushed the envelope more than twenty years ago on this very point with his groundbreaking book *Frames of Mind* (Gardner, 1983), arguing for what he called *multiple intelligences*. My own Gifted Rating Scales, which will be discussed in Chapter 7, were developed specifically with the goal of enabling practitioners to assess up to five types of gifts: intellectual, academic, artistic, creativity, and leadership (Pfeiffer & Jarosewich, 2003).

I also believe that irrespective of whatever type of gift we are assessing, we should not forget that there are *different levels or degrees of giftedness*. This is equally true whether we are assessing giftedness from a high intelligence, academically exceptional, or potential for outstanding accomplishments perspective (Pfeiffer, 2013b). This viewpoint is grounded in my early training, experience over the years working with exceptionally bright and outstanding students, and deep respect for individual differences in human abilities. Students with IQ scores above 145, for example, are quite different in a number of educationally relevant (and assessable!) ways from students with IQ scores in the 120–130 range. Elite soccer players on the Brazilian, German, Spanish, Ghanian, Australian, or USA national teams, as another example, are also quite different in a number of athletically relevant ways from Division I college soccer players. All of these groups are arguably gifted, but it should be apparent to the reader from these two examples that students with IQ scores above 145 and soccer players competing at the international level are appreciably "more gifted" in their respective domains than their less elite but nonetheless gifted counterparts.

Recall from the previous chapter that Françoys Gagné posits five levels of giftedness: the mildly gifted (top 10%; IQ of approximately 120), moderately gifted (top 1%; IQ approximately 135), highly gifted (145 IQ), exceptionally gifted (155 IQ), and the extremely gifted (165 IQ and above). Terman (1916, p. 79) provided a slightly different four-level classification system when he first published the original Stanford-Binet: 110–120 (superior intelligence), 120–140 (very superior intelligence), and above 140 (near genius or genius).

Gagné's five categories of giftedness and Terman's four categories are but two of many possible ways that one can reliably sort and distinguish the gifted by level or degree. Let's not forget that there does not exist one correct classification system or most precise number of categories that best differentiates level or degree of giftedness, whatever the domain or field (Pfeiffer, 1980).

The fourth and final fundamental belief that guides my thinking about gifted assessment is that *there exist technically adequate gifted assessment tests and procedures*. The following four chapters describe many of the more popular ones. There is still considerable work to be done by researchers and test authors to develop new and better psychological tests and procedures for gifted assessment. But we are at a point

CAUTION
....
Don't use a test or procedure for gifted identification if it is not scientifically defensible.

where the field already has many carefully developed and scientifically sound tests that can and should be used in gifted identification and assessment. This is good news for the practitioner working with high-ability students.

KEY PRINCIPLES IN GIFTED ASSESSMENT

Next we turn to seven key principles that should guide gifted assessment. These principles serve as the foundation for *best practices in gifted identification and assessment*. The principles are based on my review of the extant gifted and assessment literatures, the authoritative opinion of experts in the field, and my own experience as a psychologist working with high-ability students for many years (Pfeiffer, 2013a, 2013b).

How We Define Gifted Is Important

The first principle is that *how we define giftedness is important*. For over one hundred years, gifted students have been identified by scores obtained on IQ tests (Nisbett, 2009; Pfeiffer, 2002, 2012, 2013b). The majority of states still rely primarily, in some instances almost exclusively, on an IQ test score to determine whether or not a student is gifted (McClain & Pfeiffer, 2012).

Contemporary thinking challenges this timeworn thinking. As we explored in the last chapter, there are many different ways to conceptualize and define giftedness. No one way is correct. The old thinking was based on the premise that "being gifted" was something real and permanent, that students were either gifted if their IQ scores fell above a certain score or they were not gifted. Most authorities now discount this old view. There is no scientific basis or biophysiological justification

⟰ *Rapid Reference 3.1   Best Practices*
....
Here are five best practices in gifted assessment:

- Work from an explicit operational definition of giftedness.
- Use multiple measures.
- Consider using local norms.
- Be guided by available gifted programs and services when making decisions.
- Reevaluate periodically.

for dichotomizing students into two distinct, mutually exclusive groups—gifted and nongifted (Bronfenbrenner & Ceci, 1994; Ceci & Williams, 1997; Neisser et al., 1996). However, there is an educational and pedagogical justification. The justification speaks to the mission and goals of gifted education. Our society should be committed to challenging and inspiring educationally our brightest and most talented students. And our society should be committed to developing to their highest levels the special talents and abilities of our most promising students. To this end, it is important to consider how we define giftedness. Because how we define giftedness guides how we go about identifying and assessing students who we suspect are gifted! And it determines which students get selected for special gifted programs in the schools.

I earlier introduced the *tripartite model of giftedness* as one way to conceptualize giftedness in the schools. The tripartite model offers three different and complementary ways to define giftedness: based on exceptionally high intelligence, exceptionally impressive academic performance in the classroom, or unusually high potential to excel (Pfeiffer, 2013b). Each of these three definitions leads to alternative ways to approach gifted assessment. Stanley's *talent search model* is an example of a different approach to defining giftedness and, therefore, an alternative type of gifted assessment—the above-level talent search testing program that uses the SAT or ACT with 7th and 8th graders.

Assessment Should Consider Types of Available Gifted Programs

The second principle is that *assessment should consider the types of available gifted programs and resources.* Ultimately, gifted assessment, at least when conducted for the purpose of identification (earlier we mentioned other purposes of gifted assessment, including understanding the unique strengths and weaknesses of exceptionally bright students, assisting in the diagnosis of twice exceptionality, discerning factors that might be contributing to underachievement, and determining appropriate grade placement) has as its primary goal access to special programs or resources otherwise not available to students.

With this in mind, it is apparent that gifted assessment should consider the match or congruence between the tests and criteria that we select and what is expected in terms of the pedagogical approaches, curricular challenges, and learning outcomes available at the local level (Pfeiffer, 2013b). In other words, gifted assessment for identification purposes should never occur in a vacuum independent of context. For example, if the three available options for high school students identified as gifted in a given school district are grade skipping, AP or IB classes, and the opportunity to register for courses offered at a local community college, then it would seem apparent that gifted assessment in this school district should include assessment of social maturity.

I have previously argued that the programs, resources, and services that schools offer for gifted students must be special, unique, and effective (Pfeiffer, 2013b). Otherwise there is absolutely no valid justification or compelling reason for practitioners to spend the time and energy to conduct gifted assessment. I still recall my first experience as a parent observing the gifted program that one of my daughters participated in during her elementary school years. We were living in an affluent community on the Main Line, outside Philadelphia, and at that time students needed an IQ score of at least 130 to qualify for a gifted classification. The activities that I observed in my daughter's gifted program were fabulously interesting, highly creative, and intellectually engaging. They were what the gifted field considers *high-enrichment* activities. I was struck, however, by the fact that a great number of students attending my daughter's elementary school would likely benefit from and enjoy this special curriculum. It didn't seem that one needed to be in the top 2% or 3% of intellectual ability to benefit from these high-enrichment activities. I wondered back then, over twenty-five years ago, why an IQ test was used for the gifted assessment of my daughter to gain entrance into this wonderfully high-appeal and engaging, yet privileged and limited-access, special program. My point is that the available programs and resources at the local level should help guide the gifted assessment protocol.

Ideally, programs for the gifted should reflect the unique learning needs of high-ability students, and should be based on state and national standards and best practices in gifted education (Landrum, Callahan, & Shaklee, 2001). There are many different gifted curriculum models and programs (Dixon, 2009; Karnes & Bean, 2009; Pfeiffer, 2008; Rakow, 2008). Gifted assessment should always consider the type of programs, services, and/or resources offered by the school district and available in the community and online (Pfeiffer, 2013b). For example, if a given school district offers as part of its gifted program in the elementary grades only an academically rigorous, highly challenging, and fast-paced curriculum with higher-order, language-based analytic and critical thinking skills (Berger, 2008), then the gifted assessment test battery should include, as a key component, an individually administered IQ test. A brief, nonverbal measure of cognitive ability with lower verbal or linguistic demands would not be a prudent test of choice in a situation where the available gifted program is heavily language based (Lohman, 2005a, 2005b, 2005c, 2009; Silverman, 2013; Worrell & Erwin, 2011).

Psychometrics Count

The third principle is that *the quality of the tests and scales we use* other words, test psychometrics count! When selecting tests and procedures for a gifted assessment battery, evidence of the reliability, validity, norms, and ceiling effects of each instrument is a critically important consideration (Callahan, Renzulli, Delcourt, & Hertberg-Davis, 2013). We wouldn't want medical doctors to order diagnostic tests of suspect reliability, validity, diagnostic accuracy, or norms, and the same is true for psychological tests—including tests used in gifted assessment.

It perhaps goes without saying that quality matters in the selection of tests and procedures used for gifted assessment. Fortunately, most of the popular traditional measures of cognitive ability that are widely used for gifted identification enjoy strong psychometric qualities. The most frequently used cognitive ability tests (discussed in Chapter 4) include the Wechsler Intelligence Scale for Children— Fourth Edition (WISC-IV) and Fifth Edition (WISC-V) (Wechsler, 2003, 2014), the Stanford-Binet Intelligence Scales, Fifth Edition (SB5) (Roid, 2003), the Differential Ability Scales—Second Edition (Elliot, 2007), and the third edition and fourth edition of the Woodcock-Johnson Tests of Cognitive Abilities (Woodcock, McGrew, & Mather, 2001; Schrank, McGrew, & Mather, 2014). These measures of cognitive ability are the bread-and-butter and signature products of the test publishers, reflecting the significant cost, care, and effort that have gone into their development and revised versions (Robinson, 2008).

Many of the current cognitive ability tests have adopted the Cattell-Horn-Carroll theory of intellectual abilities (CHC theory) (Alfonso, Flanagan, & Radwan, 2005; A. S. Kaufman, 2009). More information on CHC theory and the most frequently used cognitive ability tests will appear in the next chapter.

There are also a number of widely used standardized achievement tests that also enjoy strong psychometric qualities. Popular achievement tests used in gifted assessment include the Kaufman Test of Educational Achievement, Second Edition (Kaufman & Kaufman, 2005), the KeyMath-3 Diagnostic Assessment (Connolly, 2007), the Wechsler Individual Achievement Test—Third Edition (Wechsler, 2009), and the Woodcock-Johnson III Tests of Achievement (Woodcock et al., 2001). More discussion about the most frequently used achievement tests appears in Chapter 4.

The principle of test quality should always be considered when selecting the test battery for a gifted evaluation. Recall that validity is a property of the score interpretation, not a property of the test (Impara, 2010). In terms of gifted assessment, there are very specific questions that can and should be asked in selecting one test over another. The guiding principle should be how helpful or useful interpretation of the test score is given the specific purposes and consequences of the testing. Test manuals routinely report evidence based on test content, internal structure, relations to other tests and constructs, and test-criterion relationships. What is only infrequently available, however, is *evidence based on the consequences of the testing* specific to gifted identification. No test is valid for all purposes or in all situations (American Educational Research Association, American Psychological Association, & National Council on Measurement in Education, 2014). A test that might be quite valid for assisting in the diagnosis of specific learning disabilities, for example, might be much less useful in gifted assessment.

People, Not Test Scores, Should Make Diagnostic Decisions

The fourth principle is that *gifted assessment should be guided by sound clinical judgment made by professionals*, not based on rigid adherence to test scores. Linda Silverman (2013) makes the important point that test results should be used to support clinical judgment. She writes, "in the diagnosis of giftedness, high stakes decisions frequently are made on the basis of test scores alone (sometimes even group-administered tests) . . . [whereas] accurate assessment of giftedness is dependent upon the skill and experience of the examiner in interpreting protocols" (p. 160).

I wholeheartedly agree with Silverman's position. I have written elsewhere that a scientifically defensible approach to best practices in serving the gifted should reflect the integration of three components: access to the best quality and most recent research on various assessment tests and procedures, practitioner clinical expertise, and a deep knowledge of and understanding about the gifted (Pfeiffer, 2013c). This position is equally valid when considering evidence-based practices in assessment or in the treatment of specific disorders (Norcross, Hogan, & Koocher, 2008). All three components, available research, clinician expertise, and sensitivity to and deep appreciation for the unique characteristics, concerns and preferences of the gifted, are critical if assessment (or treatment) is to be effective (Pfeiffer, 2013b). When one or more of the three components is not present, then the risk is that the practitioner will resort to boilerplate diagnostic analysis in which test scores take precedence over clinical judgment (Silverman, 2013). David Wechsler was a firm believer in IQ tests as *clinical instruments* (A. S. Kaufman, 2013). One of Wechsler's collaborators

> **CAUTION**
> ....
> People, not tests, should make decisions about students.

selected for the upcoming year. And there are always a few players who are selected but don't distinguish themselves during the year that they are on the ODP team and who may not earn an invitation for the upcoming year.

I hope that the reader understands the point that I am making in terms of the advantage and logic of local norms and recurring assessment in the gifted world of academics. Local norms make perfectly good sense at the school district level because the goal of gifted education is to serve the most capable students in the local school population—compared to local competition, not to bright students nationally. The size of a gifted program at the school district level should be dictated by the vision, mission statement, and goals (ideally, explicitly stated) at the local school district level (Pfeiffer, 2013b). And it is to be hoped that the local school district and state see a real benefit to allocating ample fiscal resources to our brightest and most able students.

My sports example implies that we should not necessarily be forced to use cut scores set nationally or even by the state in making gifted decisions at the local level. Decisions on cut scores can be guided by the number of high-ability students that the school district can serve. To return to the example, the state ODP has determined this number based on a number of logistical, human resource, and fiscal considerations; they have decided that they can effectively handle approximately twenty-four state players, at each age level, beginning at age 10, each year in their elite gifted youth soccer program. This number guides the local decisions and local cut scores that the ODP coaches use each season during tryouts.

Lohman (2012) provides an example in which students who score in the top 3% on an ability test will be considered by a hypothetical school district as strong candidates for whole-grade acceleration, and students who score in the top 10% but not the top 3%, will be considered as strong candidates for enrichment. From this defined pool, the practitioner can determine, based on local school district resources, which students are the best candidates for each of these two gifted programs. The idea of using local norms to help guide gifted assessment decisions is really no different from how schools across the United States go about selecting the most talented students to join the school band, orchestra, debate team, theatre productions, school newspaper, and athletic teams (Pfeiffer, 2013b). If local schools used national norms to select students for their swim teams, for example, one high school might find that it has only two swimmers in the school who qualify for the varsity swim team based on preestablished national times, whereas another high school might be overwhelmed because it has over eighty swimmers who all qualify based on the same national times. This, of course, makes no sense at the local level. However, when swimmers compete for a place on the Olympic team—moving from a local to a national competition—then national norms on measures relevant to swimming performance become quite relevant. The same is true in gifted education. When our brightest students in schools across the United States compete for highly select positions in the most elite colleges nationwide, they are assessed by the common yardstick of national norms on tests such as the SAT or ACT. This makes a whole lot of sense for assisting college admissions departments.

For some readers this principle may run counter to what you were taught in your graduate school assessment classes. Many of us were admonished to *always* use nationally representative norms when evaluating a client. And of course there is justification for this recommendation. For example, when attempting to determine whether a young student you might be evaluating presents with autism spectrum disorder or an adolescent presents with a substance-induced mental disorder, it is imperative that you adhere to established diagnostic criteria based on national norms. Any tests that you might select to assist in the clinical diagnosis of autism spectrum disorder or substance-induced mental disorder should be based on nationally established norms, of course, not local norms (Pfeiffer, 2013b).

However, the diagnostic question is different in gifted assessment. It is interesting and in many cases quite important to know where a student falls compared to other students nationally. This is certainly the case when administering an IQ test or achievement test, as will be discussed in the next chapters. It certainly was the case when I was executive director of the Duke TIP program and we looked closely at the SAT and ACT test scores of 7th and 8th graders nationwide who applied to our talent search and competed with other students from around the United States for admissions to our competitive summer programs. We needed to know where each applicant's score fell compared to the entire community of 7th and 8th graders nationwide who were potential selectees for admission to our gifted programs.

The situation is different, however, for gifted programs in local school districts across the nation. The selection of gifted students at the local level should be based, at least in part, on local and not national considerations. Gifted programs in school districts are local, not national. The available number of slots in any gifted classroom is finite and a local school district, not a national, matter (Pfeiffer, 2013b).

Moving on to the seventh principle—gifted assessment in the schools should be a recurring, periodic process—the soccer example speaks to this very point. Many highly talented players are not selected for the ODP state program in a given year but are permitted, in fact encouraged by the coaches who oversee the selection process, to try out again the following year. Tryouts are held annually, and it is not unusual for a number of new players to be added to the state roster each year.

Similar to this approach of recurring assessment, which is embrace performing arts and in most elite youth sports, *students identified as academically or intellectually gifted in the schools should be reevaluated at least every two years.* This is consistent with a talent development model (Subotnik, 2009). It is also consistent with the "successive hurdles approach" to assessment, pointed out in the previous chapter as recommended by Meehl and Rosen (1955) to mitigate errors of prediction when base rates are low, as they are, by definition, among the gifted.

The purpose of recurring, periodic assessment is multifaceted. First, all students identified as gifted should be reevaluated for evidence that they continue to demonstrate outstanding performance when facing increasingly challenging academic hurdles. Second, all students identified as gifted should be reevaluated in the schools at least every two years to determine the extent to which they are benefiting from the special gifted services or programs that they are receiving. This is essentially an assessment of response to intervention (RTI) and program compatibility.

Third, for those gifted students who are not evidencing expected progress or exceptional performance in the classroom or gifted program, the reevaluation should focus on determining the root reasons why—and developing an intervention plan to ameliorate the underlying root causes of the problem, which are likely multidetermined (Pfeiffer, 2012, 2013b).

Regularly scheduled, recurring gifted assessment in the schools should also be available to students who may not have been identified as gifted at an earlier time but who demonstrate recent and compelling evidence that they now should be considered for the gifted program(s) offered in the school district. Recurring gifted assessment represents a more valid prediction of future, out-of-school, real-world success than a single assessment does. Recurring gifted assessment also increases the base rate for success of the gifted identification enterprise from a talent development perspective (Ackerman, 2013; A. S. Kaufman, 2013; Pfeiffer, 2012, 2013b).

BELIEFS AND PRINCIPLES CONCLUSION

The previous sections of this chapter serve as a prelude to and foundation for the next chapters. I have advocated that gifted assessment should be guided by a set of fundamental beliefs and core principles. The four fundamental beliefs are that giftedness is a useful construct; that we are able to differentiate high-ability and high-performing students from other, less-bright and less accomplished students; that there are different types and different levels of giftedness; and that there exist technically adequate gifted assessment tests and procedures at our disposal.

The chapter also proposed seven key principles that, along with the funda-mental beliefs, constitute *best practices in gifted assessment*. These principles are that how we define giftedness is important; that gifted assessment should consider the unique gifted programs and resources available to the student; that the quality of the tests that we use is important; that gifted classification decisions should be guided by sound clinical judgment, not based on inflexibly adhering to rigid cut scores; that multiple measures provide more data to assist in making good decisions; that there is an advantage to considering local norms; and that gifted assessment should be recurring.

DECISION-MAKING OR SELECTION MODELS

Before moving on to the next chapter, one additional consideration bears comment. There are alternative decision-making or selection models that we use to determine whether a student qualifies for the gifted classification. Because giftedness is a social construction, and not something real, like a medical disease, there is no truly scientific or statistical algorithm to ensure that the classification decision is correct or maximizes the "hits" (true positives and true negatives) and minimizes the "misses" (false positives and false negatives). I wish that this were not the case; it would make gifted assessment a less messy enterprise.

Related to the cautionary note that giftedness is not something real is this reminder for practitioners: we frequently misrepresent as categorical the construct of giftedness even though we identify giftedness, in most instances, based on a test score that represents a continuously varying score distribution (Lohman, 2009). The point I am making is perhaps best illustrated by the example of a practitioner using two well-respected cognitive ability tests, the Stanford-Binet and the Wechsler Intelligence Scale for Children, as part of a gifted assessment test battery. The question is this: what should the practitioner do if the student obtains a score falling above the school district's gifted category cut score on the first of the two tests but below the gifted cutoff on the second test? Is the student gifted? Should we administer a third test? Use the test with the higher score? Take the average of the two scores?

That example is not a rare occurrence in the real world of gifted assessment. For example, the correlation between the scores on the WISC-IV and SB5 is $r = .84$ (Roid, 2003). This means that if a school district is defining gifted as those students who fall in the top 3% on an individually administered IQ test, then only about half of the students who score in the top 3% on one of these IQ tests will score in the top 3% on the second test (Lohman & Korb, 2006). What should we do about the other 50% of students who don't obtain scores in the gifted range on both highly reputable cognitive ability tests?

Shaunessy, Karnes, and Cobb (2004) compared scores from three tests administered to 196 predominantly African American students living in a poor, rural school district: the Culture Fair Intelligence Test (Cattell & Cattell, 1960), Raven's Progressive Matrices (Raven, 2000; Raven, Court, & Raven, 1983), and the Naglieri Nonverbal Ability Test (NNAT) (Naglieri, 1997). The NNAT, which has the most recent norms of the three tests, identified 3 of the 196 students as having scores above the 80th percentile rank; the Progressive Matrices test, with normative data collected in the 1980s, identified 18 students from the same cohort; and the Culture Fair Intelligence Test, with the oldest norms, identified 36 of the 196 students as having scores above the 80th percentile. The question again becomes, which of these students is gifted if the school district has decided to use the 80th percentile rank as its cut score for gifted minority group students? Lohman (2009) argues that we would be ill-advised to assume that the highest score is the best estimate of a student's ability. He makes a compelling case from a measurement perspective that the best estimate of ability is usually the average of the two or more scores purportedly measuring the same construct, in this instance, intellectual ability.

There are authorities in the gifted field who argue that the judicious selection of a best cut score or some weighted combination of cut scores when using multiple tests (which I advocate since it provides the practitioner with additional data to consider) maximizes diagnostic accuracy in identifying gifted students (Lohman, 2012). Unfortunately, this is not necessarily always the case. As I have stated elsewhere, this is the case when a clinical practitioner is attempting to correctly diagnose or identify a real phenomenon in nature, such as patients with early stage ovarian cancer or air passengers who might be carrying a hidden and illegal weapon onto a plane. In these two examples, we can unequivocally calculate the diagnostic accuracy of the test or tests using different cut scores or combination of cut scores— adjusting for Type I and Type II errors, based on whether we are more concerned with invading travelers' privacy with overly intrusive but more accurate searches at airport security, on the one hand, or more concerned with failing to identify even one passenger carrying a weapon with possible ill intent, on the other.

Unfortunately, decision-making models for gifted assessment can never provide the same degree of scientific precision that exists in clinical medicine or airport security. This limitation is similar to the one that exists when selecting youth at tryouts for the ODP soccer program, because the line demarcating elite soccer players selected at tryout from those athletes not selected is at best fuzzy and will always remain, to a degree, subjective. The same diagnostic accuracy limitation exists when considering applicants to elite Ivy League colleges. College admissions officers have long recognized the subjective nature of their often very difficult deliberations when selecting from a large pool of exquisitely bright and accomplished applicants.

Recognizing that decision-making or selection models are indeed imperfect in the gifted education world, they still need to be considered. Explicit decision rules increase the fairness and equity and even the diagnostic rigor of our clinical decisions. And they reflect ethical clinical practice—which requires establishing rules a priori that are then applied equally to all students. Sternberg and Subotnik (2000) propose five decision models that school districts and individual practitioners can consider to determine whether a student is gifted. (Examples of these five alternative models are presented in my book *Serving the Gifted* [Pfeiffer, 2013b].)

The *single cutoff decision model* has enjoyed a long history of popularity in the gifted field. Presently no state endorses selection or classification based on the score from a single test (McClain & Pfeiffer, 2012). However, at invited presentations and workshops that I give, I still hear stories from school psychologists who describe just this practice: a score of 120, 125, or 130 on an individually administered IQ test is exactly all that is required in their local school district for a student to qualify for the gifted program.

The two most popular decision-making models are the *multiple cutoff model* and the *averaging decision-making model*. Lohman (2012) explains the subtle but important differences between these two popular decision-making models. For example, if a practitioner is administering two tests as part of the gifted assessment, she could combine scores from the two tests or select the higher score from the two tests as better representative of the student's ability. Lohman reminds us that these two approaches lead to slightly different outcomes. As mentioned earlier, Lohman (2012) contends that combining scores is more accurate than selecting the higher score. *Convergent evidence scaling* is a newly emerging procedure for quantifying assessment data from multiple sources that can be applied to gifted diagnostic decision making, progress monitoring, and even evaluating the efficacy of gifted interventions (Stoiber & Kratochwill, 2002). Convergent evidence scaling has not yet been used in the gifted field, but it has shown great promise in planning, monitoring, and evaluating behavioral interventions for special needs students.

It is important to remember that regardless of which decision-making model one uses, employing prescribed cut scores on one or two or more tests (*multiple cutoff* or *averaging decision-making models*) presumes that we are viewing the construct giftedness as something real and treating it as categorical, when in fact this is not accurate and the boundaries demarcating gifted from not-gifted are anything but precise and can also be expected to change over time. Decisions on which students are gifted involve at best an inexact science and are perhaps better viewed as at least partly an art. Let's not forget that many students who fall just short of selection may be every bit as precocious, bright, and special as those who are selected. The same is true in the selection for the youth ODP soccer program. Many very talented young

DON'T FORGET

There are at least five different gifted decision-making or selection models. Each will generate a slightly different outcome.

soccer players do not get selected in a given year by the state ODP. There are many disappointed young athletes and parents each year when the ODP announces its selection.

The four fundamental beliefs and seven core principles discussed in this chapter serve to guide *why* we undertake gifted assessment, *how* we approach gifted identification and assessment, *which* tests and procedures we might select (or not select) as part of a comprehensive gifted assessment battery, and *when* gifted testing should occur. In the following chapters we move on to look at the more popular tests used in gifted assessment of intelligence, academic competence, and creativity.

 TEST YOURSELF

1. **Giftedness is not a useful psychological construct and should be discarded.**
   a. True
   b. False

2. **The author believes that we are unable to differentiate high-ability students from other, less-bright students in the schools.**
   a. True
   b. False

3. **There are different levels of giftedness.**
   a. True
   b. False

4. **The author believes, at the present time, that there are few technically adequate tests that are available for gifted assessment.**
   a. True
   b. False

5. **When initiating a gifted assessment in the schools, it is important to consider the gifted programs and resources available in the school district and community.**
   a. True
   b. False

(continued)

(continued)

6. **The author advocates for multiple measures since they provide the practitioner with additional data to corroborate other information.**

   a. True

   b. False

Answers: 1. False;   2. False;   3. True;   4. False;   5. True;   6. True.

Four

MEASURING INTELLECTUAL AND ACADEMIC ABILITY

M any people still believe in the magical IQ score, a single number that indicates a person's mental ability. There remains a myth in education, perpetuated by the popular media, that a person is born with a certain IQ, which is fixed and immutable, a part of that person from birth and resulting from predetermined biological and genetic factors (Pfeiffer, 2012, 2013b). Alan Kaufman, an internationally recognized authority on IQ testing, reminds us, however, that this is far from true. "Well, it's a crock, a common misconception. There's no such thing as a person's IQ. It varies. Change the IQ test and you change the IQ. Change the examiner, the day of the test, the person's mood, or the examiner's alertness, and you change the IQ. Test the person twelve times and you might get a dozen different IQs" (A. S. Kaufman, 2009, p. 3).

Although most of us still call tests of cognitive ability or mental processing IQ tests, these tests no longer provide "intelligence quotients." The quotient was replaced with standard scores when it became clear that the original IQ, a ratio of mental age divided by chronological age and multiplied by 100, didn't work very well developmentally because one year's growth in mental ability was not perfectly linear across the age ranges measured by the tests (A. S. Kaufman, 2009). David Wechsler revised the quotient and replaced it with standard scores in 1939, although he continued to call the overall scores IQs. The Stanford-Binet changed to standard scores in 1962, but like the Wechsler scales, also continued to use the term IQ until the fourth edition.

Well, then, where does that leave us in terms of gifted assessment and IQ testing? This chapter will examine in some detail this very important question and also issues related to cognitive testing and gifted assessment. The chapter will also briefly discuss tests of academic achievement and their role in gifted assessment.

WHY AND WHEN TO USE TESTS OF COGNITIVE AND ACADEMIC ABILITY

Recall from the previous chapter the key principles of gifted assessment. The fifth principle is that gifted assessment should include measures of different psychological constructs, based on the reason for the referral. And gifted assessment should include measures of different constructs based on how we define and conceptualize giftedness and how extraordinary talent develops across the lifespan (Horowitz, Subotnik, & Matthews, 2009; Nicpon & Pfeiffer, 2011; Pfeiffer, 2013b). For example, measuring student interests, motivation, self-regulation, passion for learning, frustration tolerance, and comfort with competition is appropriate as part of a comprehensive gifted assessment protocol in middle school and high school. These domains help explain the reasons why high-ability persons reach remarkable levels of expertise and achieve extraordinary accomplishments.

One psychological construct that I did not mention in the previous chapter is intellectual ability, a very important construct indeed. Almost all theories of giftedness and talent development view intellectual or cognitive ability as a central feature, if not the central feature, of giftedness (Dai, 2010; Feldman, 1986; Gagné, 2009; Gallagher, 2008; Humphreys, 1985; S. B. Kaufman & Sternberg, 2008; Lohman, 2006; Mönks, 1992; Renzulli, 1978; Robinson, 2008; Stanley, 2000). In other words, *measuring intellectual abilities is important*, in fact critically important, in understanding, explaining, and even predicting the unfolding of expertise and eminence in almost all fields and professions (Pfeiffer, 2013b; Simonton, 2008). It would be a gross clinical mistake to neglect to measure cognitive abilities as part of gifted assessment. Of course, historically the IQ score was considered synonymous with giftedness. Many now argue that this is an antiquated or even obsolete view, as I've discussed in an earlier chapter, but some ideas are highly resistant to change.

Recall the earlier discussion on the tripartite model of giftedness. The tripartite model proposes three alternative ways to view giftedness; one way is to view giftedness through the lens of intellectual ability. This view directs the practitioner to obtain one or multiple sound and scientifically defensible estimates of intellectual ability as an integral component of a gifted test battery. In my opinion, viewing giftedness through the lens of intellectual ability is particularly compelling when conducting gifted assessments with young children—ages 3 to 12. Most young children haven't yet had

DON'T FORGET

....
IQ testing and gifted assessment are not synonymous.

much opportunity to develop or refine skills specific to particular fields or domains, making the assessment of intellectual abilities particularly relevant.

Also recall that the tripartite model offers two additional ways of viewing giftedness, including giftedness viewed through the lens of outstanding accomplishments. Measures of academic performance fit quite nicely when giftedness is viewed through this lens.

Intellectual ability is typically viewed as "the ability to reason, solve problems, think abstractly, and acquire knowledge" (Gottfredson, 1997, p. 93). Most tests of intellectual ability—certainly the multidimensional intelligence tests that will be covered in this chapter, such as the Stanford-Binet, Wechsler scales, and Woodcock-Johnson—deliberately measure a wide variety of cognitive abilities and skills. In this regard, individually administered IQ tests represent a range of measures of a heterogeneous set of cognitive abilities (Kranzler & Floyd, 2013).

WHERE DOES ABSTRACT REASONING FIT IN?

Some authorities in the gifted field, for example, Linda Silverman, propose that, "an appropriate IQ test for gifted assessment should be an excellent measure of abstract reasoning." Silverman (2013) contends that "tests that emphasize working memory, processing speed, and nonmeaningful material are likely to produce less relevant results for . . . [the gifted] population than instruments designed to measure general intelligence (g)" (p. 164). In other words, Silverman believes that abstract reasoning is the sine qua non of what constitutes giftedness and what should be the focus of gifted assessment. She argues that practitioners should rely on subtests "highly saturated" with g loadings as representing better indicators of giftedness. The implication underlying this position is that giftedness is real and that hypothetically there is only one kind of gifted person—the individual with extraordinary intellectual capacity, and especially with highly developed abstract reasoning ability.

As the reader by now recognizes, I don't agree with this viewpoint: the proposition that giftedness is something real, something inherent within only certain individuals, present at birth and reflected in demonstrations of precocious abstract reasoning. By extension, I don't completely agree with Silverman's view that g-loadings should *always* be the predominant or primary guiding principle in how much weight a practitioner places on gifted IQ test score results. Most authorities certainly agree that

DON'T FORGET
....
Some authorities in the gifted field believe that tests of abstract reasoning are the most valuable in gifted assessment.

abstract reasoning is an important aspect of intelligence. I belong to this camp. However, contrary to Silverman's position, processing speed and working memory are also extraordinarily important cognitive processes in many fields, and should not necessarily be ignored or relegated to a second-tier position in favor of always giving preeminence to abstract reasoning when interpreting IQ test performance in gifted assessment. Finally, some authorities in the intelligence testing field argue, rather persuasively I might add, that interpretation of composite scores should always take a second seat to first considering the full scale IQ score—in part because it yields the highest reliability coefficients (Kranzler & Floyd, 2013).

From a talent development perspective, many in the gifted field have come to appreciate that different domains and professions have slightly and, in some instances, substantially different cognitive demands (Horowitz et al., 2009). Success in the academic world of scientific research, for example, requires a high level of abstract reasoning. Most highly successful and even eminent theoreticians and academic researchers don't need to make quick decisions or even retain millions of facts. Processing speed and working memory aren't critically important in their fields or for them to be recognized as gifted.

Processing speed and working memory, however, are important for success and for making one's mark as gifted or eminent in many other professions. For example, it is inconceivable to consider any highly gifted surgeon, anesthesiologist, emergency room physician, airline pilot, trial attorney, ordnance handling expert, air traffic controller, or infantry officer, to name but a few professions, who doesn't possess uncanny processing speed and working memory. I certainly wouldn't want my surgeon or the pilot of the next flight that I am about to take to be only average in processing speed!

I've often wondered if Silverman, whose writings I greatly respect,[1] and others in the gifted field formulated their views of giftedness from one specific frame of reference—their personal conception about what constitutes a gifted person—examples that come to mind include Einstein, Freud, and Darwin and, more recently, Stephen Hawking. These individuals epitomize the intellectually gifted stereotype. Abstract reasoning is clearly hugely important relative to processing speed, for example, among these four extraordinarily gifted theoreticians and scientists. But we could just as easily cite the names of other highly recognizable, extraordinarily gifted individuals whose ideas, creations, or performances reflect uniquely different profiles of cognitive abilities. My point is this: we need to

---

1. In fact, Linda Silverman contributed a chapter to my *Handbook of Giftedness in Children* (Pfeiffer, 2008).

be careful to avoid adopting an overly narrow conception of giftedness when "in the hunt" for gifted students. Also recall that giftedness is a culture-bound conceptualization, not something real in nature (Nicpon & Pfeiffer, 2011; Pfeiffer, 2002).

CAUTION
....
All students with tested high IQ scores are not the same and can, and typically do, vary tremendously across a wide range of attitudinal, social, and personality factors.

WHAT TESTS OF COGNITIVE ABILITY MEASURE

The reader will be familiar with the most popular IQ tests,[2] including the Stanford-Binet, Wechsler scales, Woodcock-Johnson Tests of Cognitive Abilities, Differential Abilities Scales, Kaufman Assessment Battery for Children, and Cognitive Assessment System, to name but a few. All of these multidimensional IQ tests are individually administered and consist of a number of subtests that sample a wide variety of cognitive skills. These and other IQ tests have gone through a number of advancements over the years in how they have been conceptualized, developed, normed, and even marketed regarding what they measure. These transformations in the IQ test date back to the time when H. H. Goddard and Lewis Terman first translated and transported the original Binet scales across the Atlantic to America at the beginning of the twentieth century (Goddard, 1908; Terman & Childs, 1912; Terman, 1916).

For more than fifty years, competing researchers and test authors have debated the question of exactly what IQ tests measure. This debate over the essence of the IQ test (e.g., Floyd, Reynolds, Farmer, & Kranzler, 2013; Watkins, 2010) parallels in many ways an ongoing debate in the scientific literature over what constitutes human intelligence (Dai, 2010; Jensen, 1998; Neisser et al., 1996; Sternberg, 1985; Sternberg, Lautrey, & Lubart, 2004).

It is beyond the scope of this chapter to detail the various arguments and positions, many quite fascinating and eloquent, on what IQ tests measure and what constitutes human intelligence. The interested reader is directed to detailed discussions in Carroll (1993), Gottfredson (2008), A. S. Kaufman (2009), S. B. Kaufman (2013), McGrew (2005), and Sternberg et al. (2004). What follows is an intentionally brief overview of the main points, particularly those distinctions relevant to our focus on gifted assessment. The bottom line is that measuring cognitive abilities is an essential component of gifted assessment and that only

---

2. For simplicity's sake, I will call these tests *IQ tests*, fully appreciating that the more accurate term is *tests of cognitive ability* (A. S. Kaufman, 2009).

scientifically sound IQ measures should be used. Fortunately, many excellent IQ tests exist to choose from. Kranzler and Floyd (2013) do a very nice job of listing the criteria that practitioners should consider in selecting the "best" IQ tests. Their criteria are based on the *Standards for Educational and Psychological Testing* (American Educational Research Association [AERA], American Psychological Association [APA], & the National Council on Measurement in Education [NCME], 2014). The criteria include quality of the norm samples (e.g., size, recency, representativeness, and developmental sensitivity), scaling (note that scale ceiling is particularly relevant in gifted assessment), and evidence for reliability and validity. I would add diagnostic accuracy and consequential validity to this list. Of course, when evaluating the best IQ tests for gifted assessment, one should pay attention to the published psychometric evidence specific to their use with high-ability students.

GENERAL AND SPECIFIC ABILITIES

There are at least four perspectives on what exactly IQ tests measure and, by extension, four different thoughts on what practitioners should emphasize when conducting IQ testing as part of gifted assessment. The most popular perspective at the moment is a hierarchical model of broad and narrow abilities based on factor analytic studies (Carroll, 1993; S. B. Kaufman, 2013; Messick, 1992).

Hierarchical Models: Cattell-Horn-Carroll

By far, the most widely cited hierarchical model is the Cattell-Horn-Carroll (CHC) theory of cognitive abilities. Precursors of the CHC model include Spearman's (1927) two-factor model of general and specific factors, Guilford's (1967) structure of intellect model, Luria's (1966) sequential-simultaneous information processing model, and Cattell-Horn's theory of fluid (Gf) and crystallized (Gc) intelligences, referred to as Gf-Gc theory (Horn & Cattell, 1966). The CHC model has a huge influence on IQ testing at this time. The CHC model recognizes the existence of general intelligence (or g, which we will discuss shortly). General intelligence, or g, is a hypothetical construct based on many factor analytic studies, theoretically conceptualized as residing at the apex of the CHC model (Stratum III). But the hierarchical model doesn't necessarily give preeminence to g.

At the base of the hierarchical model are about seventy narrowly defined and fairly specific cognitive abilities (Stratum I). Examples of these fairly specific Stratum I cognitive abilities include oral production and fluency, grammatical

≡ *Rapid Reference 4.1 CHC Theory of Cognitive Abilities*

The Cattell-Horn-Carroll (CHC) theory of cognitive abilities consists of three levels, or strata, with psychometric g at the apex.

sensitivity, and foreign language aptitude (Carroll, 1993). The real action as far as IQ test construction and interpretation goes, most now argue, is at the second level of the CHC hierarchical model—Stratum II. The second level includes ten broad cognitive abilities: fluid intelligence and crystallized intelligence (mentioned above), along with short-term memory, processing speed, visual processing, auditory processing, quantitative thinking, reading and writing, decision speed/reaction time, and long-term retrieval (McGrew, 2005).

Most of the new and many of the recently revised IQ tests, including the Wechsler Intelligence Scales for Children—Fourth Edition (WISC-IV) (Wechsler, 2003); Stanford-Binet Intelligence Scales, Fifth Edition (SB5) (Roid, 2003); Kaufman Assessment Battery for Children, Second Edition (KABC-II) (Kaufman & Kaufman, 2004a); Cognitive Assessment System (Naglieri & Das, 1997; Naglieri, Das, & Goldstein, 2012); Woodcock-Johnson Tests of Cognitive Abilities (WJ III[3] and WJ IV) (Woodcock, McGrew, & Mather, 2001; Schrank, McGrew, & Mather, 2014); and Differential Ability Scales, Second Edition (DAS-II) (Elliott, 2007), incorporate a hierarchical model of intelligence. This permits the practitioner to apply a CHC-based model for gifted test interpretation. Noted test authority Alan Kaufman asks the obvious question in his nifty little book *IQ Testing 101*: "so what is the right number of abilities [for an IQ test to measure]?" His recommendation is *not* to use the highly popular two that most of us above the age of 40 were trained on, Wechsler's Verbal and Performance IQ scales (A. S. Kaufman, 2009, p. 99).

The Wechsler scales now consist of four indexes (Wechsler's and the other IQ tests will be discussed further shortly), the same number as found in the Luria-based Cognitive Assessment System (Naglieri & Das, 1997; Naglieri et al., 2012). The KABC-II (Kaufman & Kaufman, 2004a) measures four or five broad CHC abilities, depending on the practitioner's preference for interpreting based on the Luria or CHC model. The SB5 (Roid, 2003) and DAS-II (Elliott, 2007) both measure five broad CHC abilities. And first place in the CHC-mapping

---

3. Most authorities expect and are fairly confident that the new WISC-V will incorporate a hierarchical model of cognitive abilities aligned with the CHC model; the newly published WJ IV fully incorporates the CHC model.

contest is awarded to the WJ III and IV, which both measure seven CHC ability factors.

The implication for gifted assessment that employs the CHC model is that practitioners should focus on the broad cognitive abilities now available to measure on most IQ tests. The WISC-IV (Wechsler, 2003), for example, provides four factor indexes—Verbal Comprehension Index (VCI), Perceptual Reasoning Index (PCI), Working Memory Index (WMI), and Processing Speed Index (PCI)—that, many argue, should be the first-line of interpretation in a gifted assessment. The full scale IQ score, although available on the WISC-IV and new WISC-V, should not be the primary focus when applying this first approach. A few studies have begun to examine the utility of the CHC model with high IQ and high-achievement students enrolled in gifted programs. Preliminary studies confirm the validity of CHC profiles of intellectually gifted students (subjects selected based on criteria of eligibility for gifted services, full scale IQ scores of 125 or higher, and reading and mathematics composite scores above the 75th percentile). There was also "some tendency" for gifted students to score higher on composites with higher g loadings (Margulies & Floyd, 2009, p. 9).

A second implication of applying the CHC model is the *cross-battery approach*, which advocates that practitioners select different tests to corroborate an intellectual strength (or gift) in one or more of ten broad cognitive abilities found at Stratum II. The cross-battery approach was first advocated by Richard Woodcock, then further developed by Flanagan and McGrew (1997). This approach offers the practitioner clinical flexibility in selecting from different tests to build a case that a student is gifted.

Abstract Reasoning

Recall the earlier discussion on the importance that at least one authority in the gifted field places on abstract reasoning in gifted assessment. Silverman (2013) contends that subtests that are more highly saturated with general intelligence (that load higher on g) are far better measures of abstract reasoning. And thus, she argues, these subtests are "more relevant" in gifted assessment. Focusing on measures more highly saturated with g is a second way of approaching gifted assessment test interpretation.

Silverman specifically recommends that practitioners afford greater weight to subtests such as Vocabulary (.82), Information (.79), Similarities (.79), Arithmetic (.74), Word Reasoning (.70), and Comprehension (.70) on the WISC-IV, because their g loadings are all .70 or higher. She contends that g loadings of .70 or higher are "good measures" of abstract reasoning. In contrast, she cautions practitioners against relying on subtests such as Matrix Reasoning (.68) or Block Design (.67) in gifted assessment, because they are only "fair measures of g" (Silverman, 2013, p. 165).

Silverman (2013) recommends that the Verbal Comprehension Index of the WISC-IV, composed of the Similarities, Vocabulary, and Comprehension subtests, is particularly useful in gifted assessment. The reason? Because the VCI is a better measure of abstract reasoning, based on the factor loading of its subtests, than the factor indexes: Working Memory, Processing Speed, and Perceptual Reasoning.

The implication for gifted assessment when applying this second approach is for practitioners to look for evidence in the IQ test (and of course in corroborating test and observational data) that the student being evaluated evidences advanced abstract reasoning compared to his or her peers.

General Intelligence (g)

A third perspective that has historically enjoyed wide popularity in the gifted field, and still does in many quarters, focuses on the general factor, or g, a hypothetical construct found in all IQ tests. Arthur Jensen (1998), among other notable researchers, was a staunch champion of g. Jensen argued that a general ability, or g, interpretation of IQ scores is highly justified (Dai, 2010). The general intelligence view remains widely accepted as *the* approach to gifted assessment and gifted identification in the schools and among many in gifted education (McClain & Pfeiffer, 2012). In my international travels, I have found a predominant number of gifted educators and psychologists who view the full scale IQ score as *the* criterion for gifted identification (Pfeiffer, 2013b).

As mentioned earlier, the hierarchical model of broad and narrow abilities, based on findings from literally thousands of factor analytic studies, has gained prominence in the intelligence field. Most authorities in cognitive assessment today contend that the most defensible and parsimonious model for understanding intelligence and for interpreting performance on an IQ test is found in looking at Stratum II performance, not g. By a long stretch.

However, a small but growing group of thoughtful researchers are challenging this position and asking, are we overfactoring the number of factors measured by commercial tests of cognitive ability? (e.g., Frazier & Youngstrom, 2007). A growing number of publications in top-tier measurement journals, by Gary Canivez and Marley Watkins among others, are challenging, for example, the four-factor model for the WISC-IV and WAIS-IV (Canivez & Watkins, 2010a, 2010b; Watkins, 2006). Reevaluation of the factorial/structural validity of the

SB5 similarly suggests that the Stanford-Binet may basically be a one-factor IQ test with some modest evidence for two factors at the youngest age levels (Canivez, 2008; DiStefano & Dombrowski, 2006).

The jury clearly is still out on whether these revolutionary, even radical ideas about the preeminence of g in IQ test interpretation will stand the test of more extensive scrutiny. Admittedly, the various factor analytic models that these researchers, and those who support the CHC model, employ are esoteric, cryptic, and even murky to most practitioners, myself included, and thus difficult to fully understand. My colleagues in statistics and measurement remind me that these provocative findings are open to alternative interpretations.

However, the message that this third position advocates is clear: "There is an awful lot of g in all IQ tests. The take-home message is this: "g dominates most cognitive ability tests, including the Wechsler scales, Stanford-Binet, Reynolds Intellectual Assessment Scales, and the Woodcock-Johnson Psychoeducational Battery" (Gary Canivez, personal communication, August 8, 2014; Floyd et al., 2013). When applying this third approach, the implication for gifted assessment is clear: practitioners should give close consideration to global ability (for example, General Intellectual Ability on the Woodcock-Johnson III; Full Scale IQ on the SB5 and WISC-V; and General Conceptual Ability on the Differential Ability Scales).

It is ironic given how far we've traveled in our understanding of human intelligence and the cognitive sciences that we may end up right back where we started, focusing on general intelligence! We certainly have gained a much more in-depth, sophisticated, and nuanced understanding of human abilities since the earliest IQ tests at the turn of the twentieth century. But we may also have come back full circle to an appreciation of the unerring and ubiquitous presence of g and its importance in IQ testing and gifted assessment.

David Wechsler was, according to Alan Kaufman, who worked closely with him, "a g theorist," who believed "in the reality and importance of Spearman's global or aggregate intelligence . . . he believed that a person's scores on the 10 or 12 subtests were largely a function of g, but when profile fluctuations occurred they were likely a function of differences in personality, temperament, motivation, perseverance, and so forth" (A. S. Kaufman, 2009, pp. 37–38).

My own position on the "best" approach to interpreting IQ test scores in gifted assessment is as follows: it depends on the purpose of the gifted assessment! If the purpose of the gifted assessment is to identify those students in a particular school district who are intellectually gifted (recall the first lens of the tripartite model) and the most compelling candidates for the local gifted program, then focusing on each candidate's full scale IQ score or cognitive composite scores on one or more IQ tests makes an awful lot of sense in selecting the best candidates. And it is a particularly fair and equitable, systems-wide diagnostic-identification approach.

However, if the purpose of the gifted assessment is to obtain a detailed and comprehensive understanding of the profile of strengths and possible weaknesses of one gifted student's cognitive abilities for educational or vocational planning, then test interpretation, in my opinion, benefits from examining CHC factors, narrow abilities measured by one or a few subtests, item-level score analysis, and even qualitative idiographic analysis, as will be discussed next. Sattler (2008, 2014) suggests a six successive levels approach to test interpretation that I have found useful in my clinical practice with gifted students.

Clinical Insights

A fourth approach to how we might interpret performance on an IQ test when conducting a gifted assessment was first proposed by Alan Kaufman in *Intelligent Testing with the WISC-R* (A. S. Kaufman, 1979). Kaufman introduced the concept of *intelligent testing* and advocated a clinical/diagnostic approach in which the practitioner views each child as unique and looks for contextual, familial, attitudinal, and personality explanations for observed test results. Global scores are deemphasized, and clinical observations underscored as highly relevant— especially in the hands of a skilled clinician—in helping to explain obtained test scores.

Gilman (2008) supports applying this fourth approach in gifted assessment. One component of this approach is *ipsative analysis*, essentially the analysis of subtest scores within a profile for one individual (Silverman, 2013). Sattler (2008) and Alan Kaufman (2004a), among others, describe the steps a clinician takes in conducting an ipsative profile analysis. Many practitioners, myself included, have found rich clinical utility when judiciously using intra-individual clinical inter- pretation for specific cases. Our own research indicates that when significant subtest scatter exists, the practitioner oftentimes discounts the IQ and focuses instead on interpreting the individual's profile of subtest or composite scores (Pfeiffer, Reddy, Kletzel, Schmelzer, & Boyer, 2000).

GENERAL ABILITY INDEX

Asynchronous development is an oft-cited feature of many gifted students (Webb et al., 2005). In addition, high-ability students (and by definition high-scoring

≣ Rapid Reference 4.2 General Ability Index

The General Ability Index (GAI) can be used as an estimate of a child's global intellectual ability when composite scores vary by 23 or more points.

students) evidence greater discrepancies among subtest scores (Rimm et al., 2008). Flanagan and Kaufman (2009) suggest that composite scores that vary by 23 points or more are significant and render the full scale IQ "not interpretable" (p. 128). They recommend that if the Verbal Comprehension Index and Perceptual Reasoning Index scores vary by more than 23 points, then the General Ability Index (GAI) "may be calculated and interpreted as a reliable and valid estimate of a child's global intellectual ability" (Flanagan & Kaufman, 2009, p. 128).

Many respected academics contend that ipsative profile analysis is not supported by empirical research (e.g., Kranzler & Floyd, 2013; Lovett & Lewandowski, 2006; McDermott, Fantuzzo, & Glutting, 1990; Watkins, 2000). Essentially, these critics of ipsative analysis, who raise issues such as the degraded reliability of difference scores, warn that interpretation should stop at the normative level. A. S. Kaufman (2013) challenges these critics, in an acerbic and brilliant reply to a published attack on ipsative analysis that is worth reading.

What is the implication for gifted assessment in applying this fourth approach, clinical insights guided by ipsative profile analysis? Practitioners can look into a youngster's individual profile of scores on an IQ test for evidence of unique strengths that might suggest signs of giftedness. For example, a student might not obtain a General Ability Index score or composite scores on the WISC-IV in the gifted range. But what if this same student obtained scores on the Similarities and Vocabulary subtests of 17 and 18, respectively? Do these two elevated subtest scores warrant further investigation and explanation? Or should the practitioner stop at the normative level of analysis and treat these two outliers as uninterpretable, random, or noise? I would argue for looking more closely at possible explanations for these two highly elevated scores, as well as for hypotheses why the student didn't obtain similarly impressive scores on the other subtests.

I am confident that the reader appreciates that different perspectives on how we define and conceptualize the gifted construct and the purpose of the gifted assessment can and should lead to alternative approaches to interpreting IQ test results. Before we look at some of the more popular IQ tests used in gifted assessment, this chapter briefly discusses four clinical considerations and adaptations unique to gifted assessment: tests with high ceilings, testing the limits, extended norms, and levels of intellectual giftedness.

CLINICAL CONSIDERATIONS AND ADAPTATIONS FOR HIGH-ABILITY STUDENTS

Tests with High Ceilings

When selecting IQ and achievement tests in assessing high-ability students, it is important to consider whether the tests have sufficiently high ceilings. You probably remember the measurement concepts of *scale ceiling* and *scale floor* from your graduate assessment classes. When testing children suspected of having a developmental delay or intellectual disability, recall that it is important that the tests include a number of very easy items that even the most intellectually compromised child will likely be able to answer correctly. The *floor* represents the lower boundary item-range of the test. When the IQ test floor is not low enough, then an intellectually disabled youngster may fail even the easiest items and the practitioner will be unable to determine just how intellectually delayed the child is compared with other children the same age. Two students with very different levels of intellectual deficit may obtain similar scores on an IQ test simply because the test did not have a low enough floor to differentiate them at the lower end of the ability distribution.

The same logic holds when testing gifted students who score at the upper end of the ability distribution. If a test doesn't include items that very few if any students, even the brightest students, can correctly answer, then the test doesn't have a high enough *ceiling* to discriminate at the upper end of the ability distribution. As Silverman (2013) reminds us, "when a ceiling is never reached, the full extent of the child's ability is unclear . . . it is important for the examiner to acknowledge the possibility that the child might have scored higher if there had been harder items available" (p. 171). A test with a ceiling that is too low can compromise gifted assessment, especially when testing extremely bright children in the top 1–3% of the population. The higher the ceiling, the more precisely the test functions to differentiate at the highest levels of cognitive ability.

The talent search model developed by Julian Stanley at Johns Hopkins University was based on the ingenious idea of using a test with a dizzyingly high ceiling to discriminate among even exceptionally bright 7th and 8th graders (Stanley, 1976). Stanley was familiar with Leta Hollingworth's use of *above-level testing*, in which a student is administered a test designed with norms for students several years older (Stanley, 1990). Stanley proposed using the Scholastic Aptitude Test (now the SAT-1), a test designed for college-bound 11th and 12th graders, as an above-level test for

CAUTION

When selecting IQ and achievement tests, consider high ceilings!

already very bright 7th and 8th graders who had been identified as gifted by virtue of being in the top 3–5% on grade-level standardized tests (Assouline & Lupkowski-Shopkik, 2012). As an above-level test the SAT provides a much higher ceiling that differentiates levels of cognitive abilities among even extraordinarily bright 7th and 8th graders. Using above-level testing permitted Stanley, and later others at the Johns Hopkins Center for Talented Youth, the Duke University TIP, the Northwestern University Center for Talent Development, and elsewhere, to cherry-pick the very brightest from among an already select group of high-ability students (Pfeiffer, 2013b).

Using above-level cognitive and academic achievement tests designed for older students is one approach to stretching the upper boundary limits of a test. It has been used with great success by the regional talent search programs for almost forty years (Pfeiffer, 2013b). This same approach can be used by the creative practitioner in conducting a gifted assessment.

Test publishers now recognize the importance of high test ceilings if their IQ and academic achievement tests are to be used with high-ability students as part of gifted assessment. For example, the Stanford-Binet Intelligence Scales, Fifth Edition and Reynolds Intellectual Assessment Scales both have ceilings of 160 across all ages.

Testing the Limits

The original Stanford-Binet Intelligence Scale encouraged the examiner to test all that a child knew, which is known in assessment parlance as "testing the limits." The Stanford-Binet Intelligence Scale Form L-M (SBL-M) (Terman & Merrill, 1973) embraced this idea of testing the limits, and is still in use as a supplementary test for exceptionally and profoundly gifted students (Wasserman, 2007). However, the SBL-M is the exception to the rule among modern IQ tests. Almost all cognitive ability tests today have clear *discontinue criteria* in the test manual. A ceiling is reached on a given subtest when the child fails to answer correctly a prespecified number of items. The potential problem in gifted assessment is that many high-ability students don't demonstrate their full potential on such tests. Of course, the same could be argued for any child tested following test manual discontinue criteria.

Some authorities in the gifted field recommend going beyond standardization criteria to gain additional clinical insights (Cayton, 2008; Silverman, 2013). The idea is to test the limits and challenge the high-ability child to determine just how much she knows; how far can we stretch her abilities in answering the most difficult test items beyond her ceiling—in other words, beyond where the examiner should have stopped if following directions in the test manual. Testing the limits should always be guided by experience, by a prudent clinical judgment about the child's comfort level and readiness to take on more difficult items. When testing the limits, the evaluation should report two sets of scores, *both* the scores obtained through the standardized administration and the second score obtained under the nonstandard, testing the limits administration, with a clear explanation of these scores in the report (Cayton, 2008). In my practice we frequently include a testing the limits procedure with highly intellectually precocious children. My clinical staff and I faithfully adhere to test standard administration instructions found in the test manual, since discontinue criteria are critical to standardization. However, we also find that there are times when we need to be flexible to obtain a more complete and accurate estimate of a youngster's abilities. Testing the limits is particularly useful when evaluating a gifted child's readiness for grade skipping or acceleration. Testing the limits does take additional time. One can't be in a rush when conducting a gifted assessment with a highly verbally precocious child! Testing the limits can be enjoyable and usually provides rich dividends of clinical information about a gifted child's ability profile and capacity to handle intellectual challenges.

Extended Norms

Readers familiar with the Wechsler Scale know that the maximum score a youngster can obtain on any subscale is 19 and the maximum IQ score is 160. If you've had the joy and privilege of testing exceptionally precocious students, you know that some gifted students don't top-out on one or more subtests, although their score can't exceed 19. They essentially bump their heads on the ceiling of the test! One thing a practitioner can do is use test ages from the manual as a way of providing a more precise and compelling picture of a student's intellectual prowess; for example, a 7-year 11-month-old child could be described as performing at the 16:0 years test age on the WISC-IV.

Betty Meckstroth (1989) proposed a more satisfactory and precise way of representing just how advanced a gifted student's intellectual abilities might be. She recorded the raw score points earned beyond the minimum number required to reach the subtest ceiling of 19. Pearson Assessment, publishers of the WISC-IV, reviewed scores from over 300 highly gifted children at eight different sites, and recognized the value of allowing extra credit for the number of raw score points earned. As a result, Pearson raised the maximum subtest scores from 19 to 28 and the composite scores from 160 to 210 (Gilman, 2008; Silverman, 2013). These extended norms are available on the Pearson website (http://images.pearsonclinical.com/images/assets/WISC-IV/WISCIV_Tech Report_7.pdf). It is recommended that the extended norms table be consulted when a student you are testing obtains ceiling-range scores (18 or 19) on two or more Wechsler subtests (Zhu, Cayton, Weiss, & Gabel, 2008). The topic of extended norms makes a good segue into the next topic we will briefly discuss, levels of intellectual giftedness.

Levels of Intellectual Giftedness

A brief discussion on gifted classification is in order. To prepare for that discussion, first recall that earlier in the book I argued that giftedness is a useful social construct, but not something that is actually real. Second, recognize that most practitioners who undertake gifted assessment view students as either gifted or not gifted, with those in the gifted group viewed as if were all alike (Gross, 2009). Those who work closely with gifted students, however, recognize that degree of giftedness varies among high-ability students. This idea is self-evident. I am sure you can think of two or three creative individuals that you've known in your life. Although all were creative, they undoubtedly varied with regard to their relative level of creativity. The point is this: individual differences do matter, even among the gifted. And they matter a great deal at the upper end of the ability continuum.

Lewis Terman (1916) proposed one of the first IQ classification systems. Terman's system was based on his personal views on what his IQ test was measuring; his schema wasn't based on prior research or even expert opinion or consensus. Table 4.1 depicts the three categories specific to high ability in Terman's classification system.

What exactly does an IQ score above 140 signify? Statistically, an IQ of 140 represents the 99.62th percentile rank. In other words, in the overall population, fewer than one student in a hundred of the same age will exceed an IQ of 140. An IQ score of 120 represents the 91st percentile rank. As I've already pointed out, the boundary between gifted and not-gifted is arbitrary. For the same reason, boundaries between different categories of giftedness, such as Terman suggested, are arbitrary. However, just as with intellectual disability, differences at the furthest edges are more unhesitatingly obvious (Silverman, 2013). The range

Table 4.1 Terman's Gifted IQ Classification System

Score	IQ Classification
Above 140	Near genius or genius
120–140	Very superior intelligence
110–120	Superior intelligence

Table 4.2 Proposed Categories of Intellectual Giftedness

Descriptive Term	Composite Scoring Range	Normal Curve Score Range
Profoundly gifted	175+	+5 standard deviations and above
Exceptionally gifted	160–174	+4–4.99 standard deviations
Highly gifted	145–159	+3–3.99 standard deviations
Gifted	130–144	+2–2.99 standard deviations

of scores in the top 1% on IQ tests—from 135 to above 200—is as wide as scores between the 2nd and 98th percentiles (Gross, 2009).

There is, unfortunately, a lack of consensus in the gifted field on a nomenclature that represents different degrees of intellectual giftedness. John Wasserman attempted to craft a consensus by inviting an international committee of over twenty authorities to propose descriptors that could be used in the test manual for the fifth edition of the Stanford-Binet Intelligence Scale, for which John served as project director.[4] The four gifted categories that Wasserman (2007, p. 60) came up with are displayed in Table 4.2. This classification system is a helpful reminder that not all intellectually gifted students are the same. In my consulting work with school districts, I often recommend that their gifted programs adopt a two-level intellectually gifted scheme: gifted (130–144) and highly gifted (145+). The reason why I don't routinely recommend a four-tier gifted scheme in the schools is because so very few students fall within the exceptionally gifted or profoundly gifted ranges (160+). In my experience, it is easier for school districts to design individual programs and services as they are needed for intellectually gifted students who fall four or more Standard Deviations (SD) above the mean (Pfeiffer, 2013b).

SOME POPULAR IQ TESTS USED IN GIFTED ASSESSMENT

This section provides an intentionally brief description of eight of the more popular cognitive ability tests used in gifted assessment. It is not the goal of this discussion to provide a detailed report and critical analysis of these and other IQ tests in one chapter. Recall that this is not a book on assessing intelligence; it is a book on the theory and practice of gifted assessment. The reader interested in an in-depth discussion of assessing intelligence is referred to the following excellent resources: Flanagan & Harrison (2012), Groth-Marnat (2009), A. S. Kaufman (2009), Kranzler & Floyd (2013), Neukrug & Fawcett (2014), and Sattler (2008).

---

4. I tremendously respect John Wasserman's thinking on this point; John also served as project director for the development of two tests that I developed during his tenure with PsychCorp, Pearson Assessment.

Wechsler Intelligence Scale for Children—Fifth Edition

I begin with the Wechsler Intelligence Scale for Children—Fifth Edition (WISC-V) (Wechsler, 2014) because, like previous versions of Wechsler's children scales, it will undoubtedly become hugely popular and the most widely used full-length intelligence test in gifted assessment (Pfeiffer, 2012). The WISC-V consists of twenty-one subtests and yields a Stratum III composite score called the Full Scale IQ—for all ages, 6 through 16, it is formed by seven subtests. The WISC-V also features five Stratum II primary index scores: the Verbal Comprehension Index, Visual Spatial Index, Fluid Reasoning Index, Working Memory Index, and Processing Speed Index. Substantial research supports the five factor model for the Wechsler scales (Benson, Hulac, & Kranzler, 2010; Keith, Fine, Taub, Reynolds, & Kranzler, 2006; Weiss, Keith, Zhu, & Chen, 2013a, 2013b).

Norms were collected between April 2013 and March 2014 across forty-nine states, based on the 2012 U.S. Census; internal consistency reliability is excellent. Testing time averaged across all ages is 65 minutes to obtain the five primary index scores (or less than 50 minutes if only the Full Scale IQ, Verbal Comprehension Index, and Fluid Reasoning Index are desired). For gifted children, average testing time is approximately 80 minutes to obtain the five primary index scores (or 60 minutes if only the Full Scale IQ, Verbal Comprehension Index, and Fluid Reasoning Index are desired).

Pearson is currently in the process of developing extended norms for the WISC-V. As mentioned earlier in the chapter, the WISC-IV (Wechsler, 2003), its predecessor, includes extended norms for use with children who reach the ceiling on two or more subtests (Zhu, Cayton, Weiss, & Gabel, 2008). This is a unique feature in gifted assessment. An ancillary index score, the General Ability Index, is frequently used in gifted assessment. In essence, it is an abbreviated form created by administering five subtests, which produces a Stratum III composite called the General Ability Index. Many school districts used the WISC-IV General Ability Index (Raiford, Weiss, Rolfhus, & Coalson, 2005; Saklofske, Prifitera, Weiss, Rolfhus, & Zhu, 2005) abbreviated form in gifted screening. The General Ability Index is derived from the subtests for the Verbal Comprehension, Visual Spatial, and Fluid Reasoning domains that contribute to the Full Scale IQ. Some assert that the General Ability Index should be used in placement decisions for gifted education (Rimm, Gilman, & Silverman, 2008). Some gifted children tend to obtain higher scores on the General Ability Index than on the Full Scale IQ. Among the children in the intellectually gifted special group study conducted for the WISC-V, 34% obtained higher General Ability Index scores than Full Scale IQs. Similar results were observed for the WISC-IV (Raiford et al., 2005), the Wechsler Preschool and Primary Scale of Intelligence—Fourth Edition

(WPPSI-IV) (Wechsler, 2012), and the Wechsler Adult Intelligence Scale—Fourth Edition (WAIS-IV) (Wechsler, 2008). Taken together, these results indicate that Working Memory and Processing Speed domains are frequently not particular strengths for children with scores in the gifted range.

The WISC-V offers a number of other ancillary indexes that produce useful scores. One of these of interest to the field of gifted assessment is the Quantitative Reasoning Index. Quantitative reasoning is closely related to general intellectual ability (Flanagan & Kaufman, 2009; Lichtenberger & Kaufman, 2013; Weiss et al., 2013a, 2013b) and is predictive of creativity and success in gifted programs, as well as many indicators of academic success (Lakin & Lohman, 2011; McGrew & Wendling, 2010; Robertson, Smeets, Lubinski, & Benbow, 2010; Schmidt, Homeyer, & Walker, 2009). Other ancillary indexes include the Auditory Working Memory Index, Nonverbal Index, and Cognitive Proficiency Index. The Cognitive Proficiency Index produces a useful comparison score for the General Ability Index, as it provides a summary of working memory and processing speed abilities.

Three complementary indexes for the WISC-V are additionally available. Two of these are Stratum I composites: the Naming Speed Index, which is designed to measure naming facility, and the Symbol Translation Index, which is designed to measure visual-verbal associative memory. The Storage and Retrieval Index is a Stratum II composite that measures long-term retrieval accuracy and fluency.

There is more published research on using the Wechsler scales with gifted children than is available for any other intelligence test. The interested reader will want to review a special issue of *Journal of Psychoeducational Assessment* (Volume 31, No. 2, 2013), which includes two feature articles and eight commentaries on the WISC-IV and WAIS-IV. This special issue offers valuable discussions on theoretical, psychometric, clinical, and practical issues when using the Wechsler scales for intellectual assessment (Goldstein, 2013; A. S. Kaufman, 2013; Schwartz, 2013).

The WISC-V is offered in both a paper-and-pencil format and a digital format on Q-interactive[TM], Pearson's tablet-based digital administration platform, which includes real-time automated scoring. Hand scoring and automated scoring via Q-global[TM], Pearson's web-based scoring system, is also available for those who opt for paper-and-pencil administration. Links to the Wechsler Individual Achievement Test—Third Edition (WIAT-III) and Kaufman Test of Educational Achievement, Third Edition (KTEA-3) are included.

Wechsler Preschool and Primary Scale of Intelligence—Fourth Edition

The Wechsler Preschool and Primary Scale of Intelligence—Fourth Edition (WPPSI-IV) (Wechsler, 2012) is designed for children ages 2:6 through 7:7;

it consists of seven subtests at the younger ages and fifteen primary subtests at ages 4:0 to 7:7. This recent revision of the WPPSI-III (Wechsler, 2002) samples a wider range of abilities across domains (Kranzler & Floyd, 2013). Norms were collected in the 2010 to 2012 period, based on the 2010 U.S. Census. Similar to the WISC-V, the WPPSI-IV produces a Stratum III Full Scale IQ; three Stratum II primary index scores (the Verbal Comprehension Index, Visual Spatial Index, and Working Memory Index) at the younger ages, and the same five Stratum II primary index scores as the WISC-V for older students. Internal consistency reliability is excellent. It is too soon for test reviews and research using the new revision to have appeared in publications; no peer-reviewed studies have yet been published on its use with a gifted population, although a study with fifty-six intellectual gifted children is available in the *WPPSI-IV Technical and Interpretive Manual.* Scoring and report-writing software is available through Q-global. Testing time averaged across the younger age band is 32 minutes to obtain the three primary index scores (and under 30 minutes if only the Full Scale IQ and Verbal Comprehension Index are desired). Testing time averaged across the older age band is 60 minutes to obtain the five primary index scores (and approximately 50 minutes if only the Full Scale IQ and Verbal Comprehension Index are desired). For gifted children, average testing time is 70 minutes to obtain the five primary index scores (and under 40 minutes if only the Full Scale IQ and Verbal Comprehension Index are desired).

A number of ancillary index scores are available for the older age band, including the Vocabulary Acquisition Index (a quick screener for expressive and receptive vocabulary development), the Nonverbal Index, the General Ability Index, and the Cognitive Proficiency Index. For the younger age band, the Cognitive Proficiency Index is unavailable.

Pearson is currently in the process of developing extended norms for the WISC-V. For assessment of intellectually gifted students ages 6:0–7:7, it is likely preferable to use the WISC-V.

Stanford-Binet Intelligence Scales, Fifth Edition

The Stanford-Binet Intelligence Scales, Fifth Edition (SB5) (Roid, 2003) is the second most widely used test in gifted assessment, following the WISC-IV. It enjoys, of course, a particularly long and storied history in IQ testing and gifted assessment. The SB5 consists of ten subtests and is designed for ages 2 through 90; the blueprint for its development was CHC theory. Norms were collected from 2001 to 2002, based on the 2001 U.S. Census. Like the WISC-IV, the SB5 produces a Stratum III Full Scale IQ, based on ten subtests. The SB5 also generates Verbal IQ and Nonverbal IQ composite scores, and five Stratum II composite scores (Fluid Reasoning, Knowledge, Quantitative Reasoning, Visual-Spatial Processing, and Working Memory). Similar to the Wechsler scales, the SB5 produces an abbreviated IQ score based on two subtests. It also produces a nonverbal composite IQ score based on five subtests.

The SB5 and its earlier versions have been well researched and enjoy consistently very favorable reviews and reported psychometrics in the published literature (Bain & Allin, 2005; Janzen, Obrzut, & Marusiak, 2004; Johnson & D'Amato, 2005; Williams, McIntosh, Dixon, Newton, & Youman, 2010). A few factor analytic studies have recently raised the provocative question of whether the SB5 measures much beyond psychometric g (Canivez, 2008; DiStefano & Dombrowski, 2006). This same question has been raised in factor analytic studies with the Wechsler scales (Canivez & Watkins, 2010a, 2010b). A recent factor analytic study of the SB5 with a sample of gifted students ($n = 201$) provided support for a hierarchical, four-factor model that best fit the SB5 gifted test data.

The SB5 has a number of features that practitioners appreciate. The test can be administered across a very broad age range and it provides change-sensitive ability scores based on item-response theory and also offers child-friendly manipulatives (Kranzler & Floyd, 2013). Like the WISC-IV, the SB5 is supported with scoring and report-writing software. A test bulletin published by Riverside Publishing provides detailed and useful information on features of the SB5 in the assessment of high abilities (Ruf, 2003). The bulletin notes that the SB5 features high ceilings for standard ability scores, continuous testing of abilities in a single instrument from early childhood through old age, extended IQ scores with a theoretical upper limit of a 225 IQ, and gifted composite scores that optimize gifted selection/identification.

Woodcock-Johnson IV Tests of Cognitive Abilities

The Woodcock-Johnson IV Tests of Cognitive Abilities (WJ IV COG) (Schrank, McGrew, & Mather, 2014) was very recently published; in fact, I received a sample test kit and online scoring and reporting program as I was completing this chapter. The new version replaces the Woodcock-Johnson III Tests of Cognitive Abilities Normative Update, published in 2001 and updated in 2007. Administration time for the WJ III NU was 35–45 minutes; I haven't had an opportunity to administer more than one WJ IV COG at the time of writing this chapter; I estimate that administration time is similar. The WJ has gained popularity among school psychologists over the last ten years, and is being used with increasing frequency in gifted assessment.

In my experience, the Woodcock-Johnson and Differential Ability Scales are right behind the WISC-IV and SB5, tied for the third most widely used full-length intelligence tests in gifted assessment. The WJ IV COG consists of eighteen subtests that adhere closely to CHC theory; in fact, the WJ was the first intelligence test developed based on CHC theory. Similar to the SB5, the WJ IV COG can be used with an impressive age range of 2 to 90 years. Norms were collected from 2009–2012; the normative sample consisted of 7,416 participants, based on 2010 U.S. Census projections. The examiner's manual states that the WJ IV COG is "a revised and refined version of the WJ III Tests of Cognitive Abilities, . . . [reflecting] the addition of new tests, clusters, and interpretative procedures" (Mather & Wendling, 2014).

Major highlights of the WJ IV COG include the following: ten subtests constitute the Standard Battery and eight make up the Extended Battery; seven tests are used for calculating the General Intellectual Ability (GIA) score; the Standard Battery provides a number of interpretive options, including the GIA, Brief Intellectual Ability (BIA), *Gf-Gc* Composite, three broad CHC abilities (Comprehension-Knowledge [*Gc*], Fluid Reasoning [*Gf*], and Short-Term Working Memory [*Gwm*]), and an intra-cognitive variation procedure and Scholastic Aptitude Scores. Scholastic Aptitude Scores is an option used to predict achievement in specific academic areas (reading, written language, and mathematics), based on a combination of four subtests. Not surprisingly, the new WJ includes scoring and report-writing software. The technical manual too is published as a CD.

It is, of course, way too soon to report on any research using the 2014 WJ IV COG. We will need to be patient while awaiting findings on the reliability, validity, and utility of the new WJ. The WJ IV COG produces the widest range of Stratum II composites. Factor analytic studies using the WJ III COG provided support that the seven composites line up well in measuring the CHC broad abilities (Floyd, McGrew, Barry, Rafael, & Rogers, 2009; Kranzler & Floyd, 2013; Taub & McGrew, 2014). Rizza, McIntosh, and McCunn (2001) conducted a comparative profile analysis of gifted ($n = 51$) and nongifted students ($n = 51$) using the seven CHC factors identified by the WJ III COG manual. The gifted and nongifted students were matched on gender, age, ethnicity, and father's level of education. Results of the profile analysis found similar patterns of performance across the CHC factor clusters for the gifted and nongifted students. Not surprisingly, the gifted sample, on average, scored consistently higher across the CHC factor clusters.

Differential Ability Scales, Second Edition

The Differential Ability Scales, Second Edition (DAS-II) (Elliott, 2007) consists of three age-specific cognitive ability test batteries; one for ages 2–3, a second for ages 3–6, and a third for ages 7–17. In total, the DAS-II includes a total of twenty-one subtests. Norms were collected from 2002 to 2005 following a norming plan based on the 2002 U.S. Census. As with the other IQ tests described above, reported internal consistency reliability is quite good across all three DAS batteries (for example, the average internal consistency for General Conceptual Ability was .93). Administration time is 45–60 minutes.

The DAS-II generates a General Conceptual Ability (Stratum III) composite score for all three batteries; although the test was not developed guided by a theory of cognitive processing (McGrew, 2005), it yields Stratum II composite scores labeled Verbal and Nonverbal for all three batteries, and for the older two age groups it also generates Stratum II composite scores labeled Spatial, Processing Speed, and Working Memory. Factor analytic studies provide support for the three-stratum CHC model, a parsimonious representation for the DAS scales (Sanders, McIntosh, Dunham, Rothlisberg, & Finch, 2007). Factor analytic studies also indicate that DAS-II General Conceptual Ability possesses strong *g* loadings representing Crystallized Intelligence, Fluid Reasoning, Visual Processing, Processing Speed, and Short-Term Memory (Keith, Low, Reynolds, Patel, & Ridley, 2010).

Features of the DAS-II include scores based on different subtests at varying ages, provision of ability scores based on item response theory, and child-friendly manipulatives appreciated by both children and examiners. The test is supported by scoring software, although there is no report-writing software (Dumont, Willis, & Elliott, 2008).

Kaufman Assessment Battery for Children, Second Edition

The Kaufman Assessment Battery for Children, Second Edition (KABC-II; Kaufman & Kaufman, 2004a) is designed for children ages 3 through 18; it includes eighteen subtests. The KABC-II represents the creative marriage of two theoretical models: the Luria neuropsychological model (1966, 1973), and the popular CHC theory. In this regard, the KABC-II is unique and deserves recognition for attempting an amalgam of two different models. The KABC-II departs from other cognitive ability tests in its emphasis on measuring intelligence as an individual's *style of solving problems and processing information* (A. S. Kaufman, 2009).

Norms were collected in 2001 through 2003, based on the 2001 U.S. Census. The KABC-II generates a Stratum III composite called the Fluid-Crystalized Index; this is based on ten subtests. The KABC-II also generates a Mental Processing Composite score, which omits the two subtests targeting crystallized intelligence.

The KABC-II also produces five Stratum II composites: Crystalized Intelligence, Fluid Intelligence, Long-Term Retrieval, Short-Term Memory, and Visual-Spatial Ability. Factor analysis supports the validity of the Cattell-Horn-Carroll theorized broad abilities (Reynolds, Keith, Fine, Fisher, & Low, 2007). The average internal consistency reliability value for the Fluid-Crystallized Index ranges from .96 to .97 across ages (Kranzler & Floyd, 2013); subtest reliabilities are quite good, reflective of a well-constructed test (Thorndike, 2005). Testing time is from 35–70 minutes; there is scoring software. The KABC-II includes novel and high-appeal subtest manipulatives and a language-reduced composite called the Nonverbal Index. Finally, the KABC-II is linked to a co-normed achievement test, the Kaufman Test of Educational Achievement, Second Edition (KTEA-II) (Kaufman & Kaufman, 2005). The test is not without criticism, however. Robert Sternberg wrote a critique of the original version, commenting that "(the K-ABC) is based on an inadequate conception of intelligence, and as a result, it is not a good measure of intelligence" (Sternberg, 1984, p. 277). John Carroll, of CHC fame, wrote in his classic volume on human cognitive abilities, "with respect to factorial content, there is little if anything that is new in the K-ABC test" (Carroll, 1993, p. 703). However, an article by Lichtenberger, Volker, Kaufman, and Kaufman (2006), published in a gifted journal, provides a rationale for the strengths of the KABC-II in gifted assessment. Several characteristics of the KABC-II are mentioned, including the test's ability to fairly assess children with cultural and linguistic differences, low emphasis on processing speed, high test ceilings, and above-level norms.

Cognitive Assessment System, Second Edition

The Cognitive Assessment System, Second Edition (CAS2) (Naglieri, Das, & Goldstein, 2014) is a revised and renormed update of the Cognitive Assessment System (CAS) (Naglieri & Das, 1997). It is designed for children ages 5:0 to 18:11 years and includes thirteen subtests. Administration time is 40 to 60 minutes. Development of the test was guided by Luria's neuropsychological model (see my comments above in the discussion of the KABC-II). The CAS2 translated Luria's three blocks into PASS theory, which is an expansion of the K-ABC's sequential-simultaneous processing distinction (A. S. Kaufman, 2009). The P refers to planning, the A represents attention, and the two S's refer to the simultaneous and sequential coding processes in Luria's theory. The Full Scale score from the CAS Standard Battery is an IQ; Stratum II composites include Processing, Attention, Simultaneous, and Successive. The CAS2 includes five supplemental composite scores: Executive Function with and without Working Memory, Working

Memory, Verbal Content, and Nonverbal Content. Internal consistency reliability was good but not exceptional for the original CAS (ranging from .87 to .93 for Stratum II composites, and .96 and .87 for the Full Scale (Standard and Basic Battery, respectively); the PASS Scale reliabilities (.86 to .93) and Core Battery Full Scale reliability (.95) for the CAS2 are quite good. The CAS2 deserved recognition for its ingenuity in using Luria's theory to guide test construction; the authors also are commended for developing an intervention program linked to the PASS model. The CAS2 is supported by scoring software. The new normative sample includes 1,342 children. The test emphasizes measuring important cognitive processing abilities across a broad range of differential diagnoses, including high-functioning autism spectrum disorder (formerly called Asperger's disorder), ADHD, and speech and language impairment. With its focus on serving special needs students with processing deficits, the test is not necessarily a best choice for gifted assessment. However, the test's first author, Jack Naglieri, makes a case for the application of the test and PASS theory in gifted identification. His argument appears in the gifted journal *Roeper Review*. Naglieri contends that only the CAS and K-ABC afford fair assessment of minority children with limited English language or academic skills and that the PASS theory can be utilized to examine creativity (Naglieri, 2001). Notwithstanding his thesis, many would disagree with this argument.

Reynolds Intellectual Assessment Scales

The Reynolds Intellectual Assessment Scales (RIAS) (Reynolds & Kamphaus, 2003) is designed for a wide age range: 3 through 94. The appeal of the RIAS is that it includes only six subtests. Administration time is 45–75 minutes. Although it is designed as a full-length intelligence test, many school psychologists view it as an "in-depth screener" in gifted assessment because of the small number of subtests. Norms were collected from 1999 to 2002, based on the 2001 U.S. Census. The standardization sample is smaller than is found in most other popular IQ tests (Kranzler & Floyd, 2013).

The RIAS produces a Composite Intelligence Index, formed from four subtests. The internal consistency is excellent across all ages (.97). The RIAS also produces three composite scores: Verbal Intelligence Index, Nonverbal Intelligence Index, and a Composite Memory Index. Average internal consistency for these composites was .95 across ages. Psychometric researchers have raised questions about the factorial independence of the Verbal Intelligence Index and Nonverbal Intelligence Index—essentially asking whether the Stratum II composites are measuring anything specific beyond g (Nelson & Canivez, 2012;

Nelson, Canivez, Lindstrom, & Hatt, 2007). The RIAS is supported by scoring and report-writing software and includes an abbreviated intelligence test called the Reynolds Intellectual Screening Test (RIST), consisting of two subtests.

A FEW ILLUSTRATIVE ACADEMIC MEASURES

Before concluding this chapter, I think it prudent to at least mention a few of the more popular individual achievement tests. These tests can be and often are used in gifted assessment. They certainly complement information obtained from tests of intelligence. And recall from discussion of the tripartite model that they can be instrumental in gifted identification when a school system's gifted program is based on outstanding academic accomplishments as a defining characteristic of giftedness. Individual achievement tests that enjoy wide popularity and acceptable psychometric qualities include the Diagnostic Achievement Battery-3 (Newcomer, 2001), Kaufman Test of Educational Achievement, Third Edition (KTEA-3) (Kaufman & Kaufman, 2014), Key Math-3 Diagnostic Assessment (Connolly, 2007), Wechsler Individual Achievement Test—Third Edition (WIAT-III) (Wechsler, 2009), Wide Range Achievement Test—Fourth Edition (WRAT-4) (Wilkinson & Robertson, 2006), Woodcock-Johnson IV Tests of Achievement (Schrank, Mather, & McGrew, 2014), and Woodcock Reading Mastery Tests, Third Edition (WRMT-III) (Woodcock, 2011). In addition to these individual achievement tests, the practitioner can rely on a student's performance on end-of-school-year group-administered achievement tests to obtain further data on a student's academic prowess compared to his or her peers and age-mates. Also, portfolio assessment of a student's academic work, particularly compared to other students in the class and grade, is helpful in gifted assessment.

CONCLUSION AND RECOMMENDATIONS

We have covered considerable material in this fourth chapter. Building upon the principles of gifted assessment discussed in the previous chapter, we have explored the intelligence quotient, the different purposes for gifted assessment, various uses of cognitive ability and academic ability tests in gifted assessment, and what IQ tests measure. The chapter has reminded the reader, and I hope that you are not yet tiring of my admonitions, that IQ testing and gifted assessment are not the same thing. The chapter has also looked at some of the more popular IQ tests used in gifted assessment.

It seems appropriate at this point to briefly review most of the key principles of gifted assessment, since they are central to what I have discussed in this chapter.

The first principle, remember, is that *how we define gifted is impo* example, for those who view intellectual giftedness as synonymous with abstract reasoning, certain composite scores and subtests with higher *g* loadings become particularly important in gifted assessment. The tripartite model of gifted-ness reminds us, however, that there are multiple ways to view giftedness; giftedness is not one unitary, real thing that exists in nature. Giftedness is a socially conceived construct, useful but not real. The second principle relevant to what we've covered in this chapter is that *gifted assessment should consider the types of available gifted programs.* This reminds us of the importance of linking our gifted assessment test battery with available gifted services, programs, and resources. Many gifted summer programs, for example, are based on highly advanced conceptual content presented at a very fast pace. This is the case for many summer gifted courses on the campuses of Duke University, Johns Hopkins University, and Northwestern University. Gifted assessment for admission into these programs must consider processing speed as a critical factor.

The third principle worthy of revisiting is that *psychometrics count.* Selection of IQ and academic ability tests should always be guided by evidence of the psychometric rigor of the tests in your test battery, and their clinical appropriate-ness for the population and the purpose for which you are testing. One example will suffice to highlight this important principle. When consulting with school districts across the United States, I have been impressed (and dismayed) with the number of gifted programs that continue to use homegrown, nonstandardized teacher rating scales with absolutely no evidence of reliability or validity. None whatsoever. It is quite shocking to observe that professionals in the schools make important, high-stakes decisions on the lives of students using instruments of unknown scientific precision or validity. This should never occur, but disappoint-ingly, it still does.

Another principle with relevance to this chapter is that *gifted assessment should be based on sound clinical judgment made by professionals.* Well-trained and experienced practitioners, not test scores, should make diagnostic decisions. David Wechsler was a firm believer in IQ tests as *clinical instruments* (A. S. Kaufman, 2013), and I wholeheartedly agree. School psychologists and others involved in the gifted assessment enterprise should never abdicate their role and responsibility in psychoeducational decision making. A too common practice in gifted assessment in many school districts (I also observe this in my international travels) is that gifted classification decisions are made based on one test score on one test. It's as if decision-making policy has been established that disregards what we know about error in measurement and test assessment standards (AERA et al., 2014). Most high-quality IQ test manuals provide confidence intervals and standard error of measurement; yet all too often students are proclaimed gifted or not-gifted based on a single obtained test score.

A fifth principle worth mentioning again is the *value of considering multiple measures when assessing any psychological construct*. I will not repeat what I discussed earlier about alternative decision-making models in gifted assessment. But I will restate that when the stakes are high, as they certainly are in gifted identification, multiple measures of the construct intelligence (as well as academic ability, creativity, motivation, leadership, etc.) make a whole lot of sense. This is one reason why a colleague and I developed the Gifted Rating Scales (Pfeiffer & Jarosewich, 2003)—to provide practitioners with corroborative data on intellectual, academic, and creative ability obtained from independent sources of information, teachers.

Finally, the principle of *gifted assessment being recurring, not a one-time process*, has huge relevance to the discussion of IQ tests in this chapter. For many years, I have advocated that students identified as intellectually or academically gifted in the schools should be reevaluated periodically, in my estimation at least every two years. I have also recommended that students tested but not found to qualify for a gifted classification be retested. This is fully consistent with a talent development model (Subotnik, 2009; Subotnik, Olszewski-Kubilius, & Worell, 2011). It is also fully consistent with a "successive hurdles approach" to psychological assessment to mitigate errors of prediction when base rates are low, as they are among the gifted (Meehl & Rosen, 1955). In the previous chapter, I explained the rationale and reasons for recurring, periodic gifted reassessment, so I won't repeat them here. What I will add is that practitioners should rely on the same assessment tests as they used previously when retesting a student for gifted classification or gifted programs.

🐟 TEST YOURSELF 🐟

1. **Terman's gifted classification scheme included a genius category for IQ scores above 140:**
   a. True
   b. False

2. **A test's ceiling is an important consideration in gifted assessment:**
   a. True
   b. False

3. **The RIAS is the most widely used test of intellectual ability in gifted assessment:**
   a. True
   b. False

4. **There is little or no research supporting the four Wechsler composite scores:**

   a. True

   b. False

5. **Pearson Assessment has published extended norms, available online, for the Wechsler scales:**

   a. True

   b. False

6. **The author advises against using above-level tests designed for older students in gifted assessment:**

   a. True

   b. False

7. **Research indicates that practitioners frequently use ipsative analysis in interpreting subtest scatter:**

   a. True

   b. False

Answers: 1. True; 2. True; 3. False; 4. False; 5. True; 6. False; 7. True.

Five

IDENTIFYING AND ASSESSING CREATIVITY

This chapter introduces the topic of creativity and assessment of creativity, a subject of high interest to both the lay public and those in the gifted field. Included is a discussion of how creativity is defined and conceptualized and how creativity relates to intelligence, giftedness, and talent development. The chapter also introduces measures of creativity that can be used as part of a gifted assessment.

To many people, both the lay public and academicians, creativity remains an ambiguous, vague, and even unscientific construct. Part of the reason for this view is that many of the early writings about creativity were mystical and outside of the realm of science (Sternberg & Lubart, 1999). Also, many early ideas about creativity were associated with Freudian theory and psychoanalysis (J. C. Kaufman, 2009; J. C. Kaufman, Plucker, & Baer, 2008; Makel & Plucker, 2008). Finally, a lot of popular books on creativity that appear on the bookshelves of Barnes & Noble or Books-a-Million tend to be pop psychology rather than rigorous, scientific treatises (Pfeiffer, 2013b).

DEFINING CREATIVITY

What do we mean by creativity? One popular notion that my students often suggest is "thinking outside the box." This is an alluring and widespread metaphor, but not a very useful or conceptually precise way of explaining exactly what creativity is. Dorothy Leonard (2010), author of a popular book on creativity, defines creativity as, "in its simplest terms . . . a process of developing and expressing novel ideas that are likely to be useful" (p. 4). She goes on to explain that creativity is not so much a talent as a goal-oriented process whose purpose is to solve a particular problem or satisfy a specific need. She concludes that the creative process begins with divergent thinking (generating an original idea), which is then evaluated by the individual (or group) and culminates in an innovative product, process, or service.

Note that Leonard (2010) is *not* talking about creative persons but

DON'T FORGET
....
One popular notion of creativity is "thinking outside the box."

rather creativity as a process that leads to something innovative and of value. Because she is not focusing on creative persons but rather the process driving creativity, Leonard's definition does not mention possible unique personality traits, motivational styles, or early developmental or family experiences of highly creative individuals. This is not necessarily a flaw or limitation in her definition. But it is instructive to point out that her focus is on the creative process, not the creative person.

Most explicit definitions of creativity that appear in the scientific field include two components. First, creativity should represent something unusual or innovative (Amabile, 1983; Baron, 1955). Second, creativity should not only represent something that is unusual or different, it must also represent something that is relevant, useful, or contextually appropriate (Runco, 2005; Sternberg & Kaufman, 2010). This second component eliminates the unusual but bizarre, which most would agree is not what we mean by creative.

There are alternative ways to view creativity as a psychological construct (J. C. Kaufman, 2009; Pfeiffer & Thompson, 2013). As I have indicated, Leonard (2010), for example, views creativity from one perspective, the process that leads to creative outcomes. Creativity can also be viewed from the perspective of studying creative people. Alternatively, we could view creativity based on how the classroom, the family, and even society might encourage or constrain the creativity process or creative person. Researchers have studied neurophysiological and cognitive components and social dynamics underlying the creative process. For example, investigators are experimenting with modern technologies such as the EEG and fMRI to understand how electrical and metabolic brain activity is associated with divergent thinking and creative problem solving (Fink & Neubauer, 2006; Jaušovec, 2000; Mölle, Marshall, Wolf, Fehm, & Born, 1999). Most readers are probably familiar with those who suggest that the brainstorming process leads groups to generate a greater number of creative ideas. Finally, we can view creativity from the vantage point of judging, in a scientifically defensible and rigorous way, the degree of creativity present in products that individuals create (Pfeiffer, 2013b).

In the gifted literature all four of these ways of viewing creativity have been investigated. They are called the four P's of creativity (creative person, creative process, creative press, and creative product). Like the different conceptualizations

DON'T FORGET

....

Just as there are different ways of viewing giftedness, there are different ways of viewing creativity.

of giftedness discussed in the previous chapter, there is no one correct perspective. The four perspectives are related and complementary in helping us understand what is meant by creativity. Historically, the practical classroom assessment of creativity has focused primarily on the first perspective, assessing how creative a given student might be—those judged to be highly creative are considered by many as gifted. The other three perspectives—the creative process, the creative press, and the creative product—have been the focus of research but not practice. Thus they have not enjoyed as much attention in the classroom or in gifted assessment as the creative person. In my opinion, and consistent with the tripartite model of giftedness and a talent development perspective, however, the fourth perspective—assessing the creative product—could become of value to practitioners as an element in the gifted assessment toolbox. It is not difficult, as I will discuss shortly, for practitioners to develop reliable methods to judge the level of creativity of student products. And it is enjoyable.

One of the first psychologists to bring attention to creativity and the creative process was Joy P. Guilford, who used the opportunity of his presidential address at the 1950 convention of the American Psychological Association to advocate for creativity as a relevant topic for psychological research (Guilford, 1950). Guilford (1967) viewed creativity as a component of intelligence, and conceptualized intelligence within a three-dimensional structure of intellect model that consists of operations, content, and products. If you took an intelligence testing course in graduate school, you probably recall that Guilford's model includes 120 different mental abilities. One of these operations is *divergent thinking*. For example, if we asked a group of high school students taking a cultural anthropology course, "What are the advantages of our retaining different dialects and languages?" we would obtain a sample (albeit a very limited sample based on a one-item test!) of their ability to think divergently. Guilford's structure of intellect model proposes four components of divergent thinking, which I'll explain by way of this one-item divergent thinking example.

There are a number of ways in which we could use Guilford's model to evaluate and score each student's response to the one-item hypothetical question. We could count the total number of different ideas that each student suggests. This is a measure of Guilford's first component, *fluency*. We could determine how many different categories of ideas (in this example, how many different advantages) each student generates. This is a measure of Guilford's second component, *flexibility*.

We could actually determine the unusualness of each idea; some suggested advantages will be listed by many students (in our small sample or even in a much larger representative group of high school students), whereas a few advantages will be listed by only a very few students—the very rare response. This index of rareness is a measure of Guilford's third component, *originality*. We could also measure the fourth component in Guilford's model, which is *elaboration*. Elaboration is the ability to develop and enrich (to *decorate*) each idea with greater detail, complexity, and richness.

We could even be creative (I couldn't resist the wordplay) and go beyond Guilford's four components to measure a fifth element, the *usefulness* of each suggested idea. Determining the relative usefulness of test responses is more subjective and fraught with measurement difficulties. Theoretically, however, we could design a test that allowed us to reliably measure this fifth potential component of divergent thinking.

Guilford's four components of divergent thinking serve as the foundation for one of the most popular tests of creativity, the Torrance Tests of Creative Thinking (Torrance, 1974, 2008). The TTCT, as it is commonly referred to, is a widely used test in gifted identification (Hunsaker & Callahan, 1995). If you are considering including an assessment of creativity in your gifted assessment test battery, you will want to become familiar with the TTCT. You will also want to judge how well the test might work given the model of giftedness you decide to embrace and local school district needs.

Guilford focused on the creative process. However, a number of researchers have focused on the other P's of creativity. Perhaps the most popular and widely recognized work has been writing that examines highly creative adults. As I have already mentioned, in my opinion a focus on the creative adult is less relevant or helpful and not easily translatable to our work with high-ability students in the schools. This avenue of scientific inquiry is fascinating reading, no doubt. It examines highly eminent adults who are already well established as creative in their respective field. The risk is that any implications for early parenting, family, and curriculum and instructional pedagogy in the schools that it might correlate with, much less directly facilitate, adult creativity are at best tenuous and fraught with interpretive errors. But the study of the creative person is provocative and extremely interesting. The study of the creative adult is akin to bench research. It is unquestionably fascinating and important research, which holds promise for insights into how the creative spark in adulthood is initially planted and nurtured in youth among our most highly creative geniuses. For example, Berry (1981) reported that 28% of the Nobel laureates in physics came from homes where the father had an academic background, and Simonton (2013) identified motivation, drive, and persistence as important in the early development of highly recognized creative artists and leaders.

The purported relationship between creativity and mental illness is another area of study within the creative person domain that is arguably of limited usefulness to practitioners for work in the schools. But like well-written biographies of eminent creative adults, it can make for spellbinding reading. Those of us with a fervent interest in giftedness and creativity are perhaps a tad voyeuristic in our desire to discover unique insights into the personal lives and inner worlds of the most famous eminent and creative persons—such as Beethoven, Michelangelo, Newton, and Einstein (Simonton, 2007, 2008).

However, the study of the creative process and how schooling, parenting, and environment (the creative press) affect creativity bears a more direct relationship, ultimately, to our work with high-ability students. In essence, focusing on these two P's speaks to what we as psychologists, teachers, and parents can do to foster a culture that encourages the development of creativity in the schools. However, gifted assessment in the schools does not directly align with measuring the creative process or the environment. These two P's are best left, at the moment, to the applied researcher, and not the practitioner concerned with gifted assessment in the schools. Readers interested in learning more about evidence-based ways to increase creativity in the classroom are directed to a chapter I coauthored with one of my graduate students (Pfeiffer & Thompson, 2013) and a chapter on creativity in my recent book (Pfeiffer, 2013b).

My experience suggests, and research confirms, that children and adolescents, even those who test at very high levels of intellectual ability, vary considerably in terms of their capacity for creative expression. This does not mean that students are either creative or not creative, born as either creative or uncreative (Plucker, Beghetto, & Dow, 2004). Individuals demonstrate meaningful and significant individual differences in terms of their capacity to be creative. This potential is likely based on the dynamic and synergetic interaction of multiple factors, including genetic, temperamental, personality, and attitudinal factors and early life experiences (Pfeiffer, 1978, 2013b).

Creativity can be viewed from a talent development perspective; it is an essential element and expression of expertise and eminence in any culturally valued field or domain (Pfeiffer, 1978, 2013b; Sternberg, Jarvin, & Grigorenko, 2011; Subotnik, 2003). I frequently lecture on this very idea in terms of the development of elite youth athletes (Pfeiffer, 2008a, Pfeiffer 2013b). What we observe repeatedly in the real world is that as young children of high ability develop, work hard, and are provided facilitative experiences and opportunities, they demonstrate increased likelihood for domain-specific creativity in one or more subjects or fields (Baer, 1998, 2010, 2011). This is consistent with what we observe as highly gifted young athletes develop into elite world-class competitors. They develop domain-specific creativity as they reach the highest levels in their chosen sport. This does not mean that domain-general creativity does not exist. And it does not mean that domain-general creativity can't be measured. There is research evidence for the content generality of creativity. And there is research evidence that it can be reliably measured (e.g., Plucker, 1998, 1999, 2005; Torrance, 1990; Treffinger, 1986). However, my work with many tens of hundreds of extraordinarily bright middle and high school students during my days as director of the Duke TIP program and later as codirector of the Florida Governor's School for Space Science and Technology has led me to appreciate the preeminent importance of domain-specific creativity from a talent development perspective (Pfeiffer, 2013b). This leads me to advocate that gifted assessment is more fruitful when it focuses on *domain-specific creativity*. This is in contrast to today's practice in the schools of spending time attempting to measure a student's domain-general level of creativity as part of the gifted identification process. More on this very point will shortly follow.

MEASURING CREATIVITY

We now turn to the nuts-and-bolts of this chapter, examining some of the more popular tests and procedures that measure creativity. I intentionally selected tests and procedures that, in my experience, can become tools in a gifted assessment toolbox. I should mention that the assessment of creativity is a not common practice as part of gifted assessment; McClain and Pfeiffer (2012) report, for example, that only nine states (18%) require the use of creativity tests in gifted assessment. This is an interesting finding for at least two reasons: one, because so few states require, as policy, that schools within their jurisdiction assess creativity, and two, because twenty-seven states (54%) actually include creativity in their definition of giftedness.

As mentioned earlier in this chapter, we can measure creativity from four different perspectives: the person, the process, the product, or the environment ("press"). Recall that I shared my bias earlier in the chapter; practitioners in the schools and in private practice benefit most from a practical approach that assesses the creativity of actual products that students have created. This recommendation resonates with psychologists and educators familiar with authentic assessment.

Divergent Thinking: Torrance Tests of Creative Thinking

The most popular and most widely used test of creativity is the Torrance Tests of Creative Thinking (TTCT) (Torrance, 1966, 1972, 1974, 1990, 2008). E. Paul

≋ Rapid Reference 5.1   Torrance Tests of Creative Thinking

The TTCT consists of both verbal and figural subtests.

Torrance was a leading figure in the creativity field for over half a century, and his students and followers continue to promote his ideas and his test (Hunsaker & Callahan, 1995). The TTCT is based on Guilford's (1967) structure of intellect model, described earlier. In addition to being used by practitioners in gifted identification, the TTCT is often used in efficacy studies and meta-analyses of the impact of creativity intervention programs (J. C. Kaufman et al., 2008).

The TTCT battery includes both verbal and figural subtests, each of which includes two forms, A and B. Administration and scoring is standardized, and the technical manual includes detailed norms. The Verbal forms include seven subtests:

- Asking. The student is shown a picture in this and the next two subtests. For Asking, the student is instructed by the examiner to ask as many questions as possible about the picture.
- Guessing Causes. The student is asked by the examiner to list possible causes for the action depicted in the picture.
- Guessing Consequences. The student lists possible consequences for the action depicted in the picture.
- Product Improvement. The student is asked to suggest possible changes to improve a toy.
- Unusual Uses. The student is invited by the examiner to generate many different possible uses for an ordinary item.
- Unusual Questions. The student is prompted by the examiner to ask as many questions as possible about an ordinary item (this item does not appear in the 1990 or 2008 editions).
- Just Suppose. The student is asked to "just suppose" that an improbable event has occurred, and then asked to list possible consequences.

The TTCT Figural tests include three subtests:

- Picture Construction. The student starts with a basic shape and is asked by the examiner to expand on it to create a picture.
- Picture Completion. The student is invited to finish and then title incomplete drawings.
- Lines/Circles. The student is asked to modify many different series of lines or circles.

The TTCT is easy to administer. It can be a bit tricky to score some of the categories, including originality, emotional expressiveness, and richness of imagery. Young children enjoy working on the tasks. There is a copious body of research on the psychometric qualities of the TTCT. Overall, the research is fairly consistent in supporting the reliability and concurrent validity of the Torrance Tests (J. C. Kaufman et al., 2008; Kim, 2011). However, research on the construct and predictive validity of the TTCT is less conclusive and open to widely differing interpretations. Viewing the same data, some researchers are laudatory in singing the praises of the TTCT (e.g., Cramond, Matthews-Morgan, Bandalos, & Zuo, 2005; Kim, 2011), whereas others raise compelling arguments against the use of the Torrance Tests (Almeida, Prieto, Ferrando, Oliviera, & Ferrándiz, 2008; Baer, 2011; Simonton, 2007). It is unclear, for example, how many factors the test consists of and whether it makes sense to report only a composite, or single, score, as is typically done in gifted assessment practice in the schools, rather than report score categories and profiles—as Torrance, in fact, originally proposed (Scholastic Testing Service, 2009). John Baer, a highly respected authority in the creativity field, contributed an article to a special issue of the journal *Psychology of Aesthetics, Creativity, and the Arts* on the relevance of the Torrance Tests in the twenty-first century. Baer (2011) raised a number of compelling arguments cautioning against the use of the Torrance Tests in gifted assessment. For example, Baer indicated that we lack evidence that the Torrance Tests measure anything significantly related to real-world creativity. He also argued that the TTCT distorts (or as he put it, "warps") ideas about creativity by reinforcing the notion that creativity is all about coming up with wild ideas, and by taking the view that creativity is one, monolithic thing, rather than domain specific.

My hesitation in endorsing the TTCT as a test that should routinely be included in a gifted assessment toolbox goes beyond some of the TTCT's very real psychometric limitations. My reluctance to recommend the Torrance Tests as a standard gifted assessment measure is based on the theoretical rationale underlying the test: the TTCT measures creative thinking in two (figural and verbal) domains based on a *g*-type, general, single-ability view of creativity and creative potential. This runs counter to my own thinking and that of a growing number of contemporary authorities who view creativity as multidimensional and domain specific (Pfeiffer, 2013b). No one is creative in all domains; expertise varies by domains, and so does creativity—it is highly domain specific.

In my opinion, it makes little sense to use a general test of global creativity when conducting a gifted assessment, other than perhaps in the early grades before students acquire content-specific knowledge that can be used to demonstrate creativity in specific domains.

In many states, the TTCT is quite often the only measure used for eligibility and placement in gifted programs (McClain & Pfeiffer, 2012; Scholastic Testing Service, 2009). For the reasons already mentioned, I fear that the TTCT can easily be misused in making important gifted eligibility decisions about individual students. I have long advocated, consistent with conventional psychometrics authorities (Ackerman, 2013; Mulaik, 1972), that practitioners should use at least three highly reliable and valid measures when attempting to measure a trait such as creativity. *Relying on any one measure to estimate an underlying trait or classification falls short of best practices in gifted assessment.* This, of course, is not an indictment of the TTCT but rather a cautionary measure to avoid overreliance on any popular test in gifted assessment.

I believe that the TTCT holds promise with younger students as *one* measure of global creative thinking and as a research and program evaluation tool. Its diagnostic value becomes less clear when used with older students as part of a gifted assessment battery when more authentic and more domain-specific measures of creativity exist and can be used. My inclination and recommendation (some might say bias) is to rely on more authentic assessment of creative artifacts in specific domains. At least by the 3rd or 4th grade, it seems preferable, and more fair, equitable, and valid, to assess the creativity of actual products that students produce, rather than using global and high-inference measures of creativity to make decisions on whether a student is gifted. Shortly, I will describe the Consensual Assessment Technique, which I believe provides a more authentic measure of creativity. It is based on how creativity is judged in the real world by experts. But I am getting ahead of myself. First, we will very briefly discuss two relatively new creativity scales based on Guilford's ideas and the Torrance Tests (TTCT): the Abedi Test of Creativity (Abedi, 2000) and the Profile of Creative Abilities (Ryser, 2007).

Divergent Thinking: Profile of Creative Abilities

Gail Ryser's Profile of Creative Abilities (PCA) (Ryser, 2007) is derived from Guilford's model and includes tasks similar to those found on the TTCT (J. C. Kaufman, Plucker, & Russell, 2012). One difference is that Ryser included real-world divergent thinking test items within a format that should provide a more realistic assessment of divergent thinking skills (Plucker, Runco, & Lim, 2006). The PCA consists of two subtests and two rating scales; the subtests measure two aspects of divergent production, and the rating scales (home and school versions) measure creative abilities, domain-relevant skills, creativity-relevant skills, and intrinsic motivation.

The PCA is easy to administer; in fact, the examiner's manual states that "classroom teachers, school psychologists, or any other personnel with training in standardized test administration" are qualified (Ryser, 2007, p. 9). The test is designed for students ages 5.0–14.11; subtest 1 can be administered in small groups whereas subtest 2 requires individual administration. Scoring is not simple and can be challenging, similar to scoring the TTCT. The standardization sample is relatively small ($N = 640$); split-half and alternate forms reliability, as reported in the examiner's manual, is adequate, whereas test-retest reliability is fair (.70 for drawings subtest; .74 for categories subtest; .73 for home rating scale; .86 for school rating scale). The examiner's manual presents limited research in support of construct or predictive validity; for example, the TTCT and the Scales for Identifying Gifted Students (Ryser & McConnell, 2004) were used as the two criterion measures—neither are "gold standard" options as criterion measures.

The PCA is a relatively new creativity test, and so far no articles by other researchers have been published on its reliability and diagnostic, predictive, and construct validity (Pfeiffer, 2010). It is fair to conclude that it is too soon to know how well the PCA will ultimately fare relative to the TTCT as a measure of divergent thinking. I think that it incorporates features such as real-world divergent thinking tasks that make it attractive and potentially more reliable than the TTCT. It shares the same limitations as the TTCT and other measures of divergent thinking in terms of uncertain predictive validity and because many feel its view of creativity is too narrow and excludes important aspects of creativity (J. C. Kaufman et al., 2012). I can envision a use for the PCA in the same way that I earlier suggested the TTCT could be used, as one instrument in a gifted assessment toolbox—it holds potential promise with younger students as *one* measure of global divergent thinking and as a research and program evaluation tool. Its diagnostic value becomes more suspect when used with older students as part of a gifted assessment battery when more authentic and more domain-specific measures of creativity can be used (Pfeiffer, 2010).

Self-Report: Abedi Test of Creativity

The Abedi Test of Creativity (ATC) (Abedi, 2000) is a fifty-six-item questionnaire that takes about 15 minutes to complete. It is designed to measure the same four subskills found in the TTCT. What makes the ATC unique is that it is a self-rating measure. For each item, the respondent is required to select from three options the self-description that best-fits her or him. What follows are two examples from the ATC (Abedi, 2000). The first item is designed to measure flexibility, and asks:

How do you approach a complex task?

- I come up with a single approach
- I may be able to come up with a few approaches
- I will be able to come up with a variety of approaches

The next illustrative item from the ATC is designed to measure originality:

Do people think that you come up with unique ideas?

- No, they don't
- Sometimes, they do
- Often, they do

Administration and scoring of the ATC are straightforward and do not require any training or expert judgment. The items certainly have face validity. As you can see from the two examples, selection of option 3 receives the highest score for flexibility and originality. The issue, of course, is whether a self-report measure of creativity can be valid. There is very little research to date on the ATC. The research that has been published does not, unfortunately, support the convergent, construct, or predictive validity of the ATC (Althuizen, Wierenga, & Rossiter, 2010). This is not all that surprising; it very likely is unrealistic and overreaching to expect that any self-report scale, no matter how well conceived, would be effective in measuring a person's creativity.

My research lab piloted the reliability and validity of student self-ratings and peer nominations of giftedness. We found that peer nominations were fairly reliable and correlated fairly well with teacher ratings on the Gifted Rating Scales (Pfeiffer & Jarosewich, 2003), whereas student self-ratings were hopelessly unpredictable and unreliable. J. C. Kaufman, Evans, and Baer (2010) asked 4th graders how creative they were in several areas and collected artifacts in those domains. They found, not surprisingly, that the students were quite poor judges of their own creativity. The bottom line is that self-report measures of creativity are suspect and should not be used in gifted assessment.

Teacher Checklist: Gifted Rating Scales—Creativity Scale

We next briefly turn to teacher checklists. There are a number of published creativity checklists; the two most popular are the Scales for Rating Behavioral Characteristics of Superior Students (SRBCSS) (Renzulli et al., 2002) and the

Gifted Rating Scales (GRS) (Pfeiffer & Jarosewich, 2003). Other published teacher rating scales include the Gifted Evaluation Scale, Second Edition (GES-2) (McCarney & Anderson, 1998), the Gifted and Talented Evaluation Scales (GATES) (Gilliam, Carpenter, & Christensen, 1996), and the Scales for Identifying Gifted Students (SIGS) (Ryser & McConnell, 2004).

I admit, upfront, that I am a far from unbiased commentator on the various gifted rating scales since I am the lead author of the GRS. Because of my familiarity with the Gifted Rating Scales, I will describe the GRS as illustrative of teacher checklists used to identify creativity, and I encourage the reader to seek other sources for information on the SRBCSS and other teacher checklists (e.g., Gray, McCallum, & Bain, 2009; J. C. Kaufman et al., 2012; Matthews, 2007; Renzulli, Siegle, Reis, Gavin, & Reed, 2009; Ward, 2005, 2007).

The Gifted Rating Scales (Pfeiffer & Jarosewich, 2003) is a multidimensional measure of giftedness that includes six scales. In addition to teacher ratings on creativity, the GRS rates intellectual ability, academic ability, artistic talent, leadership ability, and motivation. There are two forms of the GRS, one for preschool/kindergarten (GRS-P; ages 4.0–6.11 years) and one for school-aged students (GRS-S; ages 6.0–13.11). Each of the forms consists of twelve items rated on 9-point Likert scales; for each item, the teacher is asked to rate how the student compares to "typical" children of the same age. More detailed information on the GRS and the other five scales appears in Chapter 6. Here we focus on the Creativity scale.

Both the GRS-P and GRS-S forms include a twelve-item Creativity scale. The twelve items represent behaviors characteristic of creative thinking and productivity (e.g., "displays an active imagination, thinks or acts imaginatively"; "experiments with ideas in new or imaginative ways"). Age-based raw scores are converted to T scores and cumulative percentages by age.

The GRS was developed because of limitations in the content, technical adequacy, and diagnostic accuracy of other teacher-rated gifted scales (Jarosewich, 2003, 2007). Input from authorities in the gifted, creativity, child development, test development, and school psychology fields provided the basis for item development. Pilot testing and two field tests were conducted prior to final item revision and national standardization. The GRS is easy to complete, score,

≡ Rapid Reference 5.2 Gifted Rating Scales

The Gifted Rating Scales consist of a seventy-two-item teacher-completed rating scale that includes a twelve-item Creativity scale.

and interpret. The GRS standardization samples closely match the U.S. census in terms of ethnicity and parent education level—a proxy for socioeconomic status (SES). A large number of reliability and validation studies have been conducted in the United States and internationally (Lee & Pfeiffer, 2006; Li, Lee, Pfeiffer, & Petscher, 2008; Li, Pfeiffer, Petscher, Kumtepe, & Mo, 2008; Margulies & Floyd, 2004; Pfeiffer & Jarosewich, 2003, 2007; Pfeiffer, Kumtepe, & Rosado, 2006; Pfeiffer, Petscher, & Kumtepe, 2008; Pfeiffer, Petscher, & Jarosewich, 2007; Pfeiffer & Petscher, 2008; Ward, 2005, 2007). GRS creativity scale validation studies have compared scores to the TTCT, SRBCSS, and actual classroom performance in high-creativity subject areas (Pfeiffer & Jarosewich, 2003; Siu, 2010). Overall, research studies indicate that the GRS, including the Creativity scale, enjoys exceptionally high reliability and evidence of criterion, construct, and predictive validity. This is particularly noteworthy for a twelve-item teacher rating creativity scale, especially given the technical limitations of other rating scales reported in the literature.

The test manual warns that the GRS should *never* be used in isolation from other tests and measures as part of a gifted assessment to corroborate or rule out a gifted classification. The gifted classification ranges in the test manual based on the student's obtained *T* scores are intentionally labeled as *probabilities* of a gifted classification: low, moderate, high, and very high probability. This was designed purposely to remind practitioners to use clinical judgment and multiple pieces of evidence to classify a student as gifted or not-gifted. I recommend that the GRS become a standard part of the gifted assessment toolbox but *always* be used as part of a test battery in conjunction with other data corroborating a classification decision. Teacher ratings of creativity on the GRS work particularly well in combination with assessment of general intellectual ability and assessment of student products using the next procedure, the Consensual Assessment Technique.

Consensual Assessment Technique

The Consensual Assessment Technique (CAT) is based on the principle that the best measure of creativity of an idea, performance, or product, or any artifact for that matter, is the collective judgment of experts in that field. Panels of expert

---

≡ *Rapid Reference 5.3 Consensual Assessment Technique*

The Consensual Assessment Technique is a widely used creativity research instrument that holds promise as a clinical tool in creativity assessment.

judges are asked to rate the creativity of products such as short stories, poems, art works, science projects, drama or dance performances, or musical auditions. I must, again, disclose a personal bias: I am particularly partial to the CAT approach to creativity assessment. I used this very approach in my dissertation, along with the more traditional measures of divergent thinking and cognitive style, at the encouragement of my research mentor, Michael Wallach (Wallach, 1976), to rate creative writing products by 6th graders (Pfeiffer, 1978). I found the CAT approach easy to use although it is time consuming. In my research, I invited a group of noted authors of published short stories to rate a large sample of creative writing products of 6th graders. I provided them with a simple rubric (the Creative Writing Rating Scale) and asked them to use their own judgment and independently rate the creativity of each short story. Approximately five years after I piloted the CAT technique, Teresa Amabile (1982, 1983) first reported on its use as a research tool; many researchers have subsequently used the CAT, and it is considered the gold standard for creativity assessment (Carson, 2006; Hass, 2013). (I now routinely admonish my doctoral students to publish their dissertation research; a personal lesson learned by not publishing in 1978 my dissertation study reporting perhaps the first use of the CAT technique in creativity research!)

The CAT is considered "a powerful research tool" (Hass, 2013, p. 356). And here is the rub; it has *not* been used outside the research arena by practitioners as a viable clinical tool. I believe that this has been a missed opportunity in the gifted field. The CAT rightfully belongs in everyone's gifted assessment toolbox. Here is why.

First of all, the CAT is very easy to use. It is not weighed down by any one theory of creativity or giftedness (J. C. Kaufman et al., 2008). It employs a technique used and respected worldwide in the talent development field: internationally, the combined opinions of experts select the winners of the Pulitzer Prize, the Emmys, and the Academy Awards, the Nobel Prize, the Fields Medal in mathematics, and many Olympic events. At a more local level, the judgments of experts are routinely employed to select candidates for elite youth athletic teams and membership in competitive dance, theater, and music conservancies. The CAT is based on actual creative performances or artifacts; it reflects how creativity is viewed in the real world.

There is considerable evidence that the CAT is a highly reliable tool, especially when used by experts, and not untrained novices or neophytes, in the specific field (Baer, Kaufman, & Gentile, 2004; J. C. Kaufman, Baer, Cole, & Sexton, 2008; J. C. Kaufman, Lee, Baer, & Lee, 2007; Priest, 2006). The CAT has been successfully used as a research tool to validate poetic creativity in 4th graders (Cheng, Wang, Liu, & Chen, 2010), interior design assignments by college students (Allen, 2010), musical improvisation (Eisenberg & Thompson, 2011), and sentence captions generated by college students (J. C. Kaufman, Lee, Baer, & Lee, 2007). My research lab piloted its use in judging the creative humor of captions produced by high school students for *New Yorker* cartoons. In other words, the CAT enjoys great flexibility in its application.

Then why hasn't it been used as a clinical tool? I think the answer is twofold. First, the CAT is hampered by the time required to produce the products (or performances) that the judges will rate. In my dissertation study, I asked that each student complete two creative writing samples—this took the students considerably more time than if I had administered the TTCT, PCA, or any other published measure of divergent thinking. Second, securing a panel of local experts in a given subject area and asking them to rate the artifacts is also time consuming. Admittedly, it took my panel of experts many hours to read and rate the creative writing artifacts. Neither of these two limitations, however, should dissuade the practitioner from using the CAT. It is a proven assessment procedure with a long and rich research history. The CAT offers the practitioner the opportunity to collect valid creativity ratings on a group of students. The CAT is based on a domain-specific model of creativity, which I embrace. Two obvious uses of the CAT in creativity assessment are group screening for gifted classification as part of a broadband gifted assessment protocol, and program evaluation of a school system's or a gifted program's effectiveness in promoting creativity as part of its curriculum.

It has not yet been established just how many experts are required to produce a valid aggregate rating. In the clinical world, I would suggest at least three, which is a much smaller number than is typically reported in the research literature (e.g., Baer et al., 2004). It has also not yet been established just how much instruction or directions the experts should be given, although there is some research suggesting less is better (Kaufman & Baer, 2012). The creativity field is beginning to develop new assessment methods that rate the creativity of domain-specific products. These new tests hold promise in furthering creativity assessment from a domain-specific perspective. For example, the Creative Scientific Ability Test (C-SAT) (Sak & Ayas, 2013), designed for 6th to 8th graders, is a measure of scientific creativity in biology, chemistry, physics, and ecology.

CREATIVITY, INTELLIGENCE, AND TALENT DEVELOPMENT

We have covered a lot of territory in this chapter on creativity and creativity assessment. It is helpful to remember that just as there are many different ways to view giftedness, there are many different ways to view creativity. The great majority of authorities in the creativity field agree on two points in defining creativity. They agree that for an idea, product, or performance to be creative, it must be *original*. Second, most experts also contend that the idea, artifact, or performance must satisfy some *usefulness* or *utility* standards, whether scientific or esthetic. A third criterion, less often cited in the literature but worth mentioning, is that the creative idea, product, or performance must be *surprising* (Simonton, 2013). These three criteria focus on outcome—on judging the creativity of something produced. They are based on a domain-specific model of creativity. And they reflect a model of talent development with expertise and creative perform-ance at the pinnacle, as displayed in Figure 5.1 (Pfeiffer, 2013b; Simonton, 2013).

In contrast to this domain-specific viewpoint, there are some in the creativity and gifted fields who believe that creativity is a general ability like psychometric *g*—that an "all-purpose, domain-transcending set of creative thinking abilities exist" (Baer, 2008, p. 92). The preponderance of research does not favor this view, although admittedly the jury is still out. Tests like the TTCT fit within a creativity-general viewpoint. This leaves us with some unanswered questions about creativity assessment.

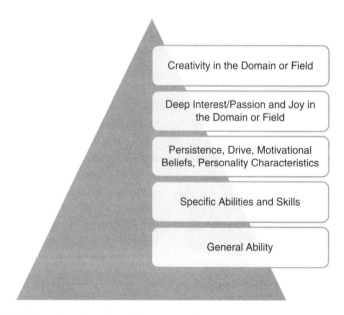

Figure 5.1 How Creativity Interfaces with Other Factors Critical to Talent Development

Source: Revised from Pfeiffer, 2013b.

Unanswered Questions

The first question is whether we should assess creative thinking using tasks that are based on a domain-general perspective or assess the creativity of products from a domain-specific perspective. This speaks to the essence of the generality-specificity issue. It may be that young children in the first few grades of school reliably vary in their levels of general creativity–relevant aptitudes, skills, and dispositions. If, on the one hand, we believe that these individual differences are valid, meaningful, and predictive of future behavior, then we can use tests such as the TTCT to help select young students for gifted programs. If, on the other hand, we believe that creative performance unfolds only *after* the acquisition of a level of foundational knowledge and skills in a specific domain or field, then it makes less sense to administer generic creativity tests to young children as part of a gifted assessment battery.

A second and related question is whether creativity assessment should be used at all for gifted identification or gifted classification. If one believes in the development of domain-specific expertise and creative performance (see Simonton, 2013), then it is logical to view creativity unfolding later rather than earlier in the child's progression toward competence and eventually expertise in any field. If this is the case, then it would seem that creativity measures should not be used as front-end, early diagnostic measures—especially in the early school grades before students have had the time or opportunity to acquire the requisite knowledge, attitudes, dispositional traits, and skills in subjects or fields. In other words, we would expect creativity to follow, not precede, developing expertise in any field, be it science, math, geography, writing, the humanities, music, dance, and so forth.

A third question is whether a creativity measure, if used in gifted identification, should ever be used alone for a gifted classification. A number of authorities in the gifted field, dating back to Guilford (1967), believe in the *threshold hypothesis* that high intellectual ability is a necessary condition for high creativity. In other words, a student is unlikely to develop into a highly creative adult if she or he doesn't possess a certain threshold of high intelligence (Pfeiffer & Thompson, 2013; Renzulli, 1978; Reis & Renzulli, 2009a, 2009b). If one believes in this relationship between intelligence and creativity, then it makes sense to administer measures of cognitive ability along with measures of creativity as part of a gifted assessment. Most researchers today believe that creativity and intelligence are conceptually related and not completely disjointed (J. C. Kaufman & Plucker, 2011).

Finally, and I alluded to this question earlier in the chapter, should creativity assessment perhaps be limited to evaluating individual students or a program's impact in fostering creativity, and *not* be used as a gifted identification measure or a measure to initially admit a student into a gifted program. This final question is not meant to suggest a diminished importance or value for the creativity construct or for creativity measurement as part of gifted assessment. Assessment of an individual student's creativity and a program's impact on creativity are important and laudatory goals. And in my opinion, they can and should become a regular part of gifted assessment in the schools. The question is whether creativity assessment in the schools should be at the front end of a program as part of gifted identification or further along in the program to help evaluate the development of creativity among high-ability students.

🪶 TEST YOURSELF 🪶

1. **Nine states (18%) require the use of creativity tests in gifted assessment:**
   a. True
   b. False

2. **The Torrance Tests of Creative Thinking (TTCT) includes figural but not verbal subtests:**
   a. True
   b. False

3. **The Profile of Creative Abilities (PCA) is derived from Guilford's model and includes tasks similar to those found on the TTCT:**
   a. True
   b. False

4. **The Creativity scale of the Gifted Rating Scale (GRS) consists of twenty-five items rated by the teacher on a 3-point Likert scale:**
   a. True
   b. False

5. **The Consensual Assessment Technique (CAT) is based on Carl Jung's theory of creativity and the collective unconscious:**
   a. True
   b. False

6. **Simonton suggests that creative products are marked by three criteria: they are unique, useful, and surprising:**
   a. True
   b. False

7. **One issue in the creativity field is the debate over generality-specificity:**
   a. True
   b. False

Answers: 1. True; 2. False; 3. True; 4. False; 5. False; 6. True; 7. True.

Six

ALTERNATIVE GIFTED ASSESSMENT METHODS

This chapter discusses alternative assessment tests and procedures that have been used in gifted identification and assessment. You will read about teacher and parent nominations, portfolio assessment, rubric scoring of student products, and teacher gifted rating scales. The chapter also includes discussion of an innovative readiness for grade acceleration scale. Many of the tests and procedures discussed in this chapter should become a part of a comprehensive test library for anyone interested in working with high-ability students.

TEACHER AND PARENT NOMINATIONS

Teacher and parent nominations have been used to screen students as the first step of a comprehensive gifted identification process. Nominations can focus on general ability or on a wide array of specific abilities and talents. Schack and Starko (1990) report that teachers consider the following four criteria particularly helpful in identifying a student as gifted: is creative, learns easily and quickly, initiates own learning, and is curious. A study by Lee and Olszewski-Kubilius (2004) examined the validity of parent nominations as part of Northwestern University's Midwest Talent Search program. They found that scores on the verbal and mathematics subtests of the SAT and ACT—above-level testing used by this talent search—were similar for applicants who qualified by standardized testing or by parent nomination. Parent nomination, however, did not significantly increase the pool of typically underrepresented applicants.

In my opinion, there is some merit in using teacher and parent nominations as a first step in a comprehensive gifted assessment protocol. The process involves parents and teachers, important stakeholders in the school system, in gifted education, and in the gifted identification process. This is clearly beneficial politically. Also, it is inexpensive and easy logistically for practitioners to implement. Finally, parent and teacher nominations can be designed to identify student interests and information on a host of related constructs, including motivation, self-regulation, persistence, and passion for learning, which might not be accessed by traditional assessment measures.

DON'T FORGET

Grade acceleration is an evidence-based intervention for many gifted students.

Parent and teacher nominations are not without potential problems, however. The most obvious problem is the lack of scientific rigor in the nomination process and in the forms that are used. Practitioners need to be cautious in how they go about inviting parents and/or teachers to nominate students; for example, the wording of the instructions on the nomination form and whether or not the practitioner provides concrete examples to assist the nominators in understanding the general or specific criteria can have a profound impact on which students are nominated (or not nominated!). Cunningham, Callahan, Plucker, Roberson, and Rapkin (1998) investigated the reliability and validity of a peer nomination form used to identify Hispanic-Latino students of outstanding talent. They concluded that the nomination scale held promise but further work was needed before recommending its use in actual practice.

A colleague and I conducted a study to determine whether students might be able to accurately nominate and rate peers from their class on dimensions relevant to gifted identification. We invited 3rd and 8th graders to nominate and rate their classmates, and compared their ratings with standardized teacher ratings (Blei & Pfeiffer, 2007). We obtained some unexpected findings. We found that popularity confounded the accuracy of the student nominations and ratings. Quite frankly, our research findings were disappointing; we did not obtain support for the use of peer nominations or ratings as part of a gifted identification process. If a practitioner decides to use parent or teacher nominations as a first stage in gifted assessment, it is highly recommended that the forms ask about specific, not general or global, behaviors (Worrell & Erwin, 2011). Even so, the research indicates that caution should be used in seeking teacher and/or parent nominations.

PORTFOLIO ASSESSMENT

A portfolio is a systematic collection of student work that provides a sample of a student's abilities, progress, and/or accomplishments in a general or specific domain (Johnsen, 1996, 2008). Many assessment experts argue that portfolios provide more authentic, naturalistic, and educationally valid records than

CAUTION

The author cautions against the use of peer nominations in gifted identification.

more traditional standardized educational assessments do (Shaklee, Barbour, Ambrose, & Hansford, 1997). Some authorities in the gifted field contend that portfolio assessment is invaluable in assessing growth in areas including creativity and critical thinking, with implications for identification, progress monitoring, curriculum development, and program evaluation (Borland & Wright, 1994).

These different assessment procedures and tests require the examinee to perform tasks that they will be expected to perform in an authentic or real-world context (Pfeiffer & Blei, 2008). Examples include composing short stories or poems, writing an editorial or opinion piece on current events, designing an experiment, solving a complicated equation, or debating an issue. Portfolio assessment entails the evaluation of a representative body of the student's academic products and accomplishments over the course of a term, year, or even the student's entire time in school. To increase the reliability and validity of judgments and the precise measurement of products, practitioners are advised to create rubrics to help rate and judge the quality of the products or performance (Van Tassel-Baska, 2008). To increase the preciseness of the portfolio assessment, it is recommended that practitioners convert the rubric to a numerical scale and quantify the ratings (Pfeiffer & Blei, 2008).

There are a number of ways in which portfolio assessment can be used as part of gifted assessment. In fact, portfolio assessment can be applied to many of the purposes of gifted assessment that were discussed in Chapter 1, including gifted identification, evaluation of student growth, and evaluation of a gifted program's curriculum and impact. Two important decisions when planning to use a portfolio as part of gifted assessment are determining the content to be included in the portfolios and how the samples or artifacts will be assessed. Let me briefly address each of these points.

The first step in a portfolio assessment process is deciding on the purpose or purposes of the assessment and the type of portfolio (Shaklee et al., 1997). This decision guides what the content will consist of. For example, Borland and Wright (1994) describe the effective application of a portfolio assessment protocol in identifying young, potentially gifted, economically disadvantaged students. These researchers used both teacher-selected samples of student work and child-selected samples—items that were "special" to the students—to assist in identifying kindergarten children for gifted programming. Borland and Wright (1994) reported that the portfolios also turned out to have predictive validity for future academic giftedness. Portfolio assessment can also be applied to monitoring an individual gifted student's growth over time and the evaluation of a gifted program— its curriculum, attainment of program goals, or impact on the gifted students' creativity, originality, higher order thinking, or group problem solving. Shaklee et al.

(1997) and Johnsen (2008) suggest the following items as possibilities for inclusion in portfolios:

- Classroom and homework assignments
- Projects, artwork, and photographs of creative work, group activities, and displays
- Audiotapes, videotapes, or CDs of performances, presentations, interviews, peer interchanges, and cooperative learning activities
- Concept webs
- Student journals, logs, or reflection papers

After deciding on the purpose and what to include in the portfolios, the practitioner's next decision is determining how the items in the portfolios will be assessed. Three related set of issues are whether the portfolios should be designed to show a student's "best" or optimal performance or "typical" performance, how many artifacts of student work are needed to produce a representative sample of a student's abilities or accomplishments, and whether the assessment is formative or summative.

Portfolios can be scored holistically or they can be scored in a detailed, more focused manner (Wiig, 2000). A more focused, fine-grained assessment is recommended; it increases reliability and provides more useful data and information (Arter & McTighe, 2001). Scoring systems can use checklists, rating scales, and rubrics to assess portfolio artifacts. For example, a rating system using a 4-point scale (with 1 representing *infrequently* or *little evidence of* and 4 representing *frequently* or *considerable evidence of*) might ask assessors to rate the degree to which the artifacts demonstrate qualities such as originality, depth of problem representation, metacognitive skills, and multiple perspectives.

Two colleagues and I used a rubric as part of a districtwide gifted screening initiative (Pfeiffer, Kumtepe, & Rosado, 2006). A school district asked us to assist it in increasing the number of typically underrepresented minority group students referred for gifted programs. Teachers were instructed to rate all the kindergarten students in the district on the Gifted Rating Scales—Preschool/ Kindergarten Form (GRS-P) (Pfeiffer & Jarosewich, 2003), a popular gifted rating scale that will be described shortly. Teachers also submitted one classroom product for each student that served as a proxy for each student's academic competence. The product was a drawing accompanied by a story told by the student and transcribed by a classroom aide. We designed a rubric to rate each of the student's products on a 1–4 scale. The school district agreed that any kindergarten student who obtained a 3 or 4 on the rubric and a T score ≥ 60 on either the GRS-P Intellectual Ability or Academic Ability scale would be recommended for a gifted evaluation. This initiative increased the number of typically underrepresented minority group students considered for gifted programs districtwide (Pfeiffer et al., 2006).

These alternative assessment procedures—performance-based assessment, authentic assessment, and portfolio assessment—hold considerable promise as part of a comprehensive gifted identification protocol. These types of assessments are representative of real-world performance and are particularly well suited to assessing giftedness through the lens of *outstanding performance*. These alternative assessment procedures also complement a *talent development model* of giftedness. Starting in middle school and in some cases earlier, authentic portfolio- and performance-based assessment for already identified gifted students makes a whole lot of sense. The practitioner, in consultation with the gifted and classroom teacher, can play an invaluable role in helping to determine how well the gifted student is progressing in specific subjects. As you will read shortly, I am a strong advocate for ongoing assessment of gifted students. Standardized achievement tests, curriculum-based measures, and authentic and portfolio assessment are among the best means by far to determine how well high-ability students are progressing in specific domains and subjects.

Recall that in Chapter 5 I introduced the Consensual Assessment Technique (CAT) as a recommended tool in creativity assessment. The CAT is very easy to use. It is not weighed down by any one theory of creativity or giftedness (J. C. Kaufman, Plucker, & Baer, 2008), and is a technique used and respected worldwide in the talent development field. The CAT is based on actual artifacts (or performances); it reflects how products or ideas are viewed by others in the real world. As I mentioned earlier, there is considerable evidence that the CAT is a highly reliable tool, especially when used by experts (and not untrained novices or neophytes) in the specific field (Baer, Kaufman, & Gentile, 2004; J. C. Kaufman, Baer, Cole, & Sexton, 2008; J. C. Kaufman, Lee, Baer, & Lee, 2007). There is no reason why the CAT should be used only to assess creativity. There is every reason to advocate that this technique be given a place in gifted assessment beyond rating creativity. The two challenges in using CAT and other scoring systems are enlisting the cooperation of local experts to rate the artifacts in the portfolios, and the time involved in rating the student products.

Some final points bear mentioning. When using portfolio assessment, those involved need to decide whether the criteria applied to rate the artifacts should relate to local, state, and/or national or even international standards or norms. It is possible for gifted programs at a local or district level to begin to collect and develop norms for gifted students that can assist in making meaningful comparisons at the local level. Additional benefits of portfolio assessment are that it contextualizes assessment. It also integrates assessment with instruction (Sternberg &

Grigorenko, 2002). As mentioned above, the challenges include enlisting the help of local experts and the time required. Two additional challenges are ensuring technical adequacy—for example, rater agreement and validity of rubrics—and stealing time away from high-stakes state assessments (Johnsen, 2008).

NONVERBAL MEASURES

Nonverbal measures have gained considerable attention and popularity in the gifted field as aids for identifying gifted students. One reason is that advocates of nonverbal measures believe these tests are more fair and equitable for culturally or linguistically diverse populations (Naglieri & Ford, 2005). Nonverbal tests refer to instruments with reduced emphasis on the use of language by the examiner and the child. Nonverbal tests are intended to have low cultural loading and linguistic demand (Athanasiou, 2000; McCallum, Bracken, & Wasserman, 2001). I discuss nonverbal measures in the last chapter, titled, "Frequently Asked Questions."

TEACHER RATINGS

Teacher rating scales are widely used screening instruments to assist in the identification of gifted students (Pfeiffer, 2002, 2013b; Pfeiffer & Blei, 2008). There are a handful of published teacher gifted rating scales: the Gifted Evaluation Scale, Second Edition (McCarney & Anderson, 1989, 1998), Gifted Rating Scales (Pfeiffer & Jarosewich, 2003), Gifted and Talented Evaluation Scales (Gilliam, Carpenter, & Christensen, 1996), Scales for Identifying Gifted Students (Ryser & McConnell, 2004), and Scales for Rating the Behavioral Characteristics of Superior Students (Renzulli et al., 2002). The remainder of this section will focus on one teacher rating scale, the Gifted Rating Scales (GRS) (Pfeiffer & Jarosewich, 2003), since I am first author and uniquely familiar with the GRS.[1] Reviews of the Gifted Evaluation Scale (McCarney & Anderson, 1998) appear in Jarosewich, Pfeiffer, and Morris (2002), Mathew (1997), and Young (2001). Reviews of the Gifted and Talented Evaluation Scales (Gilliam, Carpenter, & Christensen, 1996) can be found in Brody (2007) and Jarosewich et al. (2002). Reviews of the original and the revised Scale for Rating Behavioral Characteristics of Superior Students (Renzulli, Siegle, Reis, Gavin, & Reed, 2009) appear in

---

1. Because I developed the GRS and receive royalties from its sales, I acknowledge a conflict of interest concerning this scale. However, I promise to moderate my unconcealed enthusiasm when describing the test.

Burke, Haworth, & Ware (1982), Elliott & Argulewicz (1983), Elliott, Argulewicz, and Turco (1986), Jarosewich et al. (2002), Renzulli (1983), and Renzulli et al. (2009). Notably, the great majority of published studies on the validity of teacher gifted ratings scales have investigated the Gifted Rating Scales (GRS).

The GRS was designed to be user-friendly, requiring minimal training to administer, score, and interpret. My colleague and I wanted teachers and parents to understand what the test scores represented, and we wanted the scores to be low-inference. The GRS was developed to be scientifically rigorous and reliable. We wanted to be able to provide unequivocal evidence that the intended uses and interpretation of test scores were valid (Impara, 2010). The GRS was based on a standardization sample that matched the most recent U.S. census at the time that we developed the scale in terms of race, ethnicity, parent education level as a proxy for family socioeconomic status, and regional representation. We wanted the test to reflect recent thinking on a *multi-abilities conceptualization of giftedness* and for the scale to make sense with and complement the *tripartite model of giftedness*. We intended that the scale would be based on a clear and straightforward interpretive model that simplified the screening process for school districts and practitioners. We were committed to making the scale clinically flexible and able to complement an IQ test and other assessment procedures discussed in this book (e.g., cognitive ability tests, portfolio samples, nonverbal tests, curriculum-based measures, and achievement tests) as part of a comprehensive test battery. And finally, we envisioned that the GRS would be linked to the Wechsler Intelligence Scale for Children—Fourth Edition (WISC-IV) and Wechsler Preschool and Primary Scale of Intelligence—Third Edition (WPPSI-III), which the team of statistics experts at PsychCorp/Pearson Assessment accomplished by co-linking the GRS standardization with the standardization of the new WISC-IV and WPPSI-III (Pfeiffer & Jarosewich, 2003).

The GRS includes a Preschool/Kindergarten Form (GRS-P) for ages 4 years to 6 years, 11 months, and a School Form (GRS-S) for ages 6 years to 13 years, 11 months. The Preschool/Kindergarten version consists of five scales with twelve items each for a total of sixty items; the School Form includes a sixth scale, Leadership Ability, for a total of seventy-two items. The items on the GRS-P represent skills and behaviors developmentally appropriate for preschool and

≡ *Rapid Reference 6.1   Gifted Rating Scales*
....

The GRS-P is a seventy-two-item teacher-completed rating scale that assesses five types of giftedness and motivation.

kindergarten students, while the items on the GRS-S reflect more developmentally advanced skills and behaviors. Both forms yield raw score totals on all scales, which are converted to age-based *T*-scores and associated cumulative percentages. A recent study confirmed that an automated version of the GRS is fully compatible with the original paper-and-pencil record form and yields essentially the same ratings (Yarnell & Pfeiffer, 2014). Figure 6.1 shows the cover of the GRS record form and Figure 6.2 displays the GRS directions and the Intellectual Ability scale.

The teacher rates the items on a 9-point scale that we divided into three ranges: 1–3, Below Average; 4–6, Average; 7–9, Above Average. We intentionally shaded each of the three ranges differently, as you can see in Figure 6.2, to accentuate for the teacher our intent that the first step in the rating process is for the rater to consider which of the three broad categories best applies to the item. Next, the rater is instructed to determine, in a more discriminating and fine-grained fashion, which of the three options within that broad category to select for that item. Pilot testing and focus groups during test development confirmed that this discriminatory process works.

The test manual provides a classification system that indicates *not* whether or not a student is gifted based on scores, but rather the *likelihood* that the obtained *T* scores are indicative of a student who might be considered gifted. The higher the student's *T* score, the greater the probability that the student is gifted, compared to other same-age peers. The *T* scores were computed based on each age group and thus age adjusted so that the classificatory ranges could be applied across age bands. A *T* score between 60 and 69 suggests, in concert with other confirmatory evidence, a *high probability* that the student may be gifted. A *T* score above 70 (98th+ percentile) indicates a *very high probability*.

The GRS-S consists of six scales (five scales for the Preschool/Kindergarten version) based on a multidimensional model of giftedness. Here is a brief description of each of the scales.

- Intellectual Ability. This scale measures the student's verbal and/or nonverbal mental skills, capabilities, and intellectual competence. Items ask the teacher to rate the student's abstract reasoning, problem solving, mental speed, and memory. For example, one item asks how easily the student learns difficult concepts.
- Academic Ability. This scale measures the student's skill in dealing with factual and/or scholastic material. The items rate advanced competence and high levels of proficiency in reading, math, and other aspects of the school curriculum. For example, one item asks how well the student completes academic work unassisted.

Section 1. To be completed by the teacher/rater

Student Information

Name _____

Date of Birth ___ / ___ / ___   Today's Date ___ / ___ / ___

☐ Male ☐ Female   Grade: _____   Age: _____

Teacher Information

Name _____

Contact Number _____

School _____

School Address _____

How long have you known this child in a teaching capacity?	In general, how well do you feel you know this child?
☐ 1–3 months	☐ Not Well
☐ 4–6 months	☐ Fairly Well
☐ 7–12 months	☐ Very Well
☐ >1 year	

Additional Information

_____
_____
_____
_____
_____
_____
_____
_____
_____
_____
_____
_____
_____
_____
_____
_____
_____
_____
_____
_____

Section 2. To be completed by the examiner. See scoring instructions in the Manual

Profile of Scale Scores (T Score)

≥ 80
70
60
50
≤ 40

Scales	Intellectual	Academic	Creativity	Artistic	Leadership	Motivation
Raw Score						
*T score						
*Cumulative %						

* See Appendix B tables for T score conversion of raw scores and cumulative percentages for T scores.

Results

Strengths _____
_____
_____

Recommendations _____
_____
_____
_____

Figure 6.1 GRS-School Form: Record Form

Source: Reproduced by permission of Pearson Assessment.

The Gifted Rating Scales School Form

This Form identifies giftedness in children between the ages of 6:0–13:11. It is to be completed by classroom teachers. You will be asked to rate the child in five areas of giftedness: Intellectual Ability, Academic Ability, Creativity, Artistic Talent, and Leadership. You will also be asked to rate the child in the area of Motivation.

Scores will be based on how the child compares with other children of the *same age* in regular educational settings. It is important that you base your ratings of this child on a comparison with "typical" children of the *same age* who are in regular educational settings.

Note: If you are a teacher of the gifted; a special education teacher; a teacher of special subjects such as art, music, drama, or physical education; or if you work with children in special settings such as gifted schools, rate this child based on a comparison with "typical" children of the *same age* who are in regular educational settings.

Note: If you have not had the opportunity to observe this child's skills in the area of artistic talent, you may ask another teacher who is more familiar with the child's skills in this area to complete all of the items in the artistic scale.

To complete each item, circle the number that most closely corresponds to your impression of the child's ability relative to other children of the *same age*.

- Answer every item.
- Rate each item individually as children's skills can vary across items.
- Remember that a child may excel on some but not all items.

Example
The following example illustrates how to complete the rating form:

Rate how well this child performs the following, compared to other children of the *same age*:	Below Average			Average			Above Average		
1. Demonstrates advanced reasoning skills.	1	2	3	4	(5)	6	7	8	9
2. Demonstrates advanced reading, writing, and/or math skills.	(1)	2	3	4	5	6	7	8	9
3. Provides detail and/or elaboration in artistic work.	1	2	3	4	5	6	7	(8)	9

In this example, the teacher views the child's performance on the first item as Average, compared to children of the same age. The teacher views the child's performance on the second item as well Below Average, falling below almost all children of the same age. On the third item, the teacher views the child's performance as Above Average, above most, but not all children of the same age.

Intellectual Ability

Intellectual Ability refers to the child's verbal and/or nonverbal mental skills, capabilities, or competence. Aspects of intelligence measured by this scale include abstract learning, problem solving, reasoning, mental speed, and memory.

Rate how well this child performs the following, compared to other children of the *same age*:	Below Average			Average			Above Average		
1. Solves problems quickly.	1	2	3	4	5	6	7	8	9
2. Demonstrates advanced reasoning skills.	1	2	3	4	5	6	7	8	9
3. Thinks insightfully, intuitively understands problems.	1	2	3	4	5	6	7	8	9
4. Learns new information quickly.	1	2	3	4	5	6	7	8	9
5. Demonstrates a good memory, remembers facts and details.	1	2	3	4	5	6	7	8	9
6. Understands complex information or abstract ideas.	1	2	3	4	5	6	7	8	9
7. Answers questions in detail, with extensive information.	1	2	3	4	5	6	7	8	9
8. Makes logical inferences, draws conclusions based on sound reasoning.	1	2	3	4	5	6	7	8	9
9. Problem solves analytically, separates problems into their component parts.	1	2	3	4	5	6	7	8	9
10. Understands the essence of a problem quickly.	1	2	3	4	5	6	7	8	9
11. Applies prior knowledge to solving problems.	1	2	3	4	5	6	7	8	9
12. Learns difficult concepts easily.	1	2	3	4	5	6	7	8	9

Intellectual Ability Raw Score Total [   ]

Figure 6.2 GRS-School Form: Directions and Intellectual Ability Scale

Source: Reproduced by permission of Pearson Assessment.

- Creativity. This scale measures the student's ability to think, act, and/or produce unique, original, novel, or innovative products or ideas. For example, one creativity item asks how well a student experiments with new ideas, formulates a problem for a group project, and/or uses imagination.
- Artistic Talent. This scale measures the student's potential for or evidence of ability in drama, music, dance, drawing, painting, sculpture, singing, playing a musical instrument, and/or acting. Experience has led me to recognize that the regular classroom often feels ill-equipped to rate students on this scale. This was an unanticipated but really not a surprising finding; schools are focusing more on reading and traditional academic subjects and spending less and less time on the arts in the elementary grades. It is perfectly acceptable for school districts not to use the Artistic Talent scale when using the GRS as a gifted screening tool.
- Leadership Ability. This scale appears only on the School Form, for older students. It measures the student's ability to motivate others toward a common or shared goal. Items rate a student's conflict resolution skills, initiative in group situations, and understanding of social dynamics and interpersonal communication. An illustrative item asks how well the student inspires confidence in others. Investigations conducted by students in my research lab indicate that the Leadership Ability scale is particularly helpful in investigating the constructs of emotional intelligence (Pfeiffer, 2001a) and "strengths of the heart" (Pfeiffer, 2013a).
- Motivation. We do *not* view the Motivation scale as a measure of a type of giftedness. We included this scale because motivation is so very important in understanding the actualization of a student's gifts. The Motivation scale measures a student's drive or persistence, desire to succeed, tendency to enjoy challenging tasks, and ability to work well without encouragement or external reinforcement. An illustrative item asks how well the student strives to improve or become more proficient at school work. Feedback from practitioners indicates that the Motivation scale is particularly helpful in documenting and pinpointing specific behaviors associated with underachievement among high-ability students.

Even though we don't view motivation as a type of giftedness, the Motivation scale can certainly be used as part of the gifted identification process, particularly when assessing older students (3rd grade and above) when passion for learning, drive to achieve, frustration tolerance, and self-regulation are appropriate constructs to consider when reevaluating students already in a gifted program. Test development and validation is described in detail by Pfeiffer (2013b), Pfeiffer and Blei (2008), and Pfeiffer and Jarosewich (2003). The GRS has undergone extensive research, both in the United States and internationally, and enjoys high reliability and considerable evidence for construct and diagnostic validity (Li, Lee, Pfeiffer, Kamata, & Kumtepe, 2009; Margulies & Floyd, 2004; Pfeiffer & Jarosewich, 2003, 2007; Pfeiffer & Petscher, 2008; Pfeiffer, Petscher, & Jarosewich, 2007; Pfeiffer, Petscher, & Kumtepe, 2008; Rosado, Pfeiffer, & Petscher, 2013; Ward, 2005). For example, Pfeiffer and Jarosewich (2007) computed diagnostic efficiency statistics, including *test sensitivity*, *test specificity*, and *overall correct classification*. These diagnostic statistics are rarely conducted or reported for educational or gifted tests, although they are standard in medicine and test experts contend that diagnostic statistics should be reported for all tests (Streiner, 2003). The GRS performed exceptionally well in correctly identifying students who were, in fact, intellectually gifted based on IQ scores, and equally well in correctly identifying those students who were *not* intellectually gifted, again based on IQ scores.

The GRS is being used as a gifted screening instrument in over six hundred school districts nationwide. It is also being used as a component of a comprehensive gifted assessment battery by practitioners who value teacher input in the overall gifted diagnostic process. Figure 6.3 depicts one way in which teacher ratings from the GRS can be used in conjunction with an IQ test to help in making diagnostic decisions about gifted classification. The vertical dimension distinguishes students who score at or above the 95th percentile rank on an ability test such as the WISC-IV (Wechsler, 2003), SB5 (Roid, 2003), Woodcock-

	GRS Ratings	
	All *T* scores below 60	One or more *T* scores ≥ 60
≥ 95th percentile rank	II	I
80th–95th percentile rank	IV	III

Figure 6.3 One Method for Combining GRS Teacher Ratings on Intellectual Ability, Academic Ability, and Creativity with IQ Test Scores

Johnson IV (Schrank, McGrew, & Mather, 2014; Woodcock, McGrew, & Mather, 2001), DAS-II (Elliott, 2007), RIAS (Reynolds & Kamphaus, 2003), or KABC-II (Kaufman & Kaufman, 2004a). One can use the total score (general factor score) or one or more composite scores (Stratum II abilities), based, of course, on an a priori decision. One can use this same methodology with a brief ability screener as well, such as the Kaufman Brief Intelligence Test, Second Edition (Kaufman & Kaufman, 2004b), Wechsler Abbreviated Scale of Intelligence—Second Edition (Wechsler, 2011), or Raven's Progressive Matrices (Raven et al., 1983) as a screening protocol. Decisions on whether to use a test's total score or one or more composite scores should be made a priori and guided by the practitioner's explicit conceptualization of giftedness and consideration of the type of available gifted programs for which students are being evaluated.

The horizontal dimension of the matrix in Figure 6.3 distinguishes between students who, when compared to other students vying for the gifted classification and a position in the gifted program, obtain *T* scores on the GRS of 60 or above—indicative of a high probability of being gifted, as explained in the list below—based on teacher observations of the student. In this example, I have followed the lead of many school districts nationwide and included three GRS scales: Intellectual Ability, Academic Ability, and Creativity. In this example, a student would need to obtain a *T* score ≥ 60 on at least one of the three GRS scales to fall within the *high likelihood of being gifted* category.

Combining the two criteria—teacher ratings on the GRS and student performance on a cognitive ability test, yields four categories of gifted assessment results:

- Students in Category I are the easy decisions; their scores on *both* the IQ test and one or more of the three GRS scales reflect performance in the high-ability range indicative of *giftedness.*
- Students in Category II are a more difficult group to pigeonhole as gifted or not gifted; although their teacher ratings don't fall within the "high probability" range, their IQ test performance does fall within the top 5% for their age group—clearly indicative of a gifted classification based on the tripartite model's *high intelligence* view of giftedness (see Chapter 2). However, these same intellectually bright students might not be viewed as gifted if we were viewing giftedness through the tripartite lens of *academically gifted learners.* Clearly, if students in this second category are given a gifted classification, they require close monitoring of their progress in a gifted program to confirm that they are benefiting from its

more challenging and/or fast-paced curriculum. Obviously, students in this group have the intellectual horsepower to succeed in many gifted programs, but at the same time, they lack compelling classroom evidence, at least as perceived by one or more of their teachers, that they are performing anywhere close to their ability. Some might suggest that Category II students in the early grades should qualify for a gifted classification whereas those in the upper grades, who aren't actualizing their ability, would not necessarily qualify. This view is consistent with a talent development model.

- Students in Category III are perceived by their teachers as highly capable, engaged and motivated, bright, and/or creative. However, their test scores indicate quite respectable but not extraordinarily outstanding cognitive abilities. Quite often, these students are a conundrum for the gifted coordinator or school psychologist. If a school district has a broad array of programs for bright students, such as a schoolwide enrichment program (Renzulli, 2005a), then these students would qualify for such a program. Many bright minority group students fall into this third category—they are recognized as having a "special gift" by their teachers and test well but below the school district's IQ cut score. These are the students who are candidates for close monitoring and recommended retesting in six or twelve months. This is analogous to what I described earlier in terms of the annual tryouts used by the Youth Soccer Olympic Development Program. Local school districts could establish a 10% inclusion rule, as recommended by Ceci and Papierno (2005), for students from minority groups and financially challenged families who evidence clear and unequivocal potential but yet have test scores falling somewhat below established district cutoffs—the category III students in this example. I discuss this idea in more detail in the next chapter when answering the question about assessing typically underrepresented gifted populations.

- Finally, Children in Category IV present with respectable but not extraordinarily outstanding cognitive ability test scores but are not perceived by their teachers as distinctly bright, motivated, or creative compared to their peers. These may be good students, but not those that we typically think of in terms of gifted or talented, at least not in terms of either a high intelligence or academically gifted learner perspective. There may be other evidence that contraindicates this and suggests further testing, or a recommendation for monitoring and retesting at some future date.

THE GRS AS A MEASURE OF CHANGE

The GRS has also been used to measure *change in a student's profile of abilities*. The procedure to measure change is fairly simple and straightforward. The practitioner compares a student's original GRS scale score or scores with a range of scores that take into account the variability expected by both regression to the mean and measurement error. Standard error of prediction (SEp) scores provide confidence bands for *T* scores so that a second and more recent set of *T* scores can be compared with an earlier set or ratings on the GRS. The SEp was selected rather than the SEM because it is preferable in providing an unbiased estimate of population error (Atkinson, 1991). A simple, step-by-step description on how to use the GRS to measure change is available in Pfeiffer and Blei (2008), including easy-to-read tables that provide GRS posttest confidence ranges for pretest-posttest *T*-score comparisons.

Finally, the GRS has been used to influence the gifted curriculum by providing structured feedback on whether students are making substantial growth in the domains measured by the GRS. We piloted the GRS as a means of measuring student growth over a two-week period in a summer leadership program that I co-led at the Duke University TIP (Pfeiffer & Blei, 2008). It proved to be a valuable instrument in tracking student growth and program impact.

ASSESSING READINESS FOR GRADE ACCELERATION

This chapter concludes with a discussion of a unique scale specifically designed to assess a student's readiness for acceleration, the Iowa Acceleration Scale, Third Edition (Assouline, Colangelo, Lupkowski-Shoplik, Lipscomb, & Forstadt, 2009).

Types of Acceleration

One of the earliest definitions of acceleration was proposed more than sixty-five years ago. Pressey (1949) suggested that acceleration means allowing a student to "progress through an educational program at rates faster or at ages younger than conventional." There are a number of different types of acceleration when this idea is applied to the gifted student. What follows is a list of a few of the more popular types of acceleration:

- Single-subject acceleration. A student performing above grade level in one or more subjects is permitted to participate in one or more classes above her grade level (for example, a 5th-grade student with advanced math skills attends a 6th-grade math class every afternoon, or a musically gifted middle school student is permitted to participate in a high school orchestra).

- Curriculum compacting. For students demonstrating grade-level proficiency in a specific academic area, advanced content in this area is provided in the regular classroom.
- Dual enrollment. Highly proficient students are allowed to enroll in higher level coursework (for example, an academically gifted middle school student takes a high school honors class, or a gifted high school student registers for a university linguistics course during the school day).
- Credit by examination. If a student demonstrates mastery of course material by assessment—typically evaluated by end-of-year tests or portfolio assessment, then he can skip introductory activities and pursue more advanced course offerings.
- Special courses (Advanced Placement and International Baccalaureate®). The Advanced Placement (AP) program offers college-level coursework for students as early as middle school. Students can actually earn college credit and/or advanced university standing based on their performance on AP exams. The International Baccalaureate (IB) similarly offers university-level curricula; students complete an international exam and can receive college course credit and advanced university standing. Both AP and the IB are popular acceleration options for gifted students in high school.
- Early entrance to school/college. The two main types of early entrance options are early entrance to kindergarten (most popular) and early entrance to college (becoming increasingly popular). In addition to academic readiness, it is important to assess the student's social and emotional readiness for being placed with older peers. During my tenure at the Duke TIP, we frequently were asked by the admissions department to interview an unusually young and highly impressive applicant applying to Duke University—some applicants were as young as 15 or 16. On once occasion, we interviewed a highly precocious 13-year-old applicant (and his parents)! In addition to evaluating the applicant's intellectual and academic preparedness, it is important to assess her social skills and level of emotional intelligence (Pfeiffer, 2013a, 2013c), as well as the applicant's comfort level in interacting with considerably older peers.
- Whole-grade acceleration. An example of whole-grade acceleration is a 2nd grader skipping 3rd grade and being placed in 4th-grade classes after completing 2nd grade.

The research is quite convincing that acceleration is an empirically validated intervention for many high-ability students (Colangelo, Assouline, & Gross, 2004). The great majority of research studies confirm the academic benefits of acceleration and the lack of evidence for any negative socioemotional or behavioral issues (Neihart, 2007). However, only fifteen states have a policy that permits acceleration; the majority of states have no policy (National Association for Gifted Children & the Council of State Directors of Programs for the Gifted, 2009).

Of course, not all gifted students will benefit from acceleration. This is another important purpose of gifted assessment—to determine which high-ability students are good candidates for acceleration as an educational intervention.

Iowa Acceleration Scale

The Iowa Acceleration Scale (IAS) was developed based on the clinical research conducted at the Belin-Blank Center at the University of Iowa. According to the authors, the main purpose of the scale is to guide educators through a discussion of the academic and social characteristics of high-ability students being considered for acceleration. Essentially, the twenty-item scale is designed to improve decision making when considering acceleration as an intervention option for a gifted student. The scale is not a standardized test with national norms, and is "biased against underachievers" (Colangelo et al., n.d.).

IAS items critical to the success of whole grade level acceleration, according to the authors, are level of cognitive ability as measured by an intelligence test, grade level of sibling, and attitude of the student under consideration for acceleration. Other considerations rated on the IAS are school system support, attitude of the parent, academic proficiency, developmental considerations, and other available options. Sections on the IAS include general information on the student and family, the critical items just mentioned, school history, prior ability and achievement test data, developmental factors (e.g., physical size, age, motor coordination), interpersonal skills (e.g., relationships with peers and teachers and maturity level), and attitude and support (in relation to students, parents, and

≡ *Rapid Reference 6.2 Iowa Acceleration Scale*

The Iowa Acceleration Scale is a twenty-item scale designed to assist educators in determining whether grade acceleration is a good decision for gifted students.

the school system). The IAS yields a total score that indicates the likelihood that a student is a poor, marginal, good, or excellent candidate for acceleration.

Assouline, Colangelo, Ihrig, Forstadt, and Lipscomb (2004) report on a handful of decision-making accuracy studies using the IAS, now in its third edition (2009). The preliminary research indicates that the IAS holds promise in improving decision-making accuracy when acceleration is an option. It certainly should be considered as one tool to be included in a comprehensive gifted assessment test library.

TEST YOURSELF

1. **Portfolio assessment is ill-advised since there is no empirical support for its use:**
   a. True
   b. False

2. **Teacher ratings scales such as the GRS can assist in gifted screening and identification:**
   a. True
   b. False

3. **To increase the preciseness of portfolio assessment, it is advised to convert a rubric to a numerical scale and quantify ratings:**
   a. True
   b. False

4. **Portfolio assessment should *not* be used to monitor a gifted student's growth over time or to evaluate the effectiveness of a gifted program:**
   a. True
   b. False

5. **The Consensual Assessment Technique is an effective tool to assess creativity:**
   a. True
   b. False

6. **Portfolio assessment should always include criteria based on national norms:**
   a. True
   b. False

7. **The GRS includes a Preschool/Kindergarten Form and a School Form, together covering the age range 4.0 years to 13.11 years:**
   a. True
   b. False

(continued)

(continued)

8. The GRS can be used in conjunction with one or more other tests to help make diagnostic decisions:

   a. True

   b. False

Answers: 1. False; 2. True; 3. True; 4. False; 5. True; 6. False; 7. True; 8. True.

Seven

FREQUENTLY ASKED QUESTIONS ABOUT GIFTED ASSESSMENT

I n this final chapter, I answer six questions that are frequently raised by psychologists, gifted educators, administrators, policymakers, and researchers about gifted assessment. I have been asked these questions not only in workshops and talks that I give in the United States but also in my travels internationally. Of course, these are not all of the questions that are raised about gifted assessment and identification. However, these six questions represent what I'm most frequently asked when the topic of gifted assessment is raised by an audience. For each question, I will answer as I might if I were consulting with a colleague, standing in front of an audience of psychologists at a workshop, or responding to an e-mail from an inquiring professional. In other words, I will avoid pedantic, professorial, or doctrinaire responses. I will also minimize research citations, because that's not how I typically respond in the real world to questions from professionals, administrators, policymakers, the media, and others with an interest in gifted assessment.

SIX QUESTIONS

I hope that you find the following questions and responses helpful. Please don't hesitate to contact me if you have a gifted assessment question not covered in this chapter. And please don't hesitate to contact me if you

DON'T FORGET

For a practitioner to be effective in conducting a gifted assessment, she or he needs experience and expertise in working with gifted students.

disagree with one of my answers or if you care to share an example from your own work with high-ability students.

1. Should Nonverbal Tests Be Used As Part of Gifted Assessment, and If So, When?

As I mentioned in the previous chapter, nonverbal measures have gained considerable popularity in the gifted field in helping to identify gifted students. One reason is that advocates of nonverbal measures believe these tests are more fair and equitable for culturally or linguistically diverse populations (Naglieri & Ford, 2005). Nonverbal tests are instruments with reduced emphasis on language on the part of the examiner and the child. Nonverbal tests are intended to have low cultural loading and linguistic demand (Athanasiou, 2000; McCallum, Bracken, & Wasserman, 2001). Nonverbal tests range in terms of their coverage; some are brief and measure general ability while others are more comprehensive and measure a greater range of cognitive abilities.

Four commonly used nonverbal ability tests are the Leiter International Performance Scale—Revised (Roid & Miller, 1997), the Naglieri Nonverbal Ability Test (Naglieri, 1997, Naglieri, Das, & Goldstein, 2014), the Test of Nonverbal Intelligence, Fourth Edition (Brown, Sherbenou, & Johnson, 2010), and the Universal Nonverbal Intelligence Test (Bracken & McCallum, 1998). A number of brief intelligence tests include nonverbal scales that have been used in gifted screening, including the Kaufman Brief Intelligence Test, Second Edition (KBIT-2) (Kaufman & Kaufman, 2004b), Reynolds Intellectual Screening Test (RSIT) (Reynolds & Kamphaus, 2003), and Wechsler Abbreviated Scale of Intelligence—Second Edition (WASI-II) (Wechsler, 2011). The great attraction in nonverbal tests for gifted identification is the premise that by reducing verbal and linguistic demands, these tests will work better and be more valid for students with linguistic and cultural differences—those groups of students who typically don't perform as well on IQ tests.

However, David Lohman has challenged this premise in a series of cogent and compelling arguments (Lohman, 2005a, 2005b, 2005c). Perhaps the most telling criticism is the fact that nonverbal tests can mask the very real achievement gap that exists for certain groups of minority group students. This means that inferences one makes when using the scores from nonverbal tests in predicting future performance would be invalid (Worrell & Erwin, 2011). At this writing, there is no published research on the predictive validity of nonverbal ability measures (Pfeiffer, 2013b; Pfeiffer & Blei, 2008). Another criticism of nonverbal measures is that nonverbal test items do not match up with the skills and abilities that are part of most gifted curricula.

The appeal of using nonverbal measures to identify gifted students is based in part on the naive wish for a magic bullet that would resolve the controversies surrounding the disproportionality issue in the gifted field. However, the promise of nonverbal measures serving as the magic bullet is misleading and deceptive. Nonverbal tests have a place in psychological assessment, where they can serve a useful and specific role. But they are not, unfortunately, the panacea or universal remedy for the

DON'T FORGET

Nonverbal tests can mask the very real achievement gap that exists for certain groups of minority group students.

challenges of equity and proportionality in the gifted field. Nonverbal measures certainly are one useful tool that can and should be part of the practitioner's gifted assessment toolbox. But in my opinion, they aren't the frontline measure that should be administered to every student referred for a gifted evaluation, and they certainly should not replace individually administered cognitive ability tests.

2. How Should We Approach the Assessment and Identification of Typically Underrepresented Gifted Populations?

There is a long history of disproportionate representation of culturally, racially, and linguistically diverse students in special education programs, including programs for the gifted (NEA, 2008; O'Connor & Fernandez, 2010). *Disproportionality* is defined as a substantial overrepresentation or underrepresentation of a particular demographic group in programs, relative to the number of this group in the student population. For example, it has been amply documented that there is an overrepresentation of culturally, racially, and linguistically diverse students in specific special education categories, such as mental retardation and emotional disturbance, and a general underrepresentation of Hispanics/Latinos, African Americans, and American Indians/Alaska Natives in programs for the gifted (National Education Association, 2008; National Research Council, 2002).

Although some would like to believe otherwise, the reasons for disproportionality are complex—and not easy to remedy. Most researchers agree that poverty is a significant causal factor, with low family income increasing exposure to a host of risk factors that compromise early development (O'Connor & Fernandez, 2010). Similarly, high SES is a favorable and potentiating factor, increasing opportunities for early intellectual and educational stimulation, as well as being associated with better nutrition and certain facilitative, culture-specific values that encourage academic success (Neisser et al., 1996; Worrell & Erwin, 2011).

Some researchers have distinguished between nonjudgmental and judgmental categories as another possible factor contributing to disproportionality. A nonjudgmental category of special education is one in which the classification requires limited inference on the part of the practitioner. For example, on the one hand, the special education categories of deaf, blind, orthopedically impaired, and severe mental retardation—categories with pronounced cognitive or physiological impairment—require little inference. On the other hand, judgmental categories capture subtle disabilities for which there may be no known neurophysiological cause and for which diagnosis rests considerably on the expertise and clinical skills of the practitioner. Mild and high-functioning autism spectrum disorder and specific learning disabilities are two examples. Researchers have documented the overrepresentation of minority students in judgmental categories of special education (Hosp & Reschly, 2004). I believe that this same process may be operating for the gifted category. As you by now know, giftedness is a social construction, not something real, and the gifted represent a judgmental category, and therefore one that could well be prone to professional decision-making bias. At the moment, there is no research evidence supporting this hypothesis of bias in gifted decision making in the schools, but it is not unreasonable to speculate that it has contributed to disproportionality in gifted programs.

Three points bear on disproportionality and how we should approach the identification of typically underrepresented groups of gifted students. First, gifted identification practices should always be based on how the local school district conceptualizes giftedness and gifted students. Because giftedness is a social construct there is no one correct way to conceptualize giftedness. If, for example, High-Ability School District in Woodcock-Johnson, Tennessee, decides that its gifted program will view giftedness through the lens of high IQ, then one or more reliable measures of intelligence will likely be used to identify the students that qualify for this gifted program. Students from certain cultural, racial, and linguistic groups will be at a distinct disadvantage when competing for slots in the gifted program offered by High-Ability School District, because research confirms that certain groups of students score lower on IQ tests (Frisby & Braden, 1999; Nisbett, 2009). If High-Performance School District, in neighboring Wechsler, Kansas, decides that its gifted program will be based on a different conceptual model, viewing giftedness through the alternative lens of outstanding accomplishments, then we can expect a different proportion of students from specific cultural, racial, and linguistic groups will be identified as gifted, based on identification methods that put a greater premium on classroom and academic performance. As this example from two fictitious school districts illustrates, disproportionality is influenced by how school districts and practitioners conceptualize the construct of giftedness, because how one conceptualizes giftedness affects how one approaches identifying and assessing for giftedness.

Second, some in the gifted field contend that disproportionality is inherently problematic and needs to be directly addressed through modifications in identification and assessment practices. Donna Ford, a professor in the George Peabody College of Education at Vanderbilt University, is one of the leading proponents of this position. She has authored a number of publications on this point, including a chapter in my *Handbook of Giftedness in Children* (2008). She eloquently writes, "The field of gifted education has come under much criticism because of the consistently low representation of culturally and linguistically diverse students in gifted education. . . . [African American, Hispanic American, and Native American] students have always been inadequately represented in gifted education . . . by some 50% to 70%" (Ford & Whiting, 2008, p. 293). I wholeheartedly share Ford's concern with the underrepresentation of certain groups of minority students in gifted programs. However, I don't agree with her position that our tests are one of the primary culprits causing disproportionality and that our field needs more "culturally sensitive tests" and more wide use of "nonverbal tests"—two approaches that Ford advocates to reduce disproportionality. After carefully considering alternative arguments, I am convinced that the claim that nonverbal tests are less biased and more fair for ethnic and linguistic minority group students is unfounded (Lohman, 2005b, 2005c).

I am also fairly well convinced that our best cognitive and achievement measures work quite well and are statistically fair and unbiased in predicting academic performance and success among all groups of students. The bottom line is this: our tests are not the problem (Newman, 2008; Worrell & Erwin, 2011). Different tests of questionable validity should not replace our best measures. The problem lies, in my opinion, not in the tests that we use to identify gifted students but in the fact that different groups, based on economic and a host of sociocultural factors, vary in their readiness to compete intellectually and academically, even by the time they begin preschool (Nisbett, 2009; Pfeiffer, 2003).

Disproportionality in gifted education will be significantly reduced only when the playing field is leveled for all groups of students. Changing our tests and testing practices is not, however, the way to level the playing field. The solution is much more complex, systemic, and far-reaching. The solution reflects a societal challenge and goes way beyond what practitioners can be expected to accomplish by changing gifted identification tests or procedures. The solution requires that all infants and young children in the United States be provided safe, healthy, and supportive home and community environments with caretakers who are available and coached to stimulate early cognitive development and support values and belief systems associated with academic success. This is, of course, neither a modest nor an inexpensive societal challenge! And it is not even a realistic political goal, given the great economic challenges that our country and other nations today face. But this is the only real way that disproportionality in the gifted category will be effectively remedied.

Finally, although disproportionality among gifted students will be successfully corrected only with far-reaching and long-range societal changes, I believe and have argued elsewhere (Pfeiffer, 2013b) that we have an obligation as a society to help remedy disproportionality in gifted programs with more modest and less grandiose interventions. Ceci and Papierno (2005) offer one reasonable proposal. They recommend that we identify the top 10% of the underrepresented segments of society and ensure that they get the resources needed to develop their potential. This idea is consistent with the third way to view giftedness within the tripartite model of giftedness; giftedness through the lens of potential to excel. I have long advocated that local school districts establish a 10% admittance rule for students from minority groups who evidence clear and unequivocal potential but not yet outstanding accomplishments. Recall that this third way of viewing giftedness is based on my concern that not all students start out on equal footing. Often, children growing up in poverty, in families in which intellectual and educational activities are neither encouraged nor nurtured in the home, or in families in which English is not the primary language spoken in the home are at a distinct disadvantage when it comes to developing their potential. Selecting a top 10% of students who are almost or potentially gifted and providing them with a range of facilitative and creative resources to help mobilize their latent and as yet unrealized high potential is sound ethical practice.

3. What Constitutes a Complete Gifted Assessment Test Battery?

Unfortunately, there is no one gold standard gifted assessment test battery that is best for all students and all situations. I wish that this were the case; it would make answering this question a whole lot easier. The rule of thumb is that practitioners should customize their gifted test battery based on a number of considerations. First of all, as discussed in Chapter 3, we need to consider the scientific merit and psychometric qualities of each test that we are considering including in the test battery. Psychometrics matter! It behooves the practitioner to stay on top of

CAUTION

Nonverbal tests are not the panacea or magic bullet that will resolve the issue of racial or ethnic disproportionality in gifted programs.

the assessment research, particularly research articles that report on the reliability, validity, and diagnostic accuracy of any test that they are considering using. Relevant questions that should be asked include these: Are there articles that present research into using this test with high-ability students? If so, what do these studies report? Does the normative sample for the test include high-ability subjects? Is the test ceiling high enough for the population and purpose that we intend to use the test for?

It is very important to respect the psychometrics of every test included in a gifted assessment test battery. But psychometrics are not enough to answer the question of whether to use the test or not. It is also important to consider the specific purpose of the gifted assessment, as this too should guide test selection. Many often think of gifted assessment and gifted identification as synonymous. I hope the reader recalls from Chapter 1 that this is not the case! Gifted identification is but one of many purposes of gifted assessment.

Other purposes of gifted assessment include providing information to support admission to special schools or gifted programs; gaining a better or more comprehensive understanding of the unique learning style, strengths and/or weaknesses (asynchronies) of an exceptionally bright child; assessing growth or development in areas such as creativity or critical thinking, with implications for curriculum modification or program evaluation; assisting in the diagnosis of twice-exceptional children; discerning factors contributing to underachievement, low motivation, and/or authority issues that are compromising academic performance; providing information on homeschooling; determining appropriate grade place-ment and/or decisions about acceleration; and helping to formulate informed career choices. Each of these different purposes can lead to a slightly different test battery. For example, if the practitioner is working with a gifted high school adolescent and her parents in formulating alternative career choices—an impor-tant issue for the gifted student in terms of college choices, the test battery might include a self-concept scale and a brief vocational scale such as the Self-Directed Search (Holland & Messer, 2013), and also completing with the adolescent a CASVE Cycle (communication, analysis, synthesis, valuing, and evaluation) (Peterson, Sampson, Lenz, & Reardon, 2002; Sampson & Chason, 2008).

A final set of considerations in selecting tests to include in a gifted assessment battery addresses the unique demographic and psychosocial-developmental char-acteristics of the particular client. It is always important to consider the client's age, developmental level, ethnicity and race, proficiency with the English language, and other relevant sociocultural client characteristics when selecting a test for clinical use.

4. Should Social Competence, Passion for Learning, Motivation, and Emotional Intelligence Be Included in Gifted Assessment?

This question, like the prior one, requires a qualified response: "Well maybe, it really depends on the purpose of the assessment." Put simply, the referral question or reason for the evaluation should drive the choice of psychological constructs on which we seek clinical information and data. For example, if a school district is undertaking a large-scale, gifted screening program in the early grades, then its resources could best be allocated by selecting two scientifically sound and complementary screening tests, such as the KBIT-2 (Kaufman & Kaufman, 2004b) and the Gifted Rating Scales (Pfeiffer & Jarosewich, 2003). It would be imprudent to add measures of social competence, motivation, passion for learning, or emotional intelligence in this instance.

However, if the reason for the gifted assessment is to evaluate the impact of a pilot gifted program in a school district, and the new curriculum is based on considerable use of group learning activities, then including measures of social competence and emotional intelligence would make perfectly good sense. Finally, if the reason for the gifted assessment is to determine the reasons why an otherwise brilliant high-ability student is underachieving in the classroom, measures of the student's motivation and passion for learning would be an awfully good choice to include in the gifted assessment.

Available measures of academic motivation that I have found helpful in my clinical practice include the Academic Motivation Scale (Vallerand et al., 1992), California Measure of Mental Motivation (Giancarlo & Facione, 2000), Children's Academic Intrinsic Motivation Inventory (Gottfried, 1986), Gifted Rating Scales (Pfeiffer & Jarosewich, 2003), and Miller Motivation Scale (Miller, 1987).

The Academic Motivation Scale, developed in France and subsequently translated into English, is a self-report scale consisting of twenty-eight items subdivided into seven subscales assessing intrinsic and extrinsic motivation. The California Measure of Mental Motivation is group administered and purports to measure dispositions toward mental focus, learning orientation, creative problem solving, and cognitive integrity. The Children's Academic Intrinsic Motivation Inventory (CAIMI) and the Gifted Rating Scales (GRS) were both developed with the high-ability student in mind. The CAIMI consists of four content scales focused on attitudes toward reading, math, science, and social studies. There is also a separate global scale related to general attitudes toward school learning. The GRS, described in the previous chapter, consists of six scales, one of which is Motivation. The Motivation scale consists of twelve items rated by a teacher on a 9-point Likert scale. For example, the teacher is asked to rate the degree to which the student strives to achieve, places high value on mastery and success, and persists on tasks even when initial efforts are unsuccessful. On the GRS, across all age groups, 4:0–13:11 years, coefficient alpha internal consistency (.98–.99), test-retest reliability (.89–.97), and inter-rater reliability (.67–.73) are quite strong, higher than reliability reported for the CAIMI and other motivation measures.

5. Should We Be Concerned About Multipotentiality When Testing High-Ability Students?

Multipotentiality is defined by Barbara Kerr (1990) as "the ability to select and develop any number of career options because of a wide variety of interests, aptitudes, and abilities" (p. 1). Many in the gifted field believe (rather strongly) that multipotentiality is a very real and valid phenomenon among high-ability individuals (Pfeiffer, 2013b). Why? Because of their elevated intellectual abilities compared to their peers, the logic goes, the gifted have by their very nature a much wider net of potential career paths and opportunities to pursue.

However, the validity of this concept applied to the gifted has been challenged. For example, Achter, Benbow, and Lubinski (1997) report low differentiation of ability profiles among a large cohort of intellectually gifted students. Their research findings are impressive and can't be easily dismissed. I reconcile their findings with the generally accepted position in the gifted field that multipotentiality is very real among the gifted in this way when I work with parents of a young gifted child. The two differing positions reflect different developmental points in time and different levels of specificity in how we can measure abilities. Among young, intellectually gifted children—by the nature of their advanced cognitive abilities—it is indisputable that they have, as a group, a much greater set of potential career options than other children. However, as they get older and begin to develop more crystallized interests in specific areas, and as we can measure in a more fine-grained fashion their unique and specific profile of abilities, we can and should expect to observe a narrowing of differentiation of ability profiles (and interests), as Achter et al. (1997) report.

So, in answer to the frequently asked question about multipotentiality, yes, we should pay attention to this concept when conducting a gifted assessment! I should mention too that multipotentiality is often a mixed blessing—for the gifted child and for the child's parents. The young intellectually gifted child has more future career options than other children, which can create anxiety and confusion. The situation gets more complicated when we consider gender. There are significant gender differences in occupational interests, consistent with a sex-stereotyped model (Oppler, 1993). To help remedy this matter, the gifted field and recent federal initiatives have focused on ways to increase gifted females' interest in science, technology, engineering, and mathematics (STEM) fields and career options (Ceci, Williams, & Barnett, 2009). Well-intentioned interventions

DON'T FORGET
....
Multipotentiality is an important concept in career assessment of intellectually gifted students.

have yielded at best modest outcomes, and researchers are reexamining the potency of strategies to change strongly held cultural attitudes and values (Davies, 2011).

6. Are There Any Recommendations for Assessment of the Twice-Exceptional Learner?

This seemingly simply question is complicated and can be answered in a variety of ways. For example, we could approach the question from the perspective of the purpose of the assessment: one purpose might be to determine whether a high-ability student has a co-morbid disability such as ADHD and/or an anxiety disorder. In this instance, we already know that the client is exceptionally bright and might, in fact, have already been evaluated and found to be gifted. The diagnostic question is whether this gifted student also has a coexisting disability. A slightly different purpose might be to determine whether a student with an already established disability such as a specific learning disability is also gifted. Webb et al. (2005) offer a valuable discussion of these diagnostic conundrums in their book on misdiagnosis and dual diagnoses of the gifted. I also address the topics of misdiagnosis and missed diagnoses in my recent book (Pfeiffer, 2013b).

The National Education Association has published a white paper on the twice-exceptional student (NEA, 2006). The introduction notes that "some youngsters show a pattern of extreme strengths combined with areas of significant difficulty. . . . [These children are] commonly referred to as twice-exceptional students; students who have outstanding gifts or talents and are capable of high performance, but who also have a disability that affects some aspect of learning" (Brody & Mills, 1997, cited in NEA, 2006, p. 1). This NEA document also points out that the twice exceptional "are among the most frequently under-identified population in our schools. Twice-exceptional students present a unique identification and service delivery dilemma for educators" (p. 1). Conservative estimates suggest that approximately 360,000, or 6%, of the students served by the Individuals with Disabilities Education Improvement Act (IDEA) of 2004 are twice-exceptional: that is, academically gifted with a disability. And there are likely a considerable number of high-ability students with disabilities who have been missed and not identified.

Let's briefly consider one psychiatric disorder, ADHD. This is a difficult disorder to accurately diagnose. There are presently no objective measures or biophysiological lab tests that can confirm an ADHD diagnosis. Complicating matters, some of the symptoms that represent behavioral criteria according to the *DSM-V* (American Psychiatric Association, 2(behaviors that are reported as characteristic of some gifted children. This complicates an accurate, differential ADHD diagnosis for high-ability students. Although there are no actual epidemiological data on this point, it is reasonable to assume that an appreciable number of students with IQ scores in the gifted range are misdiagnosed with ADHD, and that an equal number of gifted students with ADHD are not correctly identified as having ADHD (a "missed diagnosis") because their high ability masks or obscures behaviors that would help in identifying the disorder (Pfeiffer, 2009, 2013b). In other words, one can expect an appreciable number of false positive and false negative ADHD diagnoses when dealing with the gifted student.

Clinical expertise and experience are required to make an accurate differential diagnosis, given the subjective nature of ADHD symptoms and the symptom overlap between characteristics of ADHD and characteristics of giftedness. Hyperactivity, impulsivity, distractibility, and inattention can be the result of multiple root causes; ADHD is only one likely cause. For example, a 2nd grader with an IQ of 135 who is bored because she has not been provided with an appropriately challenging and differentiated curriculum might be expected to display a host of inattentive and off-task behaviors that mimic ADHD. A careful assessment is necessary; we certainly don't want to misdiagnose any student as ADHD who does not have the disorder and whose behaviors are the result of other root causes. There are a number of psychological and neuropsychological tests that can assist in making a correct differential diagnosis for ADHD, including the Test of Variables of Attention (TOVA) (Greenberg, 2007, 2011), the Gordon Diagnostic System (Gordon, 1983), and the Continuous Performance Test (CPT) (Conners, 1994, 2014).

The assessment of the twice-exceptional learner is, in many ways, similar to the challenges when assessing any special population. Unfortunately, there is not a whole lot of research on the twice-exceptional gifted and also disabled student. And there is even less research on the assessment of this group of special needs students. The research that does exist suggests that students with both gifts and disabilities are more likely to be overlooked for gifted programs (Brody & Mills, 1997). One of the likely reasons is that their disability overshadows or masks (i.e., eclipses) their gifts—a diagnostic conundrum that Webb et al. (2005) and Pfeiffer (2013b) both discuss.

CAUTION

Supervision and experience should always be required before a practitioner conducts a gifted assessment.

Clinicians need to keep their antennas highly sensitive to strengths and abilities when conducting a gifted assessment on any student suspected of a disability. It is all too easy to focus on a student's deficits and weaknesses, especially when testing a student referred for learning or behavioral problems. My recommendation is to always view the client through dual lenses. The first lens requires that we adopt a rigorous and intensive clinical perspective that investigates evidence and possible root causes for the problem. The second lens reminds us to look for strengths, including emerging competencies; personal and interpersonal coping skills; resilience; motivation and interest in school and learning; and self-confidence as a learner. The assessment process, including the assessment for the twice-exceptional learner, should always include attention to student strengths. Failing to identify a student with unrecognized or latent ability, especially when the referral is to rule out a disability, is much less likely if one views children through multiple lenses, including a positive psychology lens (Seligman, 2004, 2007).

A final point bears mentioning in answering this question. The practitioner must always consider how a child's disability might affect his test-taking behavior, level of comfort and confidence, and obtained test performance. For example, most practitioners would recognize the great danger in administering a test with oral instructions to a student who has a hearing impairment or providing picture-based test stimuli to a student with a visual impairment. However, there are more subtle cases, such as the student with ADHD who may also be intellectually gifted. How would we modify the gifted assessment to evaluate this student's abilities, bearing in mind that she has considerable difficulty sustaining attention and focus? Equally challenging is the issue of how we would determine the degree to which the student's disability is moderating her self-confidence, effort, and anxiety—factors that we know can depress test scores (Sattler, 2001).

CONCLUDING COMMENTS

I hope that you have found these answers to the six frequently asked questions about gifted assessment helpful. Of course, there are many other questions that arise in the real world of gifted assessment. A book could easily be written titled "The 101 Most Frequent Questions in the Assessment of Gifted Students." In fact, that just may be my next project!

The important take-home message is this: in work with high-ability students, it is advisable to follow a scientifically defensible approach based on evidence-based practice. Recall from Chapter 3 that one of my seven principles is that gifted assessment should be guided by sound clinical judgment, not by rigid adherence to

≡ Rapid Reference 7.1 Best Practices

A scientifically defensible approach to best practices in gifted assessment integrates practitioners' access to the best quality and most recent research on the various assessment tests and procedures; their clinical expertise, and their experience with and understanding of the gifted population.

specified test scores. Linda Silverman (2013) advocates, and I agree, that test results should be used to support sound clinical judgment. When taking a scientifically defensible approach to best practices in gifted assessment, practitioners integrate these three components:

- Access to the best quality and most recent research on the various assessment tests and procedures
- Clinical expertise
- Experience with and understanding of the gifted population

This view on best practices is equally valid for both evidence-based assessment and evidence-based treatment (Norcross, Hogan, & Koocher, 2008). All three components—recent and relevant available research on tests and assessment of the gifted, clinician expertise, and sensitivity to and deep appreciation for the unique characteristics, concerns, and preferences of the gifted—are critical if gifted assessment is to be useful, effective, and scientifically defensible.

 TEST YOURSELF

1. **The author advocates that practitioners should customize their gifted test battery based on a number of considerations:**
   a. True
   b. False

2. **The author argues that disproportionality in gifted education is a simple problem: IQ tests are biased and should not be used in gifted assessment:**
   a. True
   b. False

3. **Nonverbal tests are a panacea for the problem of racial and ethnic disproportionality in gifted programs:**
   a. True
   b. False   (continued)

(*continued*)

4. **Nonverbal tests can mask the very real achievement gap that exists for certain groups of minority group students:**

   a. True

   b. False

5. **Research suggests that students with both gifts and disabilities are rarely overlooked for gifted programs:**

   a. True

   b. False

6. **Practitioners need to keep their antennas highly sensitive to strengths and abilities when conducting a gifted assessment on any student suspected of a disability:**

   a. True

   b. False

7. **Measures of self-esteem and passion for learning should always be included in a standard gifted assessment protocol:**

   a. True

   b. False

8. **A practitioner's clinical expertise and understanding of the gifted population are critical components of best practices in gifted assessment:**

   a. True

   b. False

Answers: 1. True; 2. False; 3. False; 4. True; 5. False; 6. True; 7. False; 8. True.

REFERENCES

Abedi, J. (2000). *Abedi test of creativity (ATC)*. Los Angeles: National Center for Research on Evaluation, Standards, and Student Testing, University of California, Los Angeles.

Achter, J. A., Benbow, C. P., & Lubinski, D. (1997). Multipotentiality among the gifted: Is it a pervasive problem? *Gifted Child Quarterly, 41*, 2–12.

Ackerman, P. L. (2013, May). Nonsense, common sense, and science of expert performance: Talent and individual differences. *Intelligence*. Advance online publication. doi: 10.1016/j.intell.2013.04.009

Alfonso, V. C., Flanagan, D. P., & Radwan, S. (2005). The impact of the Cattell-Horn-Carroll theory on test development and interpretation of cognitive and academic abilities. In D. P. Flanagan & P. L. Harrison (Eds.), *Contemporary intellectual assessment: Theories, tests, and issues* (2nd ed., pp. 185–202). New York: Guilford Press.

Allen, A. D. (2010). Complex spatial skills: The link between visualization and creativity. *Creativity Research Journal, 22*, 241–249.

Almeida, L. S., Prieto, F. P., Ferrando, M., Oliviera, E., & Ferrándiz, C. (2008). Torrance Test of Creative Thinking: The question of its construct validity. *Thinking Skills and Creativity, 3*, 53–58.

Althuizen, N., Wierenga, B., & Rossiter, J. (2010). The validity of two brief measures of creative ability. *Creativity Research Journal, 22*, 53–61.

Amabile, T. M. (1982). Social psychology of creativity: A consensual assessment technique. *Journal of Personality and Social Psychology, 43*, 997–1013.

Amabile, T. M. (1983). *The social psychology of creativity*. New York: Springer.

American Educational Research Association, American Psychological Association, & National Council on Measurement in Education. (2014). *Standards for educational and psychological testing*. Washington, DC: American Educational Research Association.

American Psychiatric Association. (2013). *Diagnostic and statistical manual of mental disorders* (5th ed.). Arlington, VA: American Psychiatric Association.

Arter, J., & McTighe, J. (2001). *Scoring rubrics in the classroom: Using performance criteria for assessing and improving student performance*. Thousand Oaks, CA: Corwin Press.

Assouline, S. G., Colangelo, N., Ihrig, D., Forstadt, L., & Lipscomb, J. (2004). Iowa Acceleration Scale validation studies. In N. Colangelo, S. G. Assouline, & M.U.M. Gross (Eds.), *A nation deceived: How schools hold back America's brightest students* (Vol. 1, pp. 167–172). Iowa City: Connie Belin & Jacqueline N. Blank International Center for Gifted Education and Talent Development, University of Iowa.

Assouline, S. G., Colangelo, N., Lupkowski-Shoplik, A. E., Lipscomb, J., & Forstadt, L. (2009). *The Iowa Acceleration Scale* (3rd ed.). Scottsdale, AZ: Great Potential Press.

Assouline, S. G., & Lupkowski-Shoplik, A. (2012). The talent search model of gifted identification. *Journal of Psychoeducational Assessment, 30*, 45–59.

Athanasiou, M. S. (2000). Current nonverbal assessment instruments: A comparison of psychometric integrity and test fairness. *Journal of Psychoeducational Assessment, 18*, 211–229. doi: 10.1177/073428290001800302

Atkinson, L. (1991). Three standard errors of measurement and the Wechsler Memory Scale—Revised. *Psychological Assessment, 3*, 136–138.

Baer, J. (1998). The case for domain specificity in creativity. *Creativity Research Journal, 11*, 173–177.

Baer, J. (2008). Commentary: Divergent thinking tests have problems, but this is not the solution. *Psychology of Aesthetics, Creativity, and the Arts, 2*, 89–92.

Baer, J. (2010). Is creativity domain specific? In J. C. Kaufman, & R. J. Sternberg (Eds.), *The Cambridge handbook of creativity* (pp. 321–341). New York: Cambridge University Press.

Baer, J. (2011). How divergent thinking tests mislead us: Are the Torrance Tests still relevant in the 21st century? The Division 10 debate. *Psychology of Aesthetics, Creativity, and the Arts, 5*, 309–313.

Baer, J., Kaufman, J. C., & Gentile, C. A. (2004). Extension of the Consensual Assessment Technique to nonparallel creative products. *Creativity Research Journal, 16*, 113–117.

Bain, S. K., & Allin, J. D. (2005). Review of the Stanford-Binet Intelligence Scales, Fifth Edition. *Journal of Psychoeducational Assessment, 23*, 87–95.

Baron, F. (1955). The disposition toward originality. *Journal of Abnormal and Social Psychology, 51*, 478–485.

Benson, N., Hulac, D. M., & Kranzler, J. H. (2010). Independent examination of the Wechsler Adult Intelligence Scale–Fourth Edition (WAIS–IV): What does the WAIS–IV measure? *Psychological Assessment, 22*(1), 121–130. doi: 10.1037/a0017767

Berger, S. L. (2008). *The ultimate guide to summer opportunities for teens.* Waco, TX: Prufrock Press.

Berry, C. (1981). The Nobel scientists and the origins of scientific achievement. *British Journal of Sociology, 32*, 381–391.

Binet, A., & Simon, T. (1916). *The development of intelligence in children.* Baltimore, Williams & Wilkins.

Blair, C. (2006). How similar are fluid cognition and general intelligence? A developmental neuroscience perspective on fluid cognition as an aspect of human cognitive ability. *Behavioral and Brain Sciences, 29*, 109–125.

Blei, S., & Pfeiffer, S. I. (2007). *Peer ratings of giftedness: What the research suggests.* Unpublished monograph, Florida State University, Tallahassee, FL.

Bloom, B. S. (1982). The role of gifts and markers in the development of talent. *Exceptional Children, 48*, 510–522.

Bloom, B. S. (1985). *Developing talent in young people.* New York: Ballantine Books.

Borland, J. H. (2005). Gifted education without gifted children: The case for no conception of giftedness. In R. J. Sternberg & J. E. Davidson (Eds.), *Conceptions of Giftedness* (2nd ed., pp. 1–19). New York: Cambridge University Press.

Borland, J. H. (2009). Myth 2: The gifted constitute 3% to 5% of the population. Moreover, giftedness equals high IQ, which is a stable measure of aptitude: Spinal tap psychometrics in gifted education. *Gifted Child Quarterly, 53*, 236–238.

Borland, J. H., & Wright, L. (1994). Identifying young, potentially gifted, economically disadvantaged students. *Gifted Child Quarterly, 38*, 164–171.

Bracken, B. A., & McCallum, R. S. (1998). *Universal Nonverbal Intelligence Test.* Itasca, IL: Riverside.

Brody, L. E. (2007). Review of the Gifted and Talented Evaluation Scales. In K. F. Geisinger, R. A. Spies, J. F. Carlson, & B. S. Plake (Eds.), *The seventeenth mental measurements yearbook* (pp. 343–345). Lincoln: Buros Institute of Mental Measurements, University of Nebraska-Lincoln.

Brody, L. E., & Benbow, C. P. (1987). Accelerative strategies: How effective are they for the gifted? *Gifted Child Quarterly, 31,* 105–110.

Brody, L. E., & Mills, C. J. (1997). Gifted children with learning disabilities: A review of the issues. *Journal of Learning Disabilities, 30,* 282–296.

Bronfenbrenner, U., & Ceci, S. J. (1994). Toward a more developmental behavioral genetics. *Social Development, 3,* 64–65.

Brown, L., Sherbenou, R. J., & Johnson, S. K. (2010). *Test of Nonverbal Intelligence: TONI-4.* Austin, TX: Pro-Ed.

Burke, J. P., Haworth, C. E., & Ware, W. B. (1982). Scale for Rating Behavioral Characteristics of Superior Students: An investigation of factor structure. *Journal of Special Education, 16,* 477–485.

Callahan, C. M., Renzulli, J. S., Delcourt, M.A.B., & Hertberg-Davis, H. L. (2013). Considerations for identification of gifted and talented students. In C. M. Callahan & H. L. Hertberg-Davis (Eds.), *Fundamentals of gifted education* (pp. 83–91). New York: Routledge.

Canivez, G. L. (2008). Orthogonal higher-order factor structure of the Stanford-Binet Intelligence Scales for children and adolescents. *School Psychology Quarterly, 23,* 533–541.

Canivez, G. L., & Watkins, M. W. (2010a). Exploratory and higher-order factor analyses of the Wechsler Adult Intelligence Scale—Fourth Edition (WAIS-IV) adolescent subsample. *School Psychology Quarterly, 25,* 223–235.

Canivez, G. L., & Watkins, M. W. (2010b). Investigation of the factor structure of the Wechsler Adult Intelligence Scale-Fourth Edition (WAIS-IV): Exploratory and higher-order factor analyses. *Psychological Assessment, 22,* 827–836.

Carroll, J. B. (1993). *Human cognitive abilities: A survey of factor-analytic studies.* Cambridge, UK: Cambridge University Press.

Carson, S. (2006, April). *Creativity and mental illness.* Invitational panel discussion hosted by Yale's Mind Matters Consortium, New Haven, CT.

Cattell, R. B., & Cattell, A.K.S. (1960). *Handbook for the individual or group Culture Fair Intelligence Test.* Champaign, IL: IPAT.

Cayton, T. (2008, November). *Wechsler's "ability to an extraordinary degree": Extended norms on the WISC-IV.* Paper presented at the meeting of the National Association for Gifted Children, Tampa, FL.

Ceci, S. J., & Papierno, P. B. (2005). The rhetoric and reality of gap closing: When the "have-nots" gain but the "haves" gain even more. *American Psychologist, 60,* 149–160.

Ceci, S. J., & Williams, W. M. (1997). Schooling, intelligence, and income. *American Psychologist, 52,* 1051–1058.

Ceci, S. J., Williams, W. M., & Barnett, S. M. (2009). Women's underrepresentation in science: Sociocultural and biological considerations. *Psychological Bulletin, 135,* 218–261.

Cheng, Y., Wang, W., Liu, K., & Chen, Y. (2010). Effects of association instruction on fourth graders' poetic creativity in Taiwan. *Creativity Research Journal, 22,* 228–235.

Colangelo, N., Assouline, S. G., & Baldus, C. (n.d.). The Iowa Acceleration Scale. Presentation for NHA accelerated learner teacher training [Slide show].

Colangelo, N., Assouline, S. G., & Gross, M.U.M. (Eds.). (2004). *A nation deceived: How schools hold back America's brightest students* (2 vols.). Iowa City: Connie Belin & Jacqueline N. Blank International Center for Gifted Education and Talent Development, University of Iowa. http//www/nationdeceived.org (for a free copy)

Colvin, G. (2008). *Talent is overrated: What really separates world-class performers from everybody else.* New York: Portfolio.

Conners, C. K. (1994). *The Conners' Continuous Performance Test.* Toronto: Multi-Health Systems (MHS).

Conners, C. K. (2014). *The Continuous Performance Test* (3rd ed.). North Tonawanda, NY: Multi-Health Systems (MHS).

Connolly, A. J. (2007). *Key-Math-3 Diagnostic Assessment: Manual Forms A and B.* Minneapolis, MN: Pearson.

Côté, J., Baker, J., & Abernethy, B. (2003). From play to practice: A developmental framework for the acquisition of expertise in team sports. In J. A. Starkes & K. A. Ericsson (Eds.), *Expert performance in sports: Advances in research on sport expertise* (pp. 89–114). Champaign, IL: Human Kinetics.

Coyle, D. (2009). *The talent code: Greatness isn't born, it's grown.* New York: Bantam Books.

Cramond, B., Matthews-Morgan, J., Bandalos, D., & Zuo, L. (2005). A report on the 40–year follow-up of the Torrance Tests of Creative Thinking: Alive and well in the new millennium. *Gifted Child Quarterly, 49,* 283–291.

Cunningham, C. M., Callahan, C. M., Plucker, J. A., Roberson, C., & Rapkin, A. (1998). Identifying Hispanic students of outstanding talent: Psychometric integrity of peer nomination form. *Exceptional Children, 64,* 197–210.

Dai, D. Y. (2010). *The nature and nurture of giftedness.* New York: Teachers College Press.

Davies, D. (2011). Careers education for exceptionally able girls. *Journal of the National Institute for Career Education and Counseling, 26,* 46–56.

DiStefano, C., & Dombrowski, S. C. (2006). Investigating the theoretical structure of the Stanford-Binet–Fifth Edition. *Journal of Psychoeducational Assessment, 24,* 123–136.

Dixon, F. A. (2009). *Programs and services for gifted secondary students: A guide to recommended practices.* Waco, TX: Prufrock Press.

Dumont, R., Willis, J. O., & Elliott, C. D. (2008). *Essentials of DAS-II assessment.* Hoboken, NJ: Wiley.

Durand-Bush, N., & Salmela, J. H. (2002). The development and maintenance of expert athletic performance: Perceptions of world and Olympic champions. *Journal of Applied Sport Psychology, 14,* 154–171.

The Editorial Board. (2013). Even gifted students can't keep up. *New York Times,* December 14.

Eisenberg, J., & Thompson, W. F. (2011). The effects of competition on improvisors' motivation, stress, and creative performance. *Creativity Research Journal, 23,* 129–136.

Elliot, C. D. (2007). *Differential Ability Scales, Second Edition: Administration and scoring manual.* San Antonio, TX: Pearson.

Elliott, S. N., & Argulewicz, E. N. (1983). Use of a behavior rating scale to aid in the identification of developmentally and culturally different gifted children. *Journal of Psychoeducational Assessment, 1,* 179–186.

Elliott, S. N., Argulewicz, E. N., & Turco, T. L. (1986). Predictive validity of the Scales for Rating the Behavioral Characteristics of Superior Students for gifted children from three sociocultural groups. *Journal of Experimental Education, 55,* 27–32.

Ericsson, K. A. (Ed.). (1996). *The road to excellence: The acquisition of expert performance in the arts and sciences, sports, and games.* Mahwah, NJ: Erlbaum.

Ericsson, K. A. (2103, December). Why expert performance is special and cannot be extrapolated from studies of performance in the general population: A response to criticisms. *Intelligence.* Advance online publication. doi: 10.1016/j.intell.2013.12.001

Ericsson, K. A., & Charness, N. (1995). Abilities: Innate talent or characteristics acquired through engagement in relevant activities? *American Psychologist, 50,* 803–804.

Ericsson, K. A., Krampe, R. T., & Tesch-Romer, C. (1993). The role of deliberate practice in the acquisition of expert performance. *Psychological Review, 100,* 363–406.

Ericsson, K. A., Roring, R. W., & Nandagopal, K. (2007). Giftedness and evidence for reproducibly superior performance: An account based on the expert-performance framework. *High Ability Studies, 18,* 3–56.

Feldhusen, J. F. (2005). Giftedness, talent, expertise, and creative achievement. In R. J. Sternberg & J. E. Davidson (Eds.), *Conceptions of giftedness* (2nd. ed., pp. 64–79). New York: Cambridge University Press.

Feldman, D. H. (1986). *Nature's gambit: Child prodigies and the development of human potential.* New York: Basic Books.

Feldman, D. H. (1994). An emerging paradigm for research on human creativity [Review of the book *Creating Minds* by Howard Gardner]. *American Scientist, 82,* 472–473.

Fink, A., & Neubauer, A. C. (2006). EEG alpha oscillations during the performance of verbal creativity tasks: Differential effects of sex and verbal intelligence. *International Journal of Psychophysiology, 62,* 46–53.

Flanagan, D. P., & Harrison, P. L. (2005). *Contemporary intellectual assessment: Theories, tests, and issues* (2nd ed.). New York: Guilford Press.

Flanagan, D. P., & Harrison, P. L. (2012). *Contemporary intellectual assessment: Theories, tests, and issues* (3rd ed.). New York: Guilford Press.

Flanagan, D. P., & Kaufman, A. S. (2009). *Essentials of WISC-IV assessment* (2nd ed.). Hoboken, NJ: Wiley.

Flanagan, D. P., & McGrew, K. S. (1997). A cross-battery approach to assessing and interpreting cognitive abilities: Narrowing the gap between practice and cognitive science. In D. P. Flanagan & J. L. Genshaft (Eds.), *Contemporary intellectual assessment: Theories, tests, and issues* (pp. 314–325). New York: Guilford Press.

Floyd, R., McGrew, K., Barry, A., Rafael, F., & Rogers, J. (2009). General and specific effects on Cattell-Horn-Carroll broad ability composites: Analysis of the Woodcock-Johnson III Normative Update Cattell-Horn-Carroll factor clusters across development. *School Psychology Review, 38,* 249–265.

Floyd, R. G., Reynolds, M. R., Farmer, R. L., & Kranzler, J. H. (2013). Are the general factors from different child and adolescent intelligence tests the same? Results from a five-sample, six-test analysis. *School Psychology Quarterly, 42,* 383–401.

Ford, D. Y., & Whiting, G. W. (2008). Recruiting and retaining underrepresented gifted students. In S. I. Pfeiffer (Ed.), *Handbook of giftedness in children* (pp. 293–308). New York: Springer.

Frazier, T. W., & Youngstrom, E. A. (2007). Historical increase in the number of factors measured by commercial tests of cognitive ability: Are we overfactoring? *Intelligence, 35,* 169–182.

Frisby, C. L., & Braden, J. P. (Eds.). (1999). Bias in mental testing [Special issue]. *School Psychology Quarterly, 14.*

Gagné, F. (2005). From gifts to talents: The DMGT as a developmental model. In R. J. Sternberg & J. E. Davidson (Eds.), *Conceptions of giftedness* (2nd ed., pp. 98–120). New York: Cambridge University Press.

Gagné, F. (2009). Debating giftedness: Pronat vs. antinat. In L. V. Shavinina (Ed.), *International handbook on giftedness* (pp. 155–198). New York: Springer.

Gallagher, J. J. (1960). *Analysis of research on the education of gifted children.* Springfield, IL: Office of the Superintendent of Public Instruction.

Gallagher, J. J. (2008). Psychology, psychologists, and gifted students. In S. I. Pfeiffer (Ed.), *Handbook of giftedness in children* (pp. 1–11). New York: Springer.

Galton, F. (1869). *Hereditary genius: An inquiry into its laws and consequences.* London: Macmillan.

Gardner, H. (1983). *Frames of mind.* New York: Basic Books.

Gardner, H. (1993). *Multiple intelligences: The theory in practice.* New York: Basic Books.

Giancarlo, C. A., & Facione, P. A. (2000). *The California Measure of Mental Motivation.* Millbrae: California Academic Press.

Gilliam, J. E., Carpenter, B. O., & Christensen, J. R. (1996). *Gifted and Talented Evaluation Scales*. Austin, TX: Pro-Ed.

Gilman, B. J. (2008). *Challenging highly gifted learners*. Waco, TX: Prufrock Press.

Goddard, H. H. (1908). The Binet and Simon tests of intellectual capacity. *Training School*, 3–9.

Goldstein, S. (2013). The science of intelligence testing: Commentary on the evolving nature of interpretations of the Wechsler scales. *Journal of Psychoeducational Assessment, 31*, 132–137.

Gordon, M. (1983). *Gordon Diagnostic System*. DeWitt, NY: Gordon Systems.

Gottfredson, L. S. (1997). Why *g* matters. *Intelligence, 24*, 79–132.

Gottfredson, L. S. (1998). The general intelligence factor. *Scientific American Presents, 9*, 24–30.

Gottfredson, L. S. (2008). Of what values is intelligence? In A. Prifitera, D. H. Saklofske, & L. G. Weiss (Eds.), *WISC-IV clinical assessment and intervention* (2nd ed., pp. 545–563). Amsterdam: Elsevier.

Gottfried, A. E. (1986). *Children's Academic Intrinsic Motivation Inventory*. Odessa, FL: Psychological Assessment Resources.

Gray, R., McCallum, S., & Bain, S. K. (2009). Language-reduced screening for giftedness. *Journal for the Education of the Gifted, 33*, 38–64.

Greenberg, L. M. (2007). *The Test of Variables of Attention* (Version 7.3) [Computer software]. Los Alamitos, CA: The TOVA Company.

Greenberg, L. M. (2011). *The Test of Variables of Attention* (Version 8.0) [Computer software]. Los Alamitos, CA: The TOVA Company.

Gross, M.U.M. (1994). Radical acceleration: Responding to academic and social needs of extremely gifted adolescents. *Journal of Secondary Gifted Education, 5*, 27–34.

Gross, M.U.M. (2009). Highly gifted young people: Development from childhood to adulthood. In L. V. Shavinina (Ed.), *International handbook on giftedness* (Part I, pp. 337–351). New York: Springer.

Groth-Marnat, G. (2009). *Handbook of psychological assessment* (5th ed.). Hoboken, NJ: Wiley.

Guilford, J. P. (1950). Creativity. *American Psychologist, 5*, 444–454.

Guilford, J. P. (1967). *The nature of human intelligence*. New York: McGraw-Hill.

Hass, R. W. (2013). Historiometry as extension of the Consensual Assessment Technique: A comment on Kaufman and Baer. *Creativity Research Journal, 25*, 356–360. doi: 10.1080/10400419.2013.813813

Holland, J. L., & Messer, M. A. (2013). *Self-directed search* (5th ed.). Lutz, FL: PAR.

Hollingworth, L. S. (1926). *Gifted children: Their nature and nurture*. New York: Macmillan.

Horn, J. L., & Cattell, R. B. (1966). Refinement and test of the theory of fluid and crystallized intelligence. *Journal of Educational Psychology, 57*, 253–270.

Horowitz, F. D., Subotnik, R. F., & Matthews, D. J. (Eds.). (2009). *The development of giftedness and talent across the life span*. Washington, DC: American Psychological Association.

Hosp, J. L., & Reschly, D. J. (2004). Disproportionate representation of minority students in special education: Academic, demographic and economic predictors. *Exceptional Children, 70*, 185–199.

Humphreys, L. G. (1985). A conceptualization of intellectual giftedness. In F. D. Horowitz & M. O'Brien (Eds.), *The gifted and talented: Developmental perspectives* (pp. 331–360). Washington, DC: American Psychological Association.

Hunsaker, S. L., & Callahan, C. M. (1995). Creativity and giftedness: Published instrument uses and abuses. *Gifted Child Quarterly, 39*, 110–114.

Hunsley, J., & Mash, E. J. (2008). Developing criteria for evidence-based assessment: An introduction to assessments that work. In J. Hunsley & E. J. Mash (Eds.), *A guide to assessments that work* (pp. 3–14). New York: Oxford University Press.

Impara, J. C. (2010). Assessing the validity of test scores. In R. A. Spies, J. F. Carlson, & K. F. Geisinger (Eds.), *The eighteenth mental measurements yearbook* (pp. 817–823). Lincoln: Buros Institute of Mental Measurements, University of Nebraska-Lincoln.

Individuals with Disabilities Education Improvement Act of 2004, 20 U.S.C. § 1400 et seq. (2004).

Irving, M. A., & Hudley, C. (2009). Cultural identification and academic achievement among African American males. *Journal of Advanced Academics, 19,* 676–699.

Janzen, H. L., Obrzut, J. E., & Marusiak, C. W. (2004). Review of the Stanford-Binet Intelligence Scales, Fifth Edition (SB:V). *Canadian Journal of School Psychology, 19,* 235–244.

Jarosewich, T., Pfeiffer, S. I., & Morris, J. (2002). Identifying gifted students using teacher rating scales: A review of existing instruments. *Journal of Psychoeducational Assessment, 20,* 322–336.

Jaušovec, N. (2000). Differences in cognitive processes between gifted, intelligence, creative, and average individuals while solving complex problems: An EEG study. *Intelligence, 28,* 213–237.

Jensen, A. (1998). *The g factor: The science of mental ability.* Westport, CT: Praeger.

Johnsen, S. K. (1996). What are alternative assessments? *Gifted Child Today, 19,* 12–13.

Johnsen, S. K. (2008). Portfolio assessment of gifted students. In J. VanTassel-Baska (Ed.), *Alternative assessments with gifted and talented students* (pp. 227–257). Waco, TX: Prufrock Press.

Johnson, J. A., & D'Amato, R. C. (2005). Review of the Stanford-Binet Intelligence Scales, Fifth Edition. In R. A. Spies & B. S. Plake (Eds.), *The sixteenth mental measurements yearbook* (pp. 976–979). Lincoln: Buros Institute of Mental Measurements, University of Nebraska-Lincoln.

Karnes, F. A., & Bean, S. M. (Eds.). (2009). *Methods and materials for teaching the gifted* (3rd ed.). Waco, TX: Prufrock Press.

Kaufman, A. S. (1979). *Intelligent testing with the WISC-R.* New York: Wiley.

Kaufman, A. S. (1994a). *Intelligent testing with the WISC-III.* New York: Wiley.

Kaufman, A. S. (1994b). A reply to Macmann and Barnett: Lessons from the blind men and the elephant. *School Psychology Quarterly, 9,* 199–207.

Kaufman, A. S. (2009). *IQ testing 101.* New York: Springer.

Kaufman, A. S. (2013). Intelligent testing with Wechsler's fourth editions: Perspectives on the Weiss et al. studies and the eight commentaries. *Journal of Psychoeducational Assessment, 31,* 224–234.

Kaufman, A. S., & Kaufman, N. L. (2004a). *Kaufman Assessment Battery for Children, Second Edition* (KABC-II). Circle Pines, MN: American Guidance Service.

Kaufman, A. S., & Kaufman, N. L. (2004b). *Kaufman Brief Intelligence Test, Second Edition* (KBIT-2). Circle Pines, MN: American Guidance Service.

Kaufman, A. S., & Kaufman, N. L. (2005). *Kaufman Test of Educational Achievement, Second Edition (KTEA-II).* Circle Pines, MN: American Guidance Service.

Kaufman, A. S., & Kaufman, N. L. (2014). *Kaufman Test of Educational Achievement, Third Edition* (KTEA-III). San Antonio, TX: Pearson.

Kaufman, J. C. (2009). *Creativity 101.* New York: Springer.

Kaufman, J. C., & Baer, J. (2012). Beyond new and appropriate: Who decides what is creative? *Creativity Research Journal, 24,* 83–91.

Kaufman, J. C., Baer, J., Cole, J. C., & Sexton, J. D. (2008). A comparison of expert and nonexpert raters using the Consensual Assessment Technique. *Creativity Research Journal, 20,* 171–178.

Kaufman, J. C., Evans, M. L., & Baer, J. (2010). The American Idol effect: Are students good judges of their creativity across domains? *Empirical Studies of the Arts, 28,* 3–17.

Kaufman, J. C., Lee, J., Baer, J., & Lee, S. (2007). Captions, consistency, creativity, and the Consensual Assessment Technique: New evidence of reliability. *Thinking Skills and Creativity, 2,* 96–106.

Kaufman, J. C., & Plucker, J. A. (2011). Intelligence and creativity. In R. J. Sternberg & S. B. Kaufman (Eds.), *The Cambridge handbook of intelligence* (pp. 771–783). New York: Cambridge University Press.

Kaufman, J. C., Plucker, J. A., & Baer, J. (2008). *Essentials of creativity assessment.* New York: Wiley.

Kaufman, J. C., Plucker, J. A., & Russell, C. M. (2012). Identifying and assessing creativity as a component of giftedness. *Journal of Psychoeducational Assessment, 30,* 60–73.

Kaufman, S. B. (2013). *Ungifted: Intelligence redefined.* New York: Basic Books.

Kaufman, S. B., & Sternberg, R. J. (2008). Conceptions of giftedness. In S. I. Pfeiffer (Ed.), *Handbook of giftedness in children* (pp. 71–92). New York: Springer.

Keith, T. Z., Fine, J. G., Taub, G. E., Reynolds, M. R., & Kranzler, J. H. (2006). Higher order, multisample, confirmatory factor analysis of the Wechsler Intelligence Scale for Children—Fourth Edition: What does it measure? *School Psychology Review, 15,* 108–127.

Keith, T. Z., Low, J. A., Reynolds, M. R., Patel, P. G., & Ridley, K. P. (2010). Higher-order factor structure of the Differential Ability Scale-II: Consistency across ages 4 to 17. *Psychology in the Schools, 47,* 676–697.

Kell, H. J., Lubinski, D., & Benbow, C. P. (2013). Who rises to the top? Early indicators. *Psychological Science, 24,* 648–659.

Kerr, B. (1990). *Career planning for gifted and talented youth* (ERIC Documentation Reproduction Service No. ED 321497). Alexandria, VA: ERIC Clearinghouse on Handicapped and Gifted Children.

Kim, K. H. (2011). The APA 2009 Division 10 Debate: Are the Torrance Tests of Creative Thinking still relevant in the 21st century? *Psychology of Aesthetics, Creativity, and the Arts, 5,* 302–308.

Kolitch, E. R., & Brody, L. E. (1992). Mathematics acceleration of highly talented students: An evaluation. *Gifted Child Quarterly, 36,* 78–86.

Kranzler, J. H., & Floyd, R. G. (2013). *Assessing intelligence in children and adolescents: A practical guide.* New York: Guilford Press.

Lakin, J. M., & Lohman, D. F. (2011). The predictive accuracy of verbal, quantitative, and nonverbal reasoning tests: Consequences for talent identification and program diversity. *Journal for the Education of the Gifted, 34*(4), 595–623. doi: 10.1177/016235321103400404

Landrum, M. S., Callahan, C. M., & Shaklee, B. D. (Eds.). (2001). *Aiming for excellence: Gifted program standards.* Waco, TX: Prufrock Press.

Lee, S. Y., & Olszewski-Kubilius, P. (2006). Comparison between talent search students qualifying via scores on standardized tests and via parent nomination. *Roeper Review, 28,* 157–166.

Lee, D., & Pfeiffer, S. I. (2006). The reliability and validity of a Korean-translated version of the Gifted Rating Scales. *Journal of Psychoeducational Assessment, 24,* 210–224.

Leonard, D. (2010). *Fostering creativity.* Boston: Harvard Business Press.

Li, H., Lee, D., Pfeiffer, S. I., & Petscher, Y. (2008). Parent ratings using the Chinese version of the Parent Gifted Rating Scales—School Form: Reliability and validity for Chinese students. *Educational and Psychological Measurement, 68,* 659–675.

Li, H., Pfeiffer, S. I., Petscher, Y., Kumtepe, A., & Mo, G. (2008). Validation of the Chinese Gifted Rating Scales—School Form in China. *Gifted Child Quarterly, 52,* 160–169.

Li, H., Lee, D., Pfeiffer, S. I., Kamata, A., & Kumtepe, A. T. (2009). Measurement invariance of the Gifted Rating Scales—School Form across five cultural groups. *School Psychology Quarterly, 24,* 186–198.

Lichtenberger, E. O., & Kaufman, A. S. (2013). *Essentials of WAIS–IV assessment* (2nd ed.). Hoboken, NJ: Wiley.

Lichtenberger, E. O., Volker, M. A., Kaufman, A. S., & Kaufman, N. L. (2006). Assessing gifted children with the Kaufman Assessment Battery for Children-Second Edition. *Gifted Education International, 21*, 99–126.

Lohman, D. F. (2005a). An aptitude perspective on talent: Implications for identification of academically gifted minority students. *Journal for the Education of the Gifted, 28*, 333–360.

Lohman, D. F. (2005b). Review of Naglieri and Ford (2003): Does the Naglieri Nonverbal Ability Test identify equal proportions of high-scoring white, black, and Hispanic students? *Gifted Child Quarterly, 49*, 19–28.

Lohman, D. F. (2005c). The role of nonverbal ability tests in identifying academically gifted students: An aptitude perspective. *Gifted Child Quarterly, 49*, 111–138.

Lohman, D. F. (2006). Beliefs about differences between ability and accomplishment: From folk theories to cognitive science. *Roeper Review, 29*, 32–40.

Lohman, D. F. (2009). Identifying academically talented students: Some general principles, two specific procedures. In L. V. Shavinia (Ed.), *International Handbook on Giftedness* (pp. 971–997). New York: Springer.

Lohman, D. F. (2012). Decision strategies. In S. L. Hunsaker (Ed.), *Identification: The theory and practice of identifying students for gifted and talented education services* (pp. 217–248). Mansfield, CT: Creative Learning Press.

Lohman, D. F., & Korb, K. A. (2006). Gifted today but not tomorrow? Longitudinal changes in ability and achievement during elementary school. *Journal for the Education of the Gifted, 29*, 451–484.

Lovett, B. J., & Lewandowski, L. J. (2006). Gifted students with learning disabilities: Who are they? *Journal of Learning Disabilities, 39*, 515–527.

Luria, A. R. (1966). *Higher cortical functions in man.* New York: Basic Books.

Luria, A. R. (1973). *The working brain: An introduction to neuropsychology.* London: Penguin Books.

Makel, M. C., & Plucker, J. A. (2008). Creativity. In S. I. Pfeiffer (Ed.), *Handbook of giftedness in children* (pp. 247–270). New York: Springer.

Margulies, A. S., & Floyd, R. G. (2004). Test review: The Gifted Rating Scales. *Journal of Psychoeducational Assessment, 22*, 275–282.

Margulies, A. S., & Floyd, R. G. (2009). A preliminary examination of the CHC cognitive ability profiles of children with high IQ and high academic achievement enrolled in services for intellectual giftedness. *Woodcock-Munoz Foundation Press*, No. 1, 1–12.

Mather, N., & Wendling, B. J. (2014). *Examiner's manual: Woodcock-Johnson IV Tests of Cognitive Abilities.* Rolling Meadows, IL: Riverside.

Mathew, S. T. (1997). A review of the Gifted Evaluation Scale. *Journal of School Psychology, 35*, 101–104.

Matthews, M. S. (2007). Review of the Scales for Identifying Gifted Students. In K. F. Geisinger, R. A. Spies, J. F. Carlson, & B. S. Plake (Eds.), *The seventeenth mental measurements yearbook* (pp. 729–731). Lincoln: Buros Institute of Mental Measurements, University of Nebraska-Lincoln.

Mayer, R. E. (2005). The scientific study of giftedness. In R. J. Sternberg & J. E. Davidson (Eds.), *Conceptions of giftedness* (2nd ed., pp. 437–447). New York: Cambridge University Press.

McCallum, R. S., Bracken, B. A., & Wasserman, J. D. (2001). *Essentials of nonverbal assessment.* New York: Wiley.

McCarney, S. B., & Anderson, P. D. (1989). *Gifted Evaluation Scale, Second Edition: Technical manual.* Columbia, MO: Hawthorne Educational Services.

McCarney, S. B., & Anderson, P. D. (1998). *The Gifted Evaluation Scale, Revised Second Edition: Technical manual*. Columbia, MO: Hawthorne Educational Services.

McClain, M. C., & Pfeiffer, S. I. (2012). Identification of gifted students in the U.S. today: A look at state definitions, policies, and practices. *Journal of Applied School Psychology, 28*, 59–88.

McDermott, P. A., Fantuzzo, J. W., & Glutting, J. J. (1990). Just say no to subtest analysis: A critique of Wechsler theory and practice. *Journal of Psychoeducational Assessment, 8*, 290–302.

McGrew, K. S. (2005). The Catell-Horn-Carroll theory of cognitive abilities: Past, present, and future. In D. P. Flanagan & P. L. Harrison (Eds.), *Contemporary intellectual assessment: Theories, tests, and issues* (2nd ed., pp. 136–181). New York: Guilford Press.

McGrew, K. S., & Wendling, B. J. (2010). Cattell-Horn-Carroll cognitive-achievement relations: What we have learned from the past 20 years of research. *Psychology in the Schools, 47*, 651–675. doi: 10.1002/pits.20497

Meckstroth, E. (1989). On testing. *Understanding Our Gifted, 1*, 4.

Meehl, P. E., & Rosen, A. (1955). Antecedent probability and the efficiency of psychometric signs, patterns, or cutting scores. *Psychological Bulletin, 52*, 194–216.

Messick, S. (1992). Multiple intelligences or multilevel intelligence? Selective emphasis on distinctive properties of hierarchy: On Gardner's *Frames of Mind* and Sternberg's *Beyond IQ* in the context of theory and research on the structure of human abilities. *Psychological Inquiry, 3*, 365–384.

Miller, H. J. (1987). *The Miller Motivation Scale*. Saskatchewan, Canada: Meta Development.

Mölle, M., Marshall, L., Wolf, B., Fehm, H. L., & Born, J. (1999). EEG complexity and performance measures of creative thinking. *Psychophysiology, 36*, 95–104.

Mönks, F. J. (1992). Development of gifted children: The issue of identification and programming. In F. J. Mönks & W. A. Peters (Eds.), *Talent for the future* (pp. 191–202). Proceedings of the Ninth World Conference on Gifted and Talented Children. Assen, The Netherlands: Van Gorcum.

Mönks, F. J., Heller, K. A., & Passow, H. (2000). The study of giftedness: Reflections on where we are and where we are going. In K. A. Heller, F. J. Mönks, R. J. Sternberg, & R. F. Subotnik (Eds.), *International handbook of giftedness and talent* (2nd ed., pp. 839–863). Oxford, UK: Elsevier.

Mulaik, S. A. (1972). *The foundations of factor analysis*. New York: McGraw-Hill.

Naglieri, J. A. (1997). *Naglieri Nonverbal Ability Test*. San Antonio, TX: Pearson.

Naglieri, J. A. (2001). Understanding intelligence, giftedness and creativity using the PASS theory. *Roeper Review, 23*, 151–156.

Naglieri, J. A., & Das, J. P. (1997). *Cognitive Assessment System*. Itasca, IL: Riverside.

Naglieri, J. A., Das, J. P., & Goldstein, S. (2012). PASS: A cognitive processing based theory of intelligence. In D. P. Flanagan & P. L. Harrison (Eds.), *Contemporary intellectual assessment: Theories, texts, and issues* (3rd ed.). New York: Guilford Press.

Naglieri, J. A., Das, J. P., & Goldstein, S. (2014). *Cognitive Assessment System, Second Edition*. Austin, TX: PRO-ED.

Naglieri, J. A., & Ford, D. Y. (2005). Increasing minority children's participation in gifted classes using the NNAT: A response to Lohman. *Gifted Child Quarterly, 49*, 29–36.

National Association for Gifted Children & the Council of State Directors of Programs for the Gifted. (2009). *2008–2009 state of states in gifted education: National policy and practice data*. Washington, DC: Author.

National Education Association. (2006). *The twice-exceptional dilemma*. Washington, DC: Author.

National Education Association.(2008). *Disproportionality: Inappropriate identification of culturally and linguistically diverse children* (NEA Policy Brief). Washington, DC: Author.

National Research Council.(2002). *Minority students in special and gifted education*. Washington, DC: National Academy Press.

National Science Board.(2010). *Preparing the next generation of STEM innovators: Identifying and developing our nation's human capital*. http://www.nsf.gov/nsb/publications/2010/nsb1033.pdf

Neihart, M. (2007). The socioaffective impact of acceleration and ability grouping: Recommendations for best practice. *Gifted Child Quarterly, 51*, 330–341.

Neisser, U., Boodoo, G., Bouchard, T. J., Boykin, A. W., Brody, N., Ceci, S. J., . . . Urbina, S. (1996). Intelligence: Knowns and unknowns. *American Psychologist, 51*, 77–101.

Nelson, J. M., & Canivez, G. L. (2012). Examination of the structural, convergent, and incremental validity of the Reynolds Intellectual Assessment Scales (RIAS) with a clinical sample. *Psychological Assessment, 24*, 129–140. doi: 10.1037/a0024878

Nelson, J. M., Canivez, G. L., Lindstrom, W., & Hatt, C. (2007). Higher–order exploratory factor analysis of the Reynolds Intellectual Assessment Scales with a referred sample. *Journal of School Psychology, 45*, 439–456.

Neukrug, E., & Fawcett, R. C. (2014). *Essentials of testing and assessment: A practical guide for counselors, social workers, and psychologists* (3rd ed.). Belmont, CA: Brooks/Cole, Carnage Learning.

Newcomer, P. L. (2001). *Diagnostic Achievement Battery—Third Edition*. Austin, TX: PRO-ED.

Newman, T. M. (2008). Assessment of giftedness in school-age children using measures of intelligence and cognitive abilities. In S. I. Pfeiffer (Ed.), *Handbook of giftedness in children* (pp. 161–176). New York: Springer.

Nicpon, M. F., & Pfeiffer, S. I. (2011). High ability students: New ways to conceptualize giftedness and provide psychological services in the schools. *Journal of Applied School Psychology, 27*, 293–305.

Nisbett, R. E. (2009). *Intelligence and how to get it*. New York: Norton.

No Child Left Behind Act of 2001, 20 U.S.C. 70 § 6301 et seq. (2002).

Norcross, J. C., Hogan, T. P., & Koocher, G. P. (2008). *Clinician's guide to evidence-based practice*. New York: Oxford University Press.

O'Connor, C., & Fernandez, S. D. (2010). Race, class, and disproportionality: Reevaluating the relationship between poverty and special education placement. *Educational Researcher, 35*, 6–11.

Olszewski-Kubilius, P. (2004). Talent searches and accelerated programming for gifted students. In N. Colangelo, S. G. Assouline, & M.U.M. Gross (Eds.), *A nation deceived: How schools hold back America's brightest students* (Vol. 2, pp. 69–76). Iowa City: Connie Belin & Jacqueline N. Blank International Center for Gifted Education and Talent Development, University of Iowa.

Oppler, S. H. (1993). *Career interests of academically talented seventh graders*. Paper presented at the Annual Meeting of the American Educational Research Association, Atlanta, GA.

Peterson, G. W., Sampson, J. P. Jr., Lenz, J. G., & Reardon, R. C. (2002). Becoming career problem solvers and decision makers: A cognitive information processing approach. In D. Brown (Ed.), *Career choice and development* (4th ed., pp. 312–369). San Francisco: Jossey-Bass.

Pfeiffer, S. I. (1978). The relationship between cognitive style and creative writing in children. *Dissertation Abstracts International, 201*.

Pfeiffer, S. I. (1980). The influence of diagnostic labeling on special education placement decisions. *Psychology in the Schools, 17*, 346–350.

Pfeiffer, S. I. (2001a). Emotional intelligence: Popular but elusive construct. *Roeper Review, 23*, 138–142.

Pfeiffer, S. I. (2001b). Professional psychology and the gifted: Emerging practice opportunities. *Professional Psychology: Research and Practice, 32*, 175–180.

Pfeiffer, S. I. (2002). Identifying gifted and talented students: Recurring issues and promising solutions. *Journal of Applied School Psychology, 19,* 31–50.

Pfeiffer, S. I. (2003). Challenges and opportunities for students who are gifted: What the experts say. *Gifted Child Quarterly, 47,* 161–169.

Pfeiffer, S. I. (2008). *Handbook of giftedness in children.* New York: Springer.

Pfeiffer, S. I. (2009). The gifted: Clinical challenges for child psychiatry. *Journal of the American Academy of Child and Adolescent Psychiatry, 48,* 787–790.

Pfeiffer, S. I. (2010). Review of the Profile of Creative Abilities. In K. Geisinger & R. Spies (Eds.). *The seventeenth mental measurements yearbook* (pp. 445–448). Lincoln: Buros Institute of Mental Measurements, University of Nebraska-Lincoln.

Pfeiffer, S. I. (2012). Current perspectives on the identification and assessment of gifted students. *Journal of Psychoeducational Assessment, 30,* 3–9.

Pfeiffer, S. I. (2013a). Lessons learned from working with high-ability students. *Gifted Education International, 29,* 86–97.

Pfeiffer, S. I. (2013b). *Serving the gifted: Evidence-based clinical and psychoeducational practice.* New York: Routledge.

Pfeiffer, S. I. (2013c). Treating the clinical problems of gifted children. In L. Grossman & S. Walfish (Eds.), *Translating research into practice: A desk reference for practicing mental health professionals* (pp. 57–63). New York: Springer.

Pfeiffer, S. I., & Blei, S. (2008). Gifted identification beyond the IQ test: Rating scales and other assessment procedures. In S. I. Pfeiffer (Ed.), *Handbook of giftedness in children* (pp. 177–198). New York: Springer.

Pfeiffer, S. I., & Jarosewich, T. (2003). *Gifted Rating Scales.* San Antonio, TX: Pearson.

Pfeiffer, S. I., & Jarosewich, T. (2007). The Gifted Rating Scales-School Form: An analysis of the standardization sample based on age, gender, race, and diagnostic efficiency. *Gifted Child Quarterly, 51,* 39–50.

Pfeiffer, S. I., Kumtepe, A., & Rosado, J. (2006). Gifted identification: Measuring change in a student's profile of abilities using the Gifted Rating Scales. *School Psychologist, 60,* 106–111.

Pfeiffer, S. I., & Petscher, Y. (2008). Identifying young gifted children using the Gifted Rating Scales-Preschool/Kindergarten Form. *Gifted Child Quarterly, 52,* 19–29.

Pfeiffer, S. I., Petscher, Y., & Jarosewich, T. (2007). The GRS—Preschool/Kindergarten Form: An analysis of the standardization sample based on age, gender, race. *Roeper Review, 29,* 206–211.

Pfeiffer, S. I., Petscher, Y., & Kumtepe, A. (2008). The Gifted Rating Scales—School Form: A validation study based on age, gender and race. *Roeper Review, 30,* 140–146.

Pfeiffer, S. I., Reddy, L. A., Kletzel, J. E., Schmelzer, E. R., & Boyer, L. M. (2000). The practitioner's view of IQ testing and profile analysis. *School Psychology Quarterly, 15,* 376–385.

Pfeiffer, S. I., & Thompson, T. L. (2013). Creativity from a talent development perspective: How it can be cultivated in the schools. In K. H. Kim, J. C. Kaufman, & J. Baer (Eds.), *Creatively gifted students are not like other gifted students: Research, theory, and practice* (pp. 231–255). Rotterdam, The Netherlands: Sense.

Piirto, J. (1998). *Understanding those who create* (2nd ed.). Scottsdale, AZ: Gifted Psychology Press.

Piirto, J. (2004). *Understanding creativity.* Scottsdale, AZ: Great Potential Press.

Piirto, J. (2008). Giftedness in nonacademic domains. In S. Pfeiffer (Ed.), *Handbook of giftedness in children: Psycho-educational theory, research, and best practices* (pp. 367–386). New York: Springer.

Plomin, R., & Spinath, F. M. (2004). Intelligence: Genetics, genes, and genomics. *Journal of Personality and Social Psychology, 86,* 112–129.

Plucker, J. A. (1998). Beware of simple conclusions: The case for the content generality of creativity. *Creativity Research Journal, 11*, 179–182.

Plucker, J. A. (1999). Is the proof in the pudding? Reanalysis of Torrance's (1958 to present) longitudinal data. *Creativity Research Journal, 12*, 103–114.

Plucker, J. A. (2005). The (relatively) generalist view of creativity. In J. C. Kaufman & J. Baer (Eds.), *Creativity across domains: Faces of the muse* (pp. 307–312). Mahwah, NJ: Erlbaum.

Plucker, J. A., Beghetto, R. A., & Dow, G. T. (2004). Why isn't creativity more important to educational psychologists? Potentials, pitfalls, and future directions in creativity research. *Educational Psychologist, 39*, 83–96.

Plucker, J. A., Runco, M. A., & Lim, W. (2006). Predicting ideational behavior from divergent thinking and discretionary time on task. *Creativity Research Journal, 18*, 55–63.

Pressey, S. I. (1949). *Educational acceleration: Appraisals and basic problems* (Ohio State University Studies, Bureau of Educational Research Monograph No. 31). Columbus: Ohio State University Press.

Priest, T. (2006). The reliability of three groups of judges' assessments of creativity under three conditions. *Bulletin of the Council for Research in Music Education, 167*, 47–60.

Raiford, S. E., Weiss, L. G., Rolfhus, E., & Coalson, D. (2005). *WISC-IV General Ability Index* (WISC-IV Technical Report No. 4). http://harcourtassessment.com/hai/Images/pdf/wisciv/WISCIVTechReport4.pd

Rakow, S. R. (2008). Standards-based v. standards-embedded curriculum: Not just semantics! *Gifted Child Today, 31*(1), 43–49.

Rakow, S. (2011). *Educating gifted students in middle school.* Waco, TX: Prufrock Press.

Raven, J. C. (2000). The Raven's Progressive Matrices: Change and stability over culture and time. *Cognitive Psychology, 41*, 1–48.

Raven, J. C., Court, J. H., & Raven, J. (1983). *Manual for Raven's Progressive Matrices and Vocabulary Scales: Advanced Progressive Matrices Sets I and II.* London: H. K. Lewis.

Reis, S. M. (2006). Comprehensive program design. In J. H. Purcell & R. D. Eckert (Eds.), *Designing services and programs for high-ability learners* (pp. 73–86). Thousand Oaks, CA: Corwin Press.

Reis, S. M., & Renzulli, J. S. (2009a). Developing talents and gifted behaviors in children. In B. MacFarlane & T. Stambaugh (Eds.), *Leading change in gifted education* (pp. 107–118). Waco, TX: Prufrock Press.

Reis, S. M., & Renzulli, J. S. (2009b). The schoolwide enrichment model: A focus on student strengths and interests. In J. S. Renzulli, E. J. Gubbins, K. McMillen, R. Eckert, & C. Little (Eds.), *Systems and models for developing programs for the gifted and talented* (2nd ed., pp. 323–352). Mansfield Center, CT: Creative Learning Press.

Renzulli, J. S. (1978). What makes giftedness? Reexamining a definition. *Phi Delta Kappan, 60*, 180–184.

Renzulli, J. S. (1983). Rating the behavioral characteristics of superior students. *Gifted Child Today, 29*, 30–35.

Renzulli, J. S. (1984). The triad/revolving door system: A research-based approach to identification and programming for the gifted and talented. *Gifted Child Quarterly, 28*, 163–171.

Renzulli, J. S. (2005a). *Equity, excellence, and economy in a system for identifying students in gifted education: A guidebook* (RM05208). Storrs: National Research Center on the Gifted and Talented, University of Connecticut.

Renzulli, J. S. (2005b). The three-ring conception of giftedness: A developmental model for promoting creative productivity. In R. J. Sternberg & J. E. Davidson (Eds.), *Conceptions of giftedness* (2nd ed., pp. 246–279). New York: Cambridge University Press.

Renzulli, J. S. (2009). The multiple menu model for developing differentiated curriculum. In J. S. Renzulli, E. J. Gubbins, K. S. McMillen, R. D. Eckert, & C. A. Little (Eds.), *Systems and models for developing the gifted and talented* (2nd ed., pp. 353–381). Mansfield Center, CT: Creative Learning Press.

Renzulli, J. S. (2011). Theories, actions, and change: An academic journey in search of finding and developing high potential in young people. *Gifted Child Quarterly, 55*, 305–308.

Renzulli, J. S., Siegle, D., Reis, S. M., Gavin, M. K., & Reed, R. E. S. (2009). An investigation of the reliability and factor structure of four new scales for rating the behavioral characteristics of superior students. *Journal of Advanced Academics, 21*, 84–108.

Renzulli, J. S., Smith, L. H., White, A. J., Callahan, C. M., Hartman, R. K., & Westberg, K. L. (2002). *Scales for rating the behavioral characteristics of superior students: revised edition.* Mansfield Center, CT: Creative Learning Press.

Reynolds, C. R., & Kamphaus, R. W. (2003). *RIAS: Reynolds intellectual assessment scales.* Lutz, FL: Psychological Assessment Resources. doi: 10.1177/0734282907300381

Reynolds, M., Keith, R., Fine, J., Fisher, M., & Low, J. (2007). Confirmatory factor structure of the Kaufman Assessment Battery for Children–Second Edition: Consistency with the Cattell-Horn-Carroll theory. *School Psychology Quarterly, 22*, 511–539.

Rimm, S. B. (2008). Underachievement syndrome: A psychological defensive pattern. In S. I. Pfeiffer (Ed.), *Handbook of giftedness in children* (pp. 139–160). New York: Springer.

Rimm, S. B., Gilman, B. J., & Silverman, L. K. (2008). Non-traditional applications of traditional testing. In J. VanTassel-Baska (Ed.), *Alternative assessments with gifted and talented students* (pp. 175–202). Waco, TX: Prufrock.

Rizza, M. G., McIntosh, D. E., & McCunn, A. (2001). Profile analysis of the Woodcock-Johnson III Tests of Cognitive Abilities with gifted students. *Psychology in the Schools, 38*, 447–455.

Robertson, K. F., Smeets, S., Lubinski, D., & Benbow, C. P. (2010). Beyond the threshold hypothesis: Even among the gifted and top math/science graduate students, cognitive abilities, vocational interests, and lifestyle preferences matter for career choice, performance, and persistence. *Current Directions in Psychological Science, 19*, 346–351. doi: 10.1177/0963721410391442

Robertson, S. G., Pfeiffer, S. I., & Taylor, N. (2011). Serving the gifted: A national survey of school psychologists. *Psychology in the Schools, 48*, 786–799.

Robinson, A., & Clinkenbeard, P. R. (2008). History of giftedness: Perspectives from the past presage modern scholarship. In S. I. Pfeiffer (Ed.), *Handbook of giftedness in children* (pp. 13–31). New York: Springer.

Robinson, N. M. (2008). The value of traditional assessments as approaches to identifying academically gifted students. In J. L. VanTassel-Baska (Ed.), *Alternative assessments with gifted and talented students* (pp. 157–174). Waco, TX: Prufrock Press.

Roeper, A. (1982). How the gifted cope with their emotions. *Roeper Review, 5*, 21–24.

Roid, G. H. (2003). *Stanford-Binet Intelligence Scales, Fifth Edition.* Itasca, IL: Riverside.

Roid, G. H., & Miller, L. J. (1997). *Leiter International Performance Scale—Revised.* Wood Dale, IL: Stoelting.

Rosado, J., Pfeiffer, S. I., & Petscher, Y. (2008). The reliability and validity of a Spanish translated version of the Gifted Rating Scales. *Gifted and Talented International, 23*, 102–111.

Rosado, J., Pfeiffer, S. I., & Petscher, Y. (2013). Validation of a Spanish translation of the Gifted Rating Scales. *Gifted Education International.* Advance online publication. doi: 10.1177/0261429413507178

Ruf, D. L. (2003). *Use of the SB5 in the assessment of high abilities* (Stanford-Binet Intelligence Scales, Fifth Edition, Assessment Service Bulletin No. 3). Itasca, IL: Riverside.

Runco, M. A. (2005). Creative giftedness. In R. J. Sternberg & J. E. Davidson (Eds.), *Conceptions of giftedness* (2nd ed., pp. 295–249). New York: Cambridge University Press.

Ryser, G. R. (2007). *Profile of Creative Abilities: Examiner's manual.* Austin, TX: Pro-Ed.

Ryser, G. R., & McConnell, R. (2004). *Scales for Identifying Gifted Students: Ages 5 through 18.* Waco, TX: Prufrock Press.

Sak, U., & Ayas, B. (2013). Creative Scientific Ability Test (C-SAT): A new measure of scientific creativity. *Psychological Test and Assessment Modeling, 55,* 316–329.

Saklofske, D. H., Prifitera, A., Weiss, L. G., Rolfhus, E., & Zhu, J. (2005). Clinical interpretation of the WISC–IV FSIQ and GAI. In A. Prifitera, D. H. Saklofske, & L. G. Weiss (Eds.), *WISC–IV clinical use and interpretation: Scientist practitioner perspectives* (pp. 33–65). New York: Academic Press.

Sampson, J. P., & Chason, A. K. (2008). Helping gifted and talented adolescents and young adults make informed and careful career choices. In S. I. Pfeiffer (Ed.), *Handbook of giftedness in children* (pp. 327–346). New York: Springer.

Sanders, S., McIntosh, D. E., Dunham, M., Rothlisberg, B. A., & Finch, H. (2007). Joint confirmatory factor analysis of the Differential Ability Scales and the Woodcock-Johnson Tests of Cognitive Abilities–Third Edition. *Psychology in the Schools, 44,* 119–138.

Sattler, J. M. (2001). *Assessment of children: Cognitive applications* (4th ed.). San Diego, CA: Author.

Sattler, J. M. (2008). *Assessment of children: Cognitive foundations* (5th ed.). San Diego, CA: Author.

Sattler, J. M. (2014). *Foundations of behavioral, social, and clinical assessment of children* (6th ed.). San Diego, CA: Author.

Schack, G. D., & Starko, A. J. (1990). Identification of gifted students: An analysis of criteria preferred by pre-service teachers, classroom teachers, and teachers of the gifted. *Journal for the Education of the Gifted, 13,* 346–363.

Schmidt, E. A., Homeyer, L. E., & Walker, J. L. (2009). Counselor preparation: Predictors of success on the Counselor Preparation Comprehensive Examination. *Counselor Education & Supervision, 48,* 226–238.

Scholastic Testing Service. (2009). *Gifted education: Torrance Tests of Creative Thinking.* http://www.ststesting.com/ngifted.html

Schrank, F. A., Mather, N., & McGrew, K. S. (2014). *Woodcock-Johnson IV Tests of Achievement.* Rolling Meadows, IL: Riverside.

Schrank, F. A., McGrew, K. S., & Mather, N. (2014). *Woodcock-Johnson IV Tests of Cognitive Abilities.* Rolling Meadows, IL: Riverside.

Schwartz, D. M. (2013). A four- and five-factor structural model for Wechsler tests: Does it really matter clinically? *Journal of Psychoeducational Assessment, 31,* 175–185.

Seligman, M.E.P. (2004). *Authentic happiness: Using the new positive psychology to release your potential for lasting fulfillment.* New York: Free Press.

Seligman, M.E.P. (2007). *The optimistic child.* New York: Houghton Mifflin.

Shaklee, B. D., Barbour, N. E., Ambrose, R., & Hansford, S. J. (1997). *Designing and using portfolios.* Needham Heights, MA: Allyn & Bacon.

Shaunessy, E., Karnes, F. A., & Cobb, Y. (2004). Assessing potentially gifted students from lower SES with nonverbal measures of intelligence. *Perceptual and Motor Skills, 98,* 1129–1138.

Shaw, P., Greenstein, D., Lerch, J., Clasen, L., Lenroot, R., Gogtay, N., . . . Giedd, J. (2006). Intellectual ability and cortical development in children and adolescents. *Nature, 440,* 676–679. doi: 10.1038/nature04513

Silverman, L. K. (2013). *Giftedness 101.* New York: Springer.

Simonton, D. K. (2007). Creativity: Specialized expertise or general cognitive processes? In M. J. Roberts (Ed.), *Integrating the mind: Domain general versus domain specific processes in higher cognition* (pp. 351–367). Hove, UK: Psychology Press.

Simonton, D. K. (2008). Scientific talent, training, and performance: Intellect, personality, and genetic endowment. *Review of General Psychology, 12*, 28–46.

Simonton, D. K. (2013, May). Creative performance, expertise acquisition, individual differences, and developmental antecedents: An integrative research agenda. *Intelligence.* Advance online publication. doi: 10.1016/j.intell.2013.04.007

Siu, A. F. Y. (2010). The reliability and validity of a Chinese-translated version of the Gifted Rating Scale—Preschool/Kindergarten Form. *Journal of Psychoeducational Assessment, 28*, 249–258. doi: 10.1177/0734282909345832

Spearman, C. (1904). "General intelligence," objectively determined and measured. *American Journal of Psychology, 15*, 201–293.

Spearman, C. (1927). *The abilities of man.* London: Macmillan.

Stanley, J. C. (1976). The case for extreme educational acceleration of intellectually brilliant youths. *Gifted Child Quarterly, 20*, 66–75.

Stanley, J. C. (1990). Leta Hollingworth's contributions to above-level testing of the gifted. *Roeper Review, 12*, 166–171.

Stanley, J. C. (2000). Helping students learn only what they don't already know. *Psychology, Public Policy, and Law, 6*, 216–222.

Stephens, K. R. (2008). Applicable federal and state policy, law, and legal considerations in gifted education. In S. I. Pfeiffer (Ed.), *Handbook of giftedness in children* (pp. 387–408). New York: Springer.

Stephens, K. R. (2011). Federal and state response to the gifted and talented. *Journal of Applied School Psychology, 27*, 306–318.

Sternberg, R. J. (1984). Evaluation of the Kaufman Assessment Battery for Children from an information-processing perspective. *Journal of Special Education, 18*, 269–279.

Sternberg, R. J. (1985). Implicit theories of intelligence, creativity, and wisdom. *Journal of Personality and Social Psychology, 49*, 607–627.

Sternberg, R. J. (2001). Giftedness as developing expertise: A theory of the interface between high abilities and achieved excellence. *High Ability Studies, 12*, 159–179.

Sternberg, R. J., & Davidson, J. E. (1986). *Conceptions of giftedness.* New York: Cambridge University Press.

Sternberg, R. J., & Davidson, J. E. (Eds.). (2005). *Conceptions of giftedness* (2nd ed.). New York: Cambridge University Press.

Sternberg, R. J., & Grigorenko, E. L. (2002). *Dynamic testing: The nature and measurement of learning potential.* New York: Cambridge University Press.

Sternberg, R. J., Jarvin, L., & Grigorenko, E. L. (2011). *Explorations in giftedness.* New York: Cambridge University Press.

Sternberg, R. J., & Kaufman, J. C. (2010). Constraints on creativity. In J. C. Kaufman & R. J. Sternberg (Eds.), *The Cambridge handbook of creativity* (pp. 467–482). New York: Cambridge University Press.

Sternberg, R. J., Lautrey, J., & Lubart, T. I. (Eds.). (2004). *Models of intelligence: International perspectives.* Washington, DC: American Psychological Association.

Sternberg, R. J., & Lubart, T. I. (1999). The concepts of creativity: Prospects and paradigms. In R. J. Sternberg (Ed.), *Handbook of creativity* (pp. 3–15). New York: Cambridge University Press.

Sternberg, R. J., & Subotnik, R. (2000). A multidimensional framework for synthesizing disparate issues in identifying, selecting, and serving gifted students. In K. A. Heller, F. J. Mönks, R. J. Sternberg, & R. F. Subotnik (Eds.), *International handbook of giftedness and talent* (2nd ed., pp. 271–282). Oxford, UK: Elsevier.

Streiner, D. L. (2003). Diagnosing tests: Using and misusing diagnostic and screening tests. *Journal of Personality Assessment, 81*, 209–219.

Stoiber, K. C., & Kratochwill, T. R. (2002). *Outcomes PME: Planning, monitoring, evaluating.* San Antonio, TX: Pearson.

Subotnik, R. F. (2003). A developmental view of giftedness: From being to doing. *Roeper Review, 26*, 14–15.

Subotnik, R. F. (2009). Developmental transitions in giftedness and talent: Adolescence into adulthood. In F. D. Horowitz, R. F. Subotnik, & D. J. Matthews (Eds.), *The development of giftedness and talent across the life span* (pp. 155–170). Washington, DC: American Psychological Association.

Subotnik, R. F., Olszewski-Kubilius, P., & Worrell, F. C. (2011). Rethinking giftedness and gifted education: A proposed direction forward based on psychological science. *Psychological Science in the Public Interest, 12*, 3–54.

Syed, M. (2010). *Bounce: Mozart, Federer, Picasso, Beckham, and the science of success.* New York: Harper Collins.

Tannenbaum, A. J. (1983). *Gifted children: Psychological and educational perspectives.* New York: Macmillan.

Tannenbaum, A. J. (2000). A history of giftedness in school and society. In K. A. Heller, F. J. Mönks, R. J. Sternberg, & R. F. Subotnik (Eds.). *International handbook of giftedness and talent* (2nd ed., pp. 23–53). Oxford, UK: Elsevier.

Tannenbaum, A. J. (2003). Nature and nurture of giftedness. In N. Colangelo & G. A. Davis (Eds.), *Handbook of gifted education* (pp. 45–59). Boston: Allyn & Bacon.

Taub, G. E., & McGrew, K. S. (2014). The Woodcock-Johnson Tests of Cognitive Abilities III's cognitive performance model: Empirical support for intermediate factors within CHC theory. *Journal of Psychoeducational Assessment, 32*, 187–201.

Terman, L. M. (1916). *The measurement of intelligence.* Boston: Houghton Mifflin.

Terman, L. M. (1925). *Genetic studies of genius: Vol. I. Mental and physical characteristics of a thousand gifted children.* Stanford, CA: Stanford University Press.

Terman, L. M., & Childs, H. G. (1912). A tentative revision and extension of the Binet-Simon Measuring Scale of Intelligence. *Journal of Educational Psychology, 3*, 61–74, 133–143, 198–208, 277–289.

Terman, L. M., & Merrill, M. A. (1973). *The Stanford-Binet Intelligence Scale: 1973 Norms Edition.* Boston: Houghton Mifflin.

Terman, L. M., & Oden, M. H. (1951). The Stanford studies of the gifted. In P. Witty (Ed.), *The gifted child.* Boston: D. C. Heath.

Thorndike, R. M. (2005). Review of the Kaufman Assessment Battery for Children, Second Edition. In R. A. Spies and B. S. Plake (Eds.), *The sixteenth mental measurements yearbook* (pp. 520–522). Lincoln: Buros Institute of Mental Measurements, University of Nebraska-Lincoln.

Thurstone, L. (1938). *Primary mutual abilities.* Chicago: University of Chicago Press.

Torrance, E. P. (1966). *The Torrance Tests of Creative Thinking—Norms-technical manual research edition—Verbal Tests, Forms A and B—Figural Tests, Forms A and B.* Princeton, NJ: Personnel Press.

Torrance, E. P. (1972). Predictive validity of the Torrance Tests of Creative Thinking. *Journal of Creative Behavior, 6*, 236–252.

Torrance, E. P. (1974). *Torrance Tests of Creative Thinking: Directions manual and scoring guide. Verbal test booklet A.* Bensenville, IL: Scholastic Testing Service.

Torrance, E. P. (1990). *The Torrance tests of creative thinking: Norms-technical manual.* Bensenville, IL: Scholastic Testing Service.

Torrance, E. P. (2008). *The Torrance Tests of Creative Thinking: Norms-technical manual, Figural (streamlined) Forms A & B.* Bensenville, IL: Scholastic Testing Service.

Treffinger, D. J. (1986). Research on creativity. *Gifted Child Quarterly, 30,* 15–19.

Treffinger, D. J. (Ed.). (2009). Special Issue: Demythologizing gifted education. *Gifted Child Quarterly, 53,* 229–288.

Vallerand, R. J., Pelletier, L. G., Blais, M. R., Brière, N. M., Senécal, C., & Vallières, E. F. (1992). The Academic Motivation Scale: A measure of intrinsic, extrinsic, and amotivation in education. *Educational and Psychological Motivation, 52,* 1003–1017.

VanTassel-Baska, J. (Ed.). (2008). *Alternative assessments with gifted and talented students.* Waco, TX: Prufrock Press.

Vincent, J., & Glamser, F. D. (2006). Gender differences in the relative age effect among US Olympic Development Program youth soccer players. *Journal of Sports Sciences, 24,* 405–414.

Wai, J. (2013, September). Experts are born, then made: Combining prospective and retrospective data shows that cognitive ability matters. *Intelligence.* Advance online publication. doi: 10.1016/j.intell.2013.08.009

Wallach, M. A. (1976, January–February). Tests tell us little about talent. *American Scientist,* 57–63.

Ward, S. A. (2005). Review of Gifted Rating Scales. In J. F. Spies & B. S. Plake (Eds.), *The sixteenth mental measurements yearbook* (pp. 404–407). Lincoln: Buros Institute of Mental Measurements, University of Nebraska-Lincoln.

Ward, S. A. (2007). Review of Gifted Rating Scales. In K. F. Geisinger, R. A. Spies, J. F. Carlson, & B. S. Plake (Eds.), *The seventeenth mental measurements yearbook* (pp. 731–734). Lincoln: Buros Institute of Mental Measurements, University of Nebraska-Lincoln.

Wasserman, J. (2007). Intellectual assessment of exceptionally and profoundly gifted children. In K. Kay, D. Robson, & J. F. Brenneman (Eds.), *High IQ kids: Collected insights, information, and personal stories from the experts* (pp. 48–65). Minneapolis, MN: Free Spirit.

Watkins, M. W. (2000). Cognitive profile analysis: A shared myth. *School Psychology Quarterly, 15,* 465–479.

Watkins, M. W. (2006). Orthogonal higher-order structure of the WISC-IV. *Psychological Assessment, 18,* 123–125.

Watkins, M. W. (2010). Structure of the Wechsler Intelligence Scale for Children—Fourth Edition among a national sample of referred students. *Psychological Assessment, 22,* 782–787.

Webb, J. T., Amend, E. R., Webb, N. E., Goerss, J., Beljan, P., & Olenchak, F. R. (2005). *Misdiagnosis and dual diagnoses of gifted children and adults: ADHD, bipolar, OCD, Asperger's, depression and other disorders.* Scottsdale, AZ: Great Potential Press.

Webb, J. T., Meckstroth, E. A., & Tolan, S. S. (1982). *Guiding the gifted child.* Columbus, OH: Psychology Publishing.

Wechsler, D. (2002). *Wechsler Preschool and Primary Scale of Intelligence—Third Edition* (WPPSI-III). San Antonio, TX: Psychological Corporation.

Wechsler, D. (2003). *Wechsler Intelligence Scale for Children—Fourth Edition: Technical and interpretative manual.* San Antonio, TX: Pearson.

Wechsler, D. (2008). *Wechsler Adult Intelligence Scale—Fourth Edition.* Bloomington, MN: Pearson.

Wechsler, D. (2009). *Wechsler Individual Achievement Test—Third Edition.* San Antonio, TX: Pearson.

Wechsler, D. (2011). *Wechsler Abbreviated Scale of Intelligence—Second Edition (WASI-II).* San Antonio, TX: NCS Pearson.

Wechsler, D. (2012). *Wechsler Preschool and Primary Scale of Intelligence—Fourth Edition.* Bloomington, MN: Pearson.

Wechsler, D. (2014). *Wechsler Intelligence Scale for Children—Fifth Edition*. Bloomington, MN: Pearson.

Weiss, L. G., Keith, T. Z., Zhu, J., & Chen, H. (2013a). WAIS-IV clinical validation of the four- and five-factor interpretive approaches. *Journal of Psychoeducational Assessment, 31*(2, special issue), 94–113. doi: 10.1177/0734282913478030

Weiss, L. G., Keith, T. Z., Zhu, J., & Chen, H. (2013b). WISC-IV and clinical validation of the four- and five-factor interpretive approaches. *Journal of Psychoeducational Assessment, 31*(2, special issue), 114–131. doi: 10.1177/0734282913478032

Whipple, G. M. (Ed.). (1924). *The education of gifted children* (23rd Yearbook, Part I). National Society for the Study of Education. Bloomington, IL: Public School Publishing.

Wiig, E. H. (2000). Authentic and other assessments of language disabilities: When is fair? *Reading and Writing Quarterly, 16*, 179–210.

Wilkinson, G. S., & Robertson, G. J. (2006). *Wide Range Achievement Test—Fourth Edition*. Lutz, FL: Psychological Assessment Resources.

Williams, T. H., McIntosh, D. E., Dixon, F., Newton, J. H., & Youman, E. (2010). A confirmatory factor analysis of the Stanford-Binet Intelligence Scales, Fifth Edition, with a high-achieving sample. *Psychology in the Schools, 47*, 1071–1083.

Wolfenden, L. E., & Holt, N. L. (2005). Tennis development in elite junior tennis: Perceptions of players, parents and coaches. *Journal of Applied Sport Psychology, 17*, 108–126.

Woodcock, R. W. (2011). *Woodcock Reading Mastery Tests, Third Edition*. San Antonio, TX: Pearson.

Woodcock, R. W., McGrew, K. S., & Mather, N. (2001). *Woodcock-Johnson III*. Itasca, IL: Riverside.

Worrell, F. C., & Erwin, J. O. (2011). Best practices in identifying students in gifted and talented education programs. *Journal of Applied School Psychology, 27*, 319–340.

Worrell, F. C., Subotnik, R. F., & Olszewski-Kubilius, P. (2013). Giftedness and gifted education: Reconceptualizing the role of professional psychology. *Register Report, 39*, 14–22.

Yarnell, J., & Pfeiffer, S. I. (2014). Internet administration of the paper-and-pencil Gifted Rating Scale: Assessing psychometric equivalence. *Journal of Psychoeducational Assessment,* 1–10. doi: 10.1177/0734282914564039

Young, J. W. (2001). Test review of the Gifted Evaluation Scale, Second Edition. In B. S. Plake & J. C. Impara (Eds.), *The fourteenth mental measurements yearbook* [Electronic version]. http://www.unl.edu/buros

Zhu, J., Cayton, T., Weiss, L., & Gabel, A. (2008). *Wechsler Intelligence Scale for Children—Fourth Edition: WISC-IV extended norms* (Technical Report #7). Upper Saddle River, NJ: Pearson Education. http://images.pearsonclinical.com/images/assets/WISC-IV/WISCIV_TechReport_7.pdf

ABOUT THE AUTHOR

Steven Pfeiffer, PhD, ABPP, is a professor at Florida State University, where he also serves as director of clinical training. Prior to his tenure at Florida State, Dr. Pfeiffer was a professor at Duke University, where he served for five years as executive director of Duke's program for gifted students (Duke TIP). In 2012 he was a visiting distinguished professor at the National Institute of Education in Singapore. In addition to his teaching and administrative responsibilities, he has an active clinical practice and conducts numerous presentations, workshops, and consultations each year both nationally and internationally. He is a widely published author of tests, books, book chapters, and articles. His career has included serving as executive director of the Devereux Institute of Clinical and Professional Training and Research in Villanova, Pennsylvania, and holding faculty appointments at the University of Pennsylvania, Fordham University, and Tulane University. He served as a clinical psychologist in the U.S. Navy Medical Service Corps reserves for seven years and testified at the White House before the Task Force on National Health Care Reform. Dr. Pfeiffer is the lead author of the *Gifted Rating Scales*, author of *Serving the Gifted*, and editor of the *Handbook of Giftedness in Children*. Additionally he is editor-in-chief of the *APA Handbook of Giftedness and Talent*. A popular lecturer, he is a recognized authority on issues related to the mental health of gifted children and their families and on the importance of balancing "strengths of the heart" with "strengths of the head" in encouraging the success of high-ability children.

INDEX